The anthropology of ambiguity

Manchester University Press

The anthropology
of ambiguity

Edited by

Mahnaz Alimardanian and Timothy Heffernan

MANCHESTER UNIVERSITY PRESS

Published by Manchester University Press
Oxford Road, Manchester M13 9PL

www.manchesteruniversitypress.co.uk

British Library Cataloguing-in-Publication Data
A catalogue record for this book is available from the British
Library

ISBN 978 1 5261 7384 3 hardback
ISBN 978 1 5261 9577 7 paperback

First published 2024
Paperback published 2026

EU authorised representative for GPSR:
Easy Access System Europe – Mustamäe tee 50,
10621 Tallinn, Estonia
gpsr.requests@easproject.com

Typeset by Newgen Publishing UK

Contents

Part IV: Self-realisation and disjuncture

Figures

Contributors

Mahnaz Alimardanian is Research Fellow at The Mabo Centre, Faculty of Business and Economics, The University of Melbourne, and the founder and lead researcher at PiiR Consulting. Her publications are situated at the intersections of social and philosophical anthropology, with an ethnographic focus on existential and sensory experiences and performance. She also works for the Victorian State Government designing and supporting community engagement approaches on trauma- and healing-informed social projects.

Angélica Cabrera Torrecilla is a postdoctoral researcher and member of Mexico's National System of Researchers (SNI) whose research focuses on literary and cultural studies of space and time (angelicacabrera.com). Her research has been funded by The National Autonomous University of Mexico and The Japan Foundation, and she has been a Visiting Postdoctoral Researcher at Cardiff University, the University of The Ryukyus, and The College of México.

Joe Clifford is a Master's graduate from Auckland University. His research focuses on the political use of culture, state–society relations, and nationalism. He has published articles that explore these ideas in both an Aotearoa New Zealand and Indonesian context.

Alexander Emile D'Aloia is a lecturer in anthropology and development studies at the University of Melbourne and a recent graduate of The Australian National University. His doctoral thesis, 'Precarious Alternative: Sustaining the Popular Solidarity Economy in Ecuador', won the best thesis prize of the Australian National Centre of Latin American Studies. His research focuses on the interactions between entrepreneurialism and alternative economic policy and the effects of precarity on the bureaucrats who enact it.

Timothy Heffernan is Lecturer in Anthropology at the Australian National University, Canberra, Australia. His research focus is the crisis–recovery nexus after event-based hardship, including in post-economic crisis Iceland and in Australia after wildfires. His work has appeared in the journals History and Anthropology, Religions, and Conflict and Society.

Gil Hizi is a research fellow in anthropology at the Goethe University Frankfurt (PhD Sydney University, 2018). He studies social change in China with a focus on interpersonal ethics and emotions. His articles have been published in the journals *Ethos*, *Social Analysis*, *Asian Studies Review* and *Hau*. He is the editor of *Keywords for Self-Development in China Today* (Amsterdam University Press, 2024).

Mohammad Altaf Hossain is a postdoctoral research fellow at Geary Institute for Public Policy, University College Dublin, Ireland. His current project, funded by the Marie Skłodowska-Curie European Postdoctoral Fellowship, investigates housing precarity experienced by South Asian immigrants living in Dublin. His doctoral studies in anthropology at Maynooth University, Ireland, employed ethnographic methods in island villages in Bangladesh to understand disaster vulnerabilities and people's agency.

Suzi Hutchings is a member of the Central Arrernte Nation. She is professor, Indigenous Research Development, Indigenous Engagement, Swinburne University of Technology. Her anthropological research centres on Indigenous native title claims; the impacts of criminal justice on Aboriginal youth; and she collaborates with First Nations producing music and performance. She hosts *Subway Sounds* on Melbourne community radio. Suzi is co-editor of *Activist Scholarship with Indigenous Peoples in the Global South* (AlterNative, 2022).

Jonathan Paul Marshall was an Australian Research Council Future Fellow at the University of Technology, Sydney, researching the technological and social challenges of energy transition. His publications include *Living on Cybermind: Categories, Communication and Control* (Peter Lang, 2007); *Disorder and the Disinformation Society* (co-author, Routledge, 2015); *Depth Psychology, Disorder and Climate Change* (editor, JungDownunder, 2009); *Earth, Climate, Dreams* (co-editor, Depth Psychology Alliance, 2019); and special issues of *Globalisations*, *Energy Policy*, *Energy Research and Social Science* and *The Australian Journal of Anthropology*.

Anton Piyarathne is a professor of anthropology and sociology at the Open University of Sri Lanka. His research attempts to explain ethnoreligious boundary negotiations by ordinary Sri Lankans, folk religious practices, social identity, and people's adjustment to a changing global political economy. He has published two books on the plantation Tamil community in Sri Lanka and is the author of *Constructing Commongrounds: Everyday Lifeworlds Beyond Politicised Ethnicities in Sri Lanka* (Sarasavi, 2018).

Stefanie Puszka is a medical anthropologist and postdoctoral fellow in the Diabetes Across the Lifecourse: Northern Australian Partnership at the Menzies School of Health Research. She has collaborated with Australian First Nations people and healthcare providers on critical and applied research on chronic disease, disability, risk, caregiving and healthcare. She is currently undertaking research on First Nations family caregivers in managing type 2 diabetes.

David J. Rosner is associate professor of values and ethics at Metropolitan College of New York. He served as President of the International Society for the Comparative Study of Civilizations from 2013 to 2016. His work has focused on the topic of shifting values during times of crisis. He is the author of *Conservatism and Crisis: The Anti-Modernist Perspective in Twentieth-Century German Philosophy* (Lexington Books, 2012), and the editor of *Catastrophe and Philosophy* (Lexington Books, 2019).

Sabrina Steindl-Kopf is a lecturer in social and cultural anthropology at the University of Vienna. Her research focuses on activisms of the city and of marginalised groups, such as Romani communities, taking place in both postsocialist and neoliberal contexts. She has recently finished a project on participatory action of Romani migrants in Vienna, where she looked at the intersections of migratory experience, ethnicity, age and gender.

Introduction

Timothy Heffernan and Mahnaz Alimardanian

Regardless of any confusion one has about the precise definition or treatment of the term, ambiguity is usually held as something possessing more than one meaning, quality or sense; a concept, state, situation or feeling that provokes puzzlement while also resembling a holding place from which clarity can emerge. It is the attribute of something being, becoming or possessing many things at once (or perhaps being less than this or coming to be nothing at all) that is this book's focus. An anthropology of ambiguity seeks to grapple with ambiguity in individuals' lives and in the life-worlds of human societies by paying attention to that which is bewildering, incongruent, contradictory, indeterminate, incomplete or otherwise, while also asking why what is deemed as ambiguous in one context may be construed as non-ambiguous in another. It is a steadfast commitment to viewing ambiguity not as an anomaly per se but as being part and parcel of the experience and expression of life. Ambiguity thereby offers occasions to understand how the peculiarities of knowledge, action and meaning – both old and emerging, positive and negative – manifest and take on significance in the production of life as it lived in the world. Inquiring into the presence of ambiguity, or the need to reckon with it in communal life, is not new. Yet a push to treat ambiguity as more than a negative incursion on life holds ethnographic promise. The volume takes up this mantle through an adherence to *sitting and being with* ambiguity as it arises in the lives and environments of interlocutors or in the process of writing ethnography.

Today, many of the communities that anthropologists work with have undergone or, indeed, continue to undergo unwelcome change: the supremacy of grand narratives is now viewed as no longer providing suitable direction, and the stability of institutions and authorities appears to be unstable (see Knibbe, 2014: 538). Yet, given the enduring presence of such change, there is a need for anthropology to continue to embrace ambiguity and to go beyond now dominant expressions of flux and insecurity, especially in a world profoundly affected by disruptive technologies and the threat of viral contagion, climate collapse, economic instability, livelihood precarity and political tension. There is a need, moreover, to understand these and other changes with reference to the rich cultural specificity that is characteristic of the discipline to grapple with that which is labelled or experienced as 'ambiguous'. To this end, the book uses the anthropological toolkit of sociocultural analysis and ethnography to unpack and broadly examine ambiguity as it is variously experienced and encountered. It notes ambiguity's analytical fruitfulness for understanding human life in its full complexity, rather than seeking to resolve it or to dispense with ambiguity entirely in fieldnotes or in ethnographic writing.

Such a call recognises that human life is positioned between the realms of mystery and mastery, with ambiguity conceived as the unavoidable essence of being and as part of navigating the complexity of communal life and, more generally, the human condition. The volume asks: how can we understand the place of ambiguity and the ways it is understood and responded to by the communities with whom anthropologists work? This question has become pressing in recent years as compounding crises and tensions at the local and global level bring into focus concerns about how to address agitation, contradiction and the unknown (Espírito Santo, 2023). Taking the term broadly, it asks how anthropologists can position their work to produce scholarship on ambiguity, especially given the essential, sometimes slippery, always ineffable presence of ambiguity in life, beyond merely being seen as situations or contexts of underdetermination (discussed below). We begin with the premise that, if ambiguity is part of the human condition, then it is not immutable and can constantly change in how it is expressed, experienced, thought about and come to terms with. For this reason, the term requires ongoing anthropological understanding for how it is understood, addressed and endured.

Contributors approach this through ethnographies based in Australia, the United States, Iceland, Bangladesh, Serbia, Ecuador, Aotearoa New Zealand, Sri Lanka, China and Japan, providing a veritable atlas of ambiguity. *Atlas* was the name given by European geographer Mercator in 1595 to his magnum opus, the *Cosmographical meditations upon the creation of the universe and the universe as created*. The title not only highlighted the work's cartographic composition of continents but also a methodology steeped in philosophy that brought 'a world' on to a page, in this way linking the physical and cosmographical to build a coherent picture of 'the' world. In this volume, each chapter concentrates on ambiguity in a discrete locality, which builds to depict ambiguous phenomena in the lives and minds of a great many people. Ambiguity is shown to be created by and perceived through disorder, disarray, unpredictability and contradiction; how it manifests in or is projected by absence, ignorance, disengagement, silence, subversion or liminality; and how it is wrapped up in doubt, fear, failure, indecision, humour, hope, hesitation or the uncanny. Each chapter shows how ambiguity is part of self-improvisation and cultivation and the grounds on which societal transformation occurs. This is explored through the plans people put in place, the processes and structures they rely on, and the expectation of a life's continuity, which produces a dynamic whereby people search for certainty in the face of uncertainty, even if certainty is not easily achievable or its ultimate form remains unknown. The volume contributes to understanding how people contend with loss, hardship, disruption, incongruity, the unfamiliar and the unknown, as well as the tactics used to exploit ambiguity as an opportunity for individual or group benefit or transformation.

Central to this book's inquiry is the term's relationship to knowledge, experience, sense-making, trust, consensus-building and belonging. Many of the discipline's forerunners held ambiguity to be central to their work and looked beyond disciplinary boundaries to grapple with it, especially in connection with episteme, identity, belief and ritual (Martínez et al., 2021). To establish the grounds upon which ambiguity is examined in this volume, we explore early works in anthropology and then consider its subsequent interest across humanistic, pragmatic and philosophical anthropology. The dominant framework throughout the book seeks to blur the boundaries between existential, pragmatic and humanistic theories and approaches in order to understand the presence of ambiguity in life as a constant, yet one that need not be fully explained or, indeed, explained away. Life as lived in a state of being and becoming takes centre stage, noting how people live with and through ambiguity, which we explore through scholarship on collective interpretations of the unknown, the unfamiliar and incertitude, as well as the presence of ambiguity in lived experience, self-realisation, stasis and transformation.

Ambiguity in anthropology

Ambiguity has been engaged by most scholarly disciplines concerned with knowledge and knowledge production. From the classical fields of mathematics, philosophy and logic to the natural, behavioural and social sciences, each has approached ambiguity as something to be controlled, resolved or utilised. The creation of behavioural and sociocultural definitions and classifications in the form of social and cognitive structures by early ethnographers was no different, nor were such definitions and classifications immune from ambiguity by way of exception, contradiction, slippage and overlap (Eriksen and Nielsen, 2001). Early works focused on boundaries through the analysis of the sacred and profane, purity and pollution, myth and meaning-making, showing how each functioned despite often being in flux (Durkheim, 1995 [1912]; Radcliffe-Brown, 1949; Leach, 1964; Lévi-Strauss, 1969). In *Baloma: Spirits of the Dead* (1916: 355), for example, Malinowski examined two discordant beliefs that 'exist[ed] side by side in dogmatic strength; they are [each] known to be true, and they influence the actions of men [*sic*] and regulate their behaviour'. Each belief was entertained, despite antinomy, with this contradiction illustrating how beliefs, adherence and action were mutually constitutive to the building of life and death rituals in one locale. Ambiguity was in this sense insightful and depicted how contradiction, writ large, was a fundament of human experience and knowledge.

A focus on ambiguity was furthered by the Manchester School's extended case analysis of order and disorder and crisis and conflict, with the work of Gluckman (1954), Turner (1969) and Bailey (1963) notable. The situations they studied were *atypical*, particularly those that 'threw into relief the social and political tensions that were conceived as being at the heart of everyday life' (Kapferer, 2015: 2). Instructively, such situations 'reveal[ed] the social and political forces engaged in the generation or production of social life' (Kapferer, 2015: 2–3). Their work contributed to laying and extending foundational ideas in anthropology about politics, religion, mobility and migration, identity, and the realities of human life amid social complexity. The messiness of boundaries and sociality and the fragility of communal rules were acknowledged through their endeavours (Werbner, 2020). This was especially so in studies on boundary maintenance in kinship, belief, politics, language and communication: of ritual and epistemic habits being a central framing through which people came to know, participate, and act upon the world. In turn, dealing with that which is undetermined, incomprehensible, 'other' or different, and making known what is unknown, has been the preoccupation of earlier anthropological enquiry and the enquiry of anthropology. Later, these ideas were expanded in ethnographies that shone a light on risk and danger as interpretive realms of sense-making (e.g. Douglas, 1986) in attempts to derive insights about the consequences and meanings of people's actions.

Rather than contradictions and the like being mere *expressions* of sociocultural life, however, thereby reducing its specificity, early ethnographers highlighted ambiguity as always relative. What is relevant in one context may be dismissed in another, thereby exploring what it means to be human, the generation and production of social life, and the shared attributes of this cross-culturally. For Turner (1969) this was seen specifically in his analysis of liminality, through which he explored the generative and restrictive forces leading to change and the reordering that emerged. He approached this through van Gennep's (1960) rites of passage to look at how social tension and calamity were responded to through culturally sanctioned practices: 'one finds in human cultures that structural contradictions, arguments, and anomalies are overlaid by layers of myth, ritual and symbol, which stress the axiomatic value of key structural principles, with regard to the very situations where these appear to be most imperative' (Turner, 1969: 47). Disorder was thus seen as a 'charge on the whole community', becoming 'the ritual occasion for an exhibition of values that relate to the community as a whole' (Turner, 1969: 45, 92). Order was achieved via the ritual process, comprising liminality and reintegration.

In the contemporary mass societies that are the focus of this volume, Turner's liminoid thesis has influenced contributors' understandings of how ambiguity affects people, is contemplated, and sparks a reaction. However, the neatness and linearity of his ideas (i.e. order over disorder) are ultimately challenged (see chapters by Heffernan, Hutchings and Cabrera Torrecilla). This reflects the dynamism and character of the systems, processes, occurrences and relationships that are shown to be ambiguous by each contributor, noting the role of contingency and complexity in ambiguous phenomena, as explored in the chapters by Alimardanian, Rosner and Marshall.

Liminal, like other keywords explored in this book, including indecision, polysemy, ignorance, failure and in-betweenness, signifies the transition from a 'fixed' point 'through a cultural realm that has few or none of the attributes of the past or coming state' (Turner, 1969: 94). Yet as Taussig (1987) later argued, order is not always possible or warranted, particularly when set against the backdrop of colonial intervention or globalisation (see Hutchings, this volume). Further, Vigh (2008: 7) underscores the *contextual* nature of ambiguity brought about by societal tension: after the philosopher Benjamin (1999: 248), he notes that 'the tradition of the oppressed teaches us that "the state of emergency" … is not the exception but the rule'. Indeed, ambiguity is often present in systems and processes as seen in the chapters exploring political process (Marshall, this volume), corruption (Piyarathne, this volume) and 'value' (D'Aloia, this volume). Ambiguity is also present in both mainstream and vernacular healthcare (Puszka, this volume) and humanitarian aid (Hossain, this volume). These chapters treat ambiguity as central to how people minimise or distil change, or agitate for transformation.

Turner's (1982) later work on performance elucidated the constituent presence of ambiguity in life by examining 'social dramas': occasions explicating how situations and events illustrate the character of relationships and institutions, and exhibit the nuance of accustomed styles, aesthetics, skills, beliefs and their differences. Social drama is useful here in thinking not just about the ways tensions spill over to reveal the forces complicit in social reproduction, but also the less obvious aspects that play a role in this process, or the 'emotional climate' (Turner, 1982). These include disorientation, hesitation, fear, indecision, humour or failure, which this volume's contributors duly explore. Such climates reveal ambiguity as a *source* of productive tension in life but also a *reaction* to be leveraged through courting, eschewing, tolerating or becoming indifferent to it. This is examined against variables and probabilities subject to forms of knowing and certitude, but also forms of not-knowing and unpredictability, making clear the conundrum people face: of seeking stasis or new directions in life, reinterpreting their existence, or completely restructuring their surroundings. Importantly, such (re)actions are not oppositional but show the varied and contradictory responses people exhibit as they contend with ambiguity. As such, studying ambiguity requires looking to the notion of lived experience and theories of existence and self-cultivation, to which we turn now.

The essence of being and becoming

The idea that experience is embodied, relational and yet located within a world has long guided theoretical intervention into ambiguity to understand the human condition in all its complexity. This was especially so in continental philosophers' attempts to meditate on what it means to understand, respond to and shape a world by delving into the nuanced relationship between experience, meaning, action and outcome (e.g. Sartre, Kierkegaard, de Beauvoir and Merleau-Ponty). Writers sought to move beyond conceiving of ambiguity as merely the *context* or the *content* of life (de Beauvoir, 1962), instead pushing debate toward understanding the place of the human and of human agency within the systems and situations remarked on thus far in this chapter (Das et al., 2014). Anthropologists have, in turn, commented on how such inquiries have produced theoretical insights that edge closer to understanding the complexity of human existence and that mediate between 'generalization' and 'overspecialization' (Jackson, 2014: 27). To this end, philosophical anthropology has drawn on the substance of these writings over the past four decades to deal with existence and experience (Jackson and Piette, 2015). This has ranged from the affective, transitional and intersubjective aspects of experience (Jackson, 2013) to ontological concerns of being and becoming in everyday relation (Throop, 2010).

Anthropologists looked to philosophers such as Merleau-Ponty (2002) and de Beauvoir (1962) who framed ambiguity in complexity and the intricacy of perception and judgement. These philosophical works sought to respond to the tension in literature and fine arts between reality and representation, particularly in light of the ideas of freedom and oppression being explored by their contemporaries (e.g. Sartre and Kierkegaard). *Individual* freedom and experience were key foci, with the person positioned not as a passive observer to the unfolding of life but implicated in a world through action and reflection. This stressed the need to push away from the person 'depicted one-dimensionally, their lives more than allegories and instantiations of political, historical or social process' (Jackson, 2013: 4). Kierkegaard (1985), for instance, noted different stages of becoming: of the individual being bound up in how choice and contingency are handled (see chapters by Alimardanian, Marshall and Rosner). Choice and contingency, however, are based in the capacity 'to know' and 'to anticipate' through reference to an established, collective schema for making sense of the state of life. Episteme, the ways people come to know what they know, grounds knowledge as a historical and philosophical project (Foucault, 1970), but also highlights the individual's capacity to know the world around them (or not) and to act on it (or not). Existence is therefore based in the relationship between experience and knowledge, a focus taken up by Alimardanian on lived experience, action and forms of 'negative' engagement, such as non-action and anti-action.

To expand anthropology's grappling with knowledge, choice, contingency and action, a recent body of scholarship influenced by pragmatism (e.g. Boltanski, 2011) has further developed this focus by positioning certainty and uncertainty as heuristic tools (Dousset, 2022; Carey and Pedersen, 2017).[1] While all knowledge and action are contingent on their spatiotemporal, physical and social environments, this literature distinguishes between, on the one hand, the incapacity to determine whether A or B will happen, are right, appropriate and so on, which has connections with ambiguity through its focus on risk management. On the other hand, this body of research is concerned with a fundamental focus on the 'capacity' to understand what *is* happening, with reference to existing institutional, cultural and social tools (Dousset, 2022). These foci are useful for inquiring into the quality of knowledge and experience in the context of what is ambiguous and cannot easily be determined. This has been a central concern for scholars referencing the nature, origin and effect of ambiguity on making-up one's mind. Choice and contingency highlight the tendency for having things 'both-ways' (Weisbrode, 2012) or neither, or of being in 'two-minds' (Brogaard and Electra, 2021), distilling the place of multiplicity and hesitancy in the production of life (Boltanski, 2014).

While a pragmatist approach would seek, where possible, to resolve ambiguity, a point of difference in the current volume is dwelling on the power inherent in *sitting and being with ambiguity*. Ambiguity is in this way the source of the dynamic between certainty and uncertainty. In *Ethics of Ambiguity* (1962: 8), de Beauvoir notes a tendency to eliminate ambiguity by confronting it with the intention of dispensing with it 'by making oneself pure inwardness or pure externality, by escaping from the sensible world or by being engulfed in it, by yielding to eternity or enclosing oneself in the pure moment'. De Beauvoir's ethics is directed less to moral and ethical ideas and collective accountability than it is toward the development of an individual sensibility for operating within worlds where ambiguity is encountered. It is about building up in sociocultural terms the mind, the person and the collective expectancies of *being*, extending out to self-realisation and self-actualisation. In this volume, this sensibility is primarily explored with reference to the complexities and frictions encountered through a person's engagement with dominant structuring processes. This includes the advances of globalised capitalism in places like Iceland, China and Japan, as well as the ongoing legacies of socialism in Serbia or colonialism in Australia, Aotearoa New Zealand and Sri Lanka.

Humanistic, pragmatic and philosophical engagements with ambiguity are useful, then, in showing the shared yet nuanced nature of ambiguity in life, leading to explorations of how people respond to such phenomena and how individuals base their sense of being and becoming. Importantly, however, it sets the scene for establishing ambiguity as not simply a negative presence in people's lives and worlds, but one of transformation and generativity. When viewed as generative and not simply as a negative, ambiguity highlights the utility of play, drama, humour and notions of the otherwise in knowledge production and meaning-making. In more recent scholarship, the focus on human agency has been expanded to examine ambiguity in human and nonhuman relations, such as with nonhuman actants (Latour, 2005). What remains salient is the open plain ambiguity brings into view across life and in scholarship. As social theorist Donald Levine (1985: 8) points out, 'fleeing from the ambiguities of human life and utterance' fails to consider its multidimensional relation in social science: in a community's life, in ethnographic presence and fieldwork, and in scholarly language.

Toward an anthropology of ambiguity

An anthropology of ambiguity seeks to position the term at the centre of theoretical and ethnographic analysis, seeing ambiguity as both inherent to the essence of being and becoming and a pertinent term of exploration in anthropology – historically and today. Ambiguity is relational in nature, emerging through engagements with self and other (Leistle, 2017), the quality of which is mediated in ethnographic practice and writing by a proximal relation to time and space (Fabian, 1983). Yet sitting and being with ambiguity is challenging given the curious nature that ambiguity can take as being many things at once, and sometimes less than this or nothing at all, to become a feeling, state or phase to be remarked upon by interlocutors.

It is further challenging for ethnographers who contend with what they are seeing in the field (etic perspective), or what interlocutors themselves see (emic). For Rabinow, however, the problem for such anthropological concerns is the need to inquire into what is taking place without deducing it. That is, to come to terms with, but not set aside, what is producing or perpetuating ambiguity. Contemplating this 'requires sustained research, patience, and new concepts, or modified old ones. The purpose is not destruction or deconstruction but a reevaluation; its goal is not reform or revolution but rather a type of remediation' (Rabinow, 2008: 3). In bringing together discrete theoretical and ethnographic encounters with ambiguity, the volume moves across great distances in four continents, bringing together reflections on the persistence of ambiguity in varied lives and lifeways, yet making clear its potency to understanding human life.

The volume is divided into four parts, beginning with Part I, 'Theorising ambiguity'. In Chapter 1, Alimardanian explores the links between lived experience and knowledge, arguing ambiguity is an *essential force of existence* and the source of the dynamic between certainty and uncertainty, through which knowledge and experience are generated. Chapter 2 moves to the interplay between knowledge and contingency. Rosner takes the COVID-19 pandemic in the United States as an example and, while noting the difficulty involved in crisis prediction and management, argues there is utility in embracing 'open-mindedness' to pursue stability. In Chapter 3, complex systems and their ability to provide knowledge surety and consensus are explored by Marshall. He shows how politicians use complexity to *suppress* knotty challenges such as climate change, thereby allowing risk compartmentalisation to take hold. This occurs through a belief in 'the market' to block engagement with the unknown and to deny epistemological limits. The taken-for-granted terms of lived experience, contingency and complexity in this section provide the basis for producing conceptual nuance about ambiguity.

Part II, 'Navigating temporal disruption', explores disruptive phenomena that render time and meaning-making ambiguous. In Chapter 4, Heffernan explores Icelanders' attempts to make sense of a banking collapse after several years of forward-oriented economic growth. Feelings of confusion, ignorance and failure are traced; queer theory is used to show how failure and ignorance were embraced to produce meaning and challenge narratives of 'success'. Puszka's chapter further explores the ambiguous temporalities of chronic disease brought about by policies that immobilise and isolate Australian Indigenous patients. 'Strategic ignorance' is shown to be used by practitioners to control healthcare provision. In response, kin connections help to build patient alliance and wellbeing amid the open-endedness of chronic illness. Chapter 6 then explores the livelihood strategies employed by Bangladeshi *char* islanders impacted by climate change. Hossain shows how the seasons no longer act as stable temporal markers amid increasing weather extremes, affecting labour prospects. Diverse understandings of climate change are developed by local actors to produce meaning.

Part III, 'Imagining an otherwise', explores how ambiguity is manipulated or staged to challenge authorities. Chapter 7 looks to citizenry activism against a 'backward' Serbian state. Steindl-Kopf stresses that not only are protests useful for highlighting government contradictions, but that social movements themselves contain procedural ambiguity and yet are sites of individual and collective identity transformation. Moving to Ecuador, D'Aloia explores in Chapter 8 the development of an economic model that is alternative to capitalism, the Popular Solidarity Economy. The model is premised on building collaborations between those who use it, purporting to 'add value' to their work, though this value is shown to not be well understood. Chapter 9 examines Māori-enforced checkpoints into remote communities in Aotearoa New Zealand during the COVID-19 pandemic. Motivated by their historical vulnerability to introduced disease, activists are shown to exploit the 'plasticity' of the nation-state amid crisis to protect their people, thereby rendering the authority and sovereignty of the state ambiguous. In Chapter 10, Piyarathne analyses satirical cartoons aimed at censuring politicians in Sri Lanka during a moral panic stoked by the country's authoritarian government. While this panic was sparked to divert public attention away from elite impropriety, Piyarathne shows how cartoons offered a rare opportunity for political critique and public calls for reform in a depressed public sphere.

In Part IV, 'Self-realisation amid disjuncture', the individual is the centre of analysis against dominant structuring processes experienced as impinging on identity and belonging. In Chapter 11, Hutchings reflexively engages with the ambiguity of having fair skin while claiming an Indigenous identity. Drawing on racial tensions highlighting the ongoing-ness of colonialism, Hutchings argues that ambiguity of identity can allow for individual and embodied resistances which are explored through literary works, film and magical realism, to disrupt dominant views. In Chapter 12, Hizi examines 'indeterminacy' in person-making practices in contemporary China, focusing on the paradox of shifting ethical standpoints stemming from Confucianism and neoliberal self-help material. Literature and workshops are shown to come up against the 'traditions' of gender, the expectations of filial piety, and the usual course of self-realisation. In Chapter 13, Cabrera Torrecilla explores 'ontological ambiguity' from the incursion of Western imperialism into Japan in the twentieth century. Fiction is paired with cultural analysis to explore temporal disruption and disjuncture of the self amid social and technological change, which Cabrera Torrecilla explores in dreams and the uncanny to understand the effects of self-ambiguity.

The volume culminates in an Editors' Afterword. Reference to literature and creativity is extended following Hutchings' and Cabrera Torrecilla's chapters through recourse to de Beauvoir's and Turner's works on ambiguity in theatre and literature. A recapitulation of the book's major themes and the core takeaways of an anthropology of ambiguity are teased out.

Note

1 Examples include the work of Gerald Bronner, Luc Boltanski, Cyril Lemieux and Laurent Dousset for the French pragmatic approach, in connection with the pragmatist approach in the United States (J. Dewey and his contemporaries).

References

Bailey, F.G. (1963) *Politics and Social Change: Orissa in 1959* (Berkeley, CA: University of California Press).

Benjamin, W. (1999) *The Arcades Project* (Cambridge, MA: Belknap Press).

Boltanski, L. (2014) *Mysteries and Conspiracies: Detective stories, spy novels and the making of modern societies* (London: Polity Press).

Boltanski, L. (2011) *On Critique: A sociology of emancipation* (London: Polity Press).

Brogaard, B. and Electra Gatzia, D., eds (2021) *The Philosophy and Psychology of Ambivalence: Being of two minds* (New York: Routledge).

Carey, M. and Pedersen, M. (2017) 'Introduction: Infrastructures of certainty and doubt', *Cambridge Journal of Anthropology*, 35:2, 18–29.

Das, V., Jackson, M.D., Kleinman, A. and Singh, B. (2014) *The Ground Between: Anthropologists engage philosophy* (Durham, NC: Duke University Press).

De Beauvoir, S. (1962) *The Ethics of Ambiguity* (Secaucus, NJ: Citadel Press).

Durkheim, E. (1995 [1912]) *The Elementary Forms of Religious Life*, trans. K.E. Fields (New York: The Free Press).

Douglas, M. (1986) *Purity and Danger: An analysis of concepts of pollution and taboo* (London: Routledge).

Dousset, L. (2022) 'Invisible agents: Framework for a comparative approach to fundamental uncertainty', *Revue Des Sciences Sociales*, 67, 26–33.

Eriksen, T.H. and Nielsen, F.S. (2001) *A History of Anthropology* (London: Pluto Press).

Espírito Santo, D., Murray, M. and Salinas, P. (2023) 'Ways of not-knowing in neoliberal Chile: Notes towards a dark anthropology', *Social Anthropology*, 31:2, 1–18.

Fabian, J. (1983) *Time and the Other: How anthropology makes its object* (New York: Columbia University Press).

Foucault, M. (1970) *The Order of Things: An archaeology of the human sciences* (London: Tavistock).

Gluckman, M. (1954) *Rituals of Rebellion in South-east Africa* (Manchester: Manchester University Press).

Jackson, M.D. (2014) 'Ajàlá's heads: Reflections on anthropology and philosophy in a West African setting', in V. Das, M. Jackson, A. Kleinman and B. Singh (eds),

The Ground Between: Anthropologists engage philosophy (Durham, NC: Duke University Press), 27–49.

Jackson, M.D. (2013) *Lifeworlds: Essays in existential anthropology* (Chicago, IL: University of Chicago Press).

Jackson, M.D. and Piette, A. (2015) 'Introduction: Anthropology and the existential turn', in M.D. Jackson and A. Piette (eds), *What is Existential Anthropology?* (Oxford: Berghahn), 1–29.

Kapferer, B. (2015) 'Introduction', in L. Meinert and B. Kapferer (eds), *In the Event – Toward an anthropology of generic moments* (Oxford: Berghahn), 1–28.

Kierkegaard, S. (1985) *Fear and Trembling* (London: Penguin).

Knibbe, K. (2014) 'Certainty and uncertainty in contemporary spirituality and Catholicism: Finding proof versus destabilizing certainties in popular religion in the Netherlands', *Social Compass*, 61:4, 537–94.

Latour, B. (2005) *Reassembling the Social: An introduction to actor-network-theory* (Oxford: Oxford University Press).

Leach, E. (1964) 'Anthropological aspects of language: Animal categories and verbal abuse', in E.H. Lenneberg (ed.), *New Directions in the Study of Language* (Cambridge, MA: MIT Press), 23–63.

Leistle, B., ed. (2017) *Anthropology and Alterity: Responding to the other* (London: Routledge).

Lévi-Strauss, C. (1969) *The Raw and the Cooked*, trans. J. Weightman and D. Weightman (London: Penguin).

Levine, D.N. (1985) *The Flight from Ambiguity: Essays in social and cultural theory* (Chicago, IL: University of Chicago Press).

Malinowski, M. (1916) 'Baloma: Spirits of the dead in the Trobriand Islands', *Journal of the Royal Anthropological Institute*, 46, 353–430.

Martínez, F., Frederiksen, M.D. and Puppo, L. (2021) 'Introduction: Welcome to the corners of the peripheral', in F. Martínez, M.D. Frederiksen and L. Puppo (eds), *Peripheral Methodologies: Unlearning, not-knowing, and ethnographic limits* (Abingdon: Routledge), 1–14.

Merleau-Ponty, M. (2002) *The Phenomenology of Perception* (London: Taylor & Francis).

Rabinow, P. (2008) *Marking Time: On the anthropology of the contemporary* (Princeton, NJ: Princeton University Press).

Radcliff-Brown, A.R. (1949) 'A further note on joking relationships', *Journal of the International African Institute*, 19:2, 133–40.

Taussig, M. (1987) *Shamanism, Colonialism, and the Wild Man: A study in terror and healing* (Chicago, IL: University of Chicago Press).

Throop, J. (2010) *Suffering and Sentiment: Exploring the vicissitudes of experience and pain in Yap* (Berkeley, CA: University of California Press).

Turner, V. (1982) *From Ritual to Theatre: The human seriousness of play* (Cambridge, MA: PAJ Publications).

Turner, V. (1969) *The Ritual Process: Structure and anti-structure* (London: Routledge).

van Gennep, A., *The Rites of Passage* (London: Routledge).

Vigh, H. (2008) 'Crisis and chronicity: Anthropological perspectives on continuous conflict and decline', *Ethnos*, 73:1, 5–24.

Weisbrode, K. (2012) *On Ambivalence: The problems and pleasures of having it both ways* (Cambridge, MA: MIT Press).

Werbner, R. (2020) *Anthropology after Gluckman: The Manchester School, colonial and postcolonial transformations* (Manchester: Manchester University Press).

Part I

Theorising ambiguity

1

Ontology and its double: on the nature of ambiguity and lived experience

Mahnaz Alimardanian

Introduction

It has been said that Zoroastrian Iranians, known as Parsis, transferred many sacred Avestan-Pahlavi texts to India between the eighth and tenth centuries CE during their migration after the conquest of Iran by Arab Muslims and the fall of the Sassanid Empire. With the passing of centuries, the texts were still used in religious rituals; some were archived and preserved, and exist today. Ultimately, it was only in recent history that the specific content of some texts was revealed after enduring speculation. A Parsi friend once told me of a family memory which involved the discovery of a number of such ceremonial texts that turned out to be recipes (herbal or culinary), not actually prayers. The texts had been written in Averstan script and treated as sacred for years. The discovery became an entertaining story, with her Moubad brother (a Zoroastrian priest) making jokes about the topic by moving his hands in the air while reciting with ritualistic intonation: 'two spoons of cinnamon; a touch of saffron; then stir well' (repeated).

In this story of speculation and searching for meaning, there is a relationship between ambiguity, knowledge and experience. In any ceremony guided by cooking instructions, Zoroastrian participants being present in a specific space at a particular time in an event involving sanctified fire, purification rituals, aromas of espand (harmala) and sukhar (sandalwood), set to the rhythm of 'sacred' recitation and movement are the elements which incited meaningful experience. Perhaps the texts did provide a kind of 'touch of saffron' in the taste of experience but the semantics of the texts did not affect the spirit of the ceremony. In fact, interpretation of the text was under influence of the heavily contextualised action of *reading* the texts and not their *meaning*. Here, the ceremonial knowledge in question and its transcendental experience survived diaspora, regardless of the ultimate ambiguity surrounding the texts and their sacred meaning. Openness of the texts to interpretation and, as elaborated below, the dependency of knowledge *and* experience, gave the texts new life in this story of exile and diasporic migration.

Experience has always been essential to knowing and understanding. For example, from Sohrevardi's Philosophy of Illumination to Hegel's Phenomenology of Spirit and Jung's Red Book, one finds analytical and methodological engagement with the concept of experience, and with visions, the sensory and dreams being critical as both modes of inquiry and objects of study to develop knowledge. Also, from Comte's positivism to Kierkegaard's existentialism, there is a related issue pertaining to the dialectic of knowledge and experience, whether this experience is reduced to 'neutral' empirical observations or extended to 'personal' feelings.

In the wake of positivism, there has been a protracted scholarly attempt to redefine the position of experience in Western schools of thought by Dilthy, Merleau-Ponty, Husserl, Dewey, James and Schutz (Jackson, 1996; Throop, 2003a). This 'turn' in philosophy, the humanities and the social sciences moved away from absolute truth and objective knowledge toward interdependencies and relativism. It shifted to the idea of 'partial truth' (Clifford, 1986) and 'regimes of truth' (Foucault, 1980), recognising knowledge as grounded in practice and efficacious beliefs constantly in the making. This acknowledges a complicated relationship between knowledge and experience in studies of existence on the events and activities constituting 'being in the world and being with others' (Jackson, 1998; Desjarlais, 1997; Csordas, 1994a). The relationship nowadays is commonly referred to as 'lived and living experience' and recognised as a person's unique knowledge of being and becoming. In turn, it differs from the 'received' wisdom of knowledge, such as the sacred Avestan-Pahlavi texts, instead focusing on the nuanced linkage between knowledge and meaning-making through experience in life.

In order to see the essentiality of lived experience, one could imagine the 'touch of saffron' event otherwise. What if the text and the literal translations survived migration, but not the associated ceremonies? In such a scenario, one wonders how far meaning could continue to have been derived and regenerated from the text without the bodily presence and engagement of selves in full ceremony? Undoubtedly, divine meaning could have continued, and sacred feeling and presence might have been experienced from knowing the meaning of verses, but the outcome would not have been the same. The flow of the ceremony relies on its performativity. Knowledge must be lived, not only perceived, in order to be part of an ordinary and pragmatic ontology rather than a mere archive of information used to express ideas. Any form of belief in life (as meaning, feeling or ethics) is shaped through the flow of knowledge *and* experience as a continuous transformation of one to the other (see Knibbe and Versteeg, 2008). Theorising lived experience in this two-way cycle of 'worldview' and 'life-world', or 'epistemology' and 'ontology', is something of a challenge and I acknowledge that any attempt in essence is a process of minimising the complex.

In this chapter, I discuss how ambiguity is inherent in the two-way cycle of knowledge and experience and essential to meaning-making. Ambiguity is the source and force of dynamism between certainty and uncertainty and fundamental to the formation of a practical and realistic version of life.

I heard the 'touch of saffron' story while analysing ethnographic data from my PhD fieldwork (2009–13) in another context, with Bandjalang people in southeast Australia. My research project was on a local belief system constituting the relationship between humans, spirits, and ancestral land and waters and how this informs and influences everyday life and decisions. Similar to the 'touch of saffron' story, ambiguity and how it affects the quality or form of lived experience was the core of my ethnography. Ambiguity was manifested in knowing and not-knowing within a chain of certainties and uncertainties. In Bandjalang Country, I witnessed how ambiguity is mediated and navigated in bridging Indigenous and non-Indigenous worlds, the spiritual and material, and the visible (human) and invisible (spirit) realms, none of which were necessarily clear-cut. Ambiguity emerged out of competing and contradictory epistemic views and ontologies of proper action; the result of colonisation whereby knowledge loss and preservation were of concern. But importantly, ambiguity was at the heart of cultural practice when it came to Bandjalang spiritual knowledge and experience and the openness of knowledge to wider interpretation.

The importance of ambiguity resonated with my previous study (2003–05) of a healing ceremony, popular among Iranian Turkmen, where I was interested in the performative elements of healing practices. The ceremony created a space in between affliction and cure, human and spirit worlds, and used dramatic qualities to deliver healing and reinforce local healing philosophy. Surprisingly, the running force of the ceremony was embedded in the enigma of an opaque and mysterious dialogue between healer and invisible spirit world, not the quality of the performance. The fundament of ambiguity in the Bandjalang world as the poetics of being, on the one hand, and the forced colonial reality on the other, as well as the place of ambivalence in the Turkmen healing performance and outcomes, led me to think about the nature and manifestations of ambiguity. My theoretical reflections in this chapter on lived experience and on the presence of ambiguity as an essential force of existence similar to time or space, are driven out of the fundamental nature of ambiguity in Bandjalang spiritual life and the Turkmen healing world. They are further developed with reference to my applied anthropological work during the last ten years where I have engaged with Australian Indigenous communities negotiating their land and cultural rights and interests in legal and development contexts, and with community members in trauma and healing-informed social projects.

The ethnographic vignettes I refer to throughout have led me to see that the cyclicality of knowledge–experience is a process of being and becoming in the midst of lived ambiguities. By illustrating these ideas, I bring together scholarship on existential thought and humanistic anthropology, especially around knowledge, experience and action. I revisit the work of the Manchester School and their emphasis on the study of processes and attention to societal tension, particularly the later work of Turner (1987, 1986) on performance and experience. I model a detailed and nuanced version of a two-way cycle of knowledge and experience by focusing on the nature of lived experience and also on *negative* engagements with the world. My level of analysis is person-centred. It does not engage with the processes of influence driven by history, power dynamics, structural (dis)advantage, or socio-political constructs shaping personal and collective experiences. By deploying an existential and phenomenological frame of analysis, not only do I stress the critical role of ambiguity in the regeneration of ontology, but I see ambiguity as a true elementary feature of what I refer to as ontology's double: non-ontology.

The phenomenon of lived experience

Broad projections of experience as thinking and feeling and extending out to emotion, action or will open the notion up to various interpretations and analytical perspectives (Throop, 2005, 2009, 2003a,b). The framework that I use is one covering pre-objective, objective and subjective modes of experience (see Csordas, 1994a,b). This involves the process of experiencing, comprehending and communicating experience. Although access to others' experiences is commonly through narrative (Mattingly, 1998), this should not divert attention from the senses (Howes, 2014; Stoller, 1989), affect (Rosaldo, 1984; Leavitt, 1996), and embodiment and action (Korom, 2013; Laderman and Roseman, 1996). Intersubjectivity itself is not limited to dialogue but is articulated as interaction. Experience requires embodiment to be understood and comprehended motivations to occur (both subjectively and objectively). Experience cannot be analysed without attention to the complex mediations between mind and body, thought and action, presence and absence, belief and practice, and affect and decision. In the 'touch of saffron' story, the texts separated from their living context wouldn't survive without being put into practice. In the same way, the Turkmen healing experience was performative and Bandjalang spirit encounter was entangled with the sensory.

In theorising performance and experience, Turner (1985, 1986, 1987) defines experience as living through events, and identifies a kind of flow which links experience to the performance in a spiralling process, asserting that meaning and feeling are generated in this process. In developing the concept of social drama, he emphasises the sequence of experience, and the processual attributes. He explains the relation between expression and experience as structuring and restructuring one another dynamically and stresses the complexity of this dynamic, bringing the elements of being, time and order together. Turner's model is not merely applicable to experience in highly performative and collective formats, such as social dramas. For the individual, one side of the equation is all one knows, deems worthy of knowing, or believes to know (i.e. expression in its full potential, including reasoning and communication). On the other side is what happens and takes place with the direct, wishful, decisional, or incidental and receptive involvement of the self (i.e. experience in its full potential, including passive and active modes of engagement). One's competence and performance work hand in hand to shape the experience of being 'present' in and to the world, and sharing the world with others.[1] After all, experience, as Bruner (Turner and Bruner, 1986: 16) highlighted in *The Anthropology of Experience,* 'is not just passive acceptance but rather an active, volatile, creative force'.

Life experience is an infinite spiral of knowledge and competence that transforms into active and passive modes of experience. Figure 1.1 illustrates how layers of knowledge and competence regenerate each other on one side, and how active and passive experiences are linked on the other. In the complexity of living and being present in the world, some experiences are felt as 'subjection' through feeling a lack of control over what is happening while others are marked by a sense of control and autonomy. The difference was evidenced in Bandjalang's navigation of a shared human and spirit world where spirit encounters could happen anytime due to the spirit world being autonomous, capricious and immanent in the world at large. As the existential 'wheel' turns, knowledge and experience shift in relation to each other at the junction of affect and ethics, where interpretation, sense and meaning arise in negotiating with others or in one's chain of thoughts and memories. Elements of this nuanced and detailed dynamics between knowledge and experience were recognisable in both of my ethnographic studies. The Turkmen healing ceremony was a scene of interaction, acting and being acted upon between participants, healer, and spirits where the senses and ideas about wellbeing and relief from affliction were constantly in the making. Daily life in Bandjalang Country was entangled by monitoring events to identify spiritual incidents. The sensory and affective experience were the main ways of achieving spiritual knowledge.

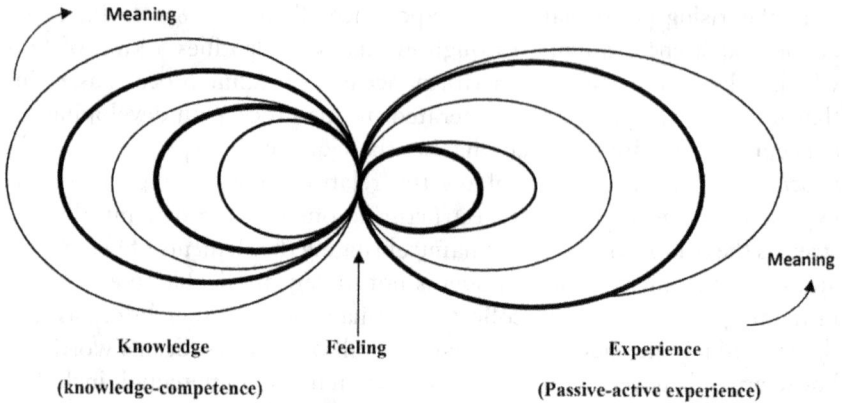

Figure 1.1 A sketch of existence as outlined in the text

An accumulation of knowledge and competence could, theoretically, be informed by an infinity of worldviews, but its relevance and meaningfulness in the flow of existence are based on transformations of knowledge and experience, competence and performance. In other words, its 'truthiness' is pragmatic. Furthermore, life is a permanent seeking of balance between passive and active modes, reflexive and habitual grounds. Knowledge covers the explanation of life, incidents and events, and competence informs performance and generates action and counteraction in life. The chain of actions and reactions creates experience and contributes to knowledge formation.

However, the reality is always more complex. The relationship between knowledge and experience in general, and knowledge and practice in particular, is neither fully ordered nor coherent due to the nature of human life and the human condition: a piece of information might be put into a fully improvised act in a meaningful, inspirational moment of faith and trust, or an anticipated reaction to some particular incident might be ignored in a moment of doubt and hesitation. Somewhere between these extreme situations the circulation of knowledge and experience happens relatively as the curves are not balanced across this hypothetical spiral. Such gaps, amplifications or tensions across knowledge and experience are illustrated in Michael Jackson's (1996: 2) phenomenological analysis of life where he stresses that 'the knowledge whereby one lives is not necessarily identical with the knowledge whereby one explains life'. Richard Schechner (2003) refers to this in his theory of performance as an ambivalence between the composed and the spontaneous. Notably, both my Bandjalang and Turkmen interlocutors were referring to knowledge and experience in interchangeable fashion. Their expressions of life showcased similar traits of complexity across expectation, expression and experience. In my fieldnotes, such complexities were surely not just appearing in the mysterious moments of leaving the self in the hands of a healer or feeling the presence of an ancestral being at a sacred site. Improvising life across inconsistencies, incomprehension or unpredictability were immanent in sense- and meaning-making and those experiences were expressed through fear, prudence, hope or excitement.

Figure 1.1 is not necessarily regenerated within a full simultaneous flow either. There are, for example, 'absences' of body or mind in the chain of thoughts and practices (see Leder, 1990), and there are disruptions caused by external factors or internal residues like memories of past experiences. Moreover, our experiences are the outcome of a dynamic relationship between circumstances over which we 'feel' in control or not. Additionally, certain experiences are only validated as sources of knowledge if a consensus with others is reached. This was significantly the case in the Bandjalang way of navigating ancestral land and waters. There, any sense- or meaning-making was a collective effort.

Importantly, there is also the necessity of balance in the struggle for being amid ups and downs, and between possibilities and impossibilities. Balance as such becomes a situation to move toward rather than being a point to reach. I saw this search at the heart of Turkmen healing philosophy and practices to maintain personal and social wellbeing where participation in a ceremony was a chance to defeat negative forces impacting wellbeing (including malevolent spirits). In one sense, balance refers to an epistemological and ontological dialectic; in a related sense, it refers to existential continuity. Taking all the nuances into account, the study of lived experience involves both passive and active qualities in their incidental and decisional formats from sensory, affective and performative experiences. The latter is a combination of active or controlled modes involving socioculturally driven habits, practices or inspired actions in both positive and negative modes.

Negative engagement and its analytical value

Being in the world is an indeterminacy of living knowledge and of experience, with a grand number of possibilities and contingencies shaping each other and shifting in moments of certainty and uncertainty. The spiral of actualities in a particular life-world arises out of an infinity of potentialities, and existence makes sense in an interplay of knowledge and ability, acting and being acted upon, emerging from a ground of limits and affordances (for example, see Edith Stein's (2009) philosophy of being). Also, the dialectics of change and stability, and the struggle to maintain balance and continuity on a day-to-day basis, take shape partly through individual decisions and personal will and partly through whatever lies beyond them, and therefore out of a person's control. This volition relates to unselected options as well as selected ones (see Jackson, 2008). A variety of imposed historical, social or political restrictions, as well as culturally sedimented taboos and prohibitions, push out the spiral of knowledge and experience. This means that the ability to understand exists alongside one's inability to understand. On the one hand, there are imperatives, possibilities and active presences; on the other hand, there are contingencies, impossibilities and passive presences. Alongside positive and active modes of existence, negative and passive modes play important roles in configuring the boundaries of people's capacities and potentialities. Sometimes, limitations serve to make sense of life, so that being-in-the-world is lived through dismissing prohibited actions, anti-actions and non-actions. This leads to a flow of faith and hesitation, improvisation and perplexity which eventually all come to shape the borders of experience.

People usually find themselves at the centre of events as subjects, actors and decision-makers. From the actor's point of view, an active experience may be recognised in terms of personal decisions or reactions. Active experiences are ensembles of action and its opposite which are both pragmatically connected to daily life. Anti-actions, non-actions and actions all give meaning to events and incidents. There exist actions that one is encouraged or obligated to perform and actions that one is prohibited from performing. There are actions one does habitually, or decides to do creatively and thoughtfully, and there are decisions to do nothing. Also, there is a passive mode of response to circumstances as well as an active mode. Accordingly, silences, prohibitions and avoidance are as critical as active engagements in generating a meaningful continuity of being. Existence is a flow of transition between potentiality and actuality, between activity and passivity, but also between positivity and negativity. If living 'is to strike a balance between being an actor and being acted upon' (Jackson, 2008: x), it also strikes a balance between action and counteraction, acting and not acting, as indicated in Figure 1.2.

The importance of negative engagement was perceptible in Bandjalang spiritual life where spiritual safety by protecting one from dangerous or unwelcome spirit encounters through, for example, intimate, close engagements with ancestral lands and waters dictated the quality of actions undertaken or recommended counteractions. Importantly, counteractions were often the subject of collective consensus in contrast to actions which might be the subject of contestation if shared with others. Turkmen healing

Passive Experience

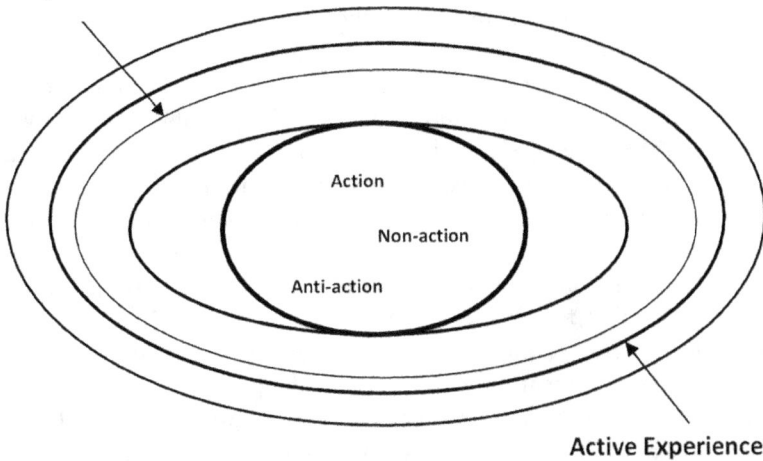

Figure 1.2 A sketch of experience

also created a space of transformation by breaking some of the ordinary norms and introducing novel ideas about accepted practice during the ceremony. A Turkmen patient might not find the reason behind their affliction by visiting a healer or be certain of being cured, but they would receive a clear instruction, entailing a list of actions and counteractions to adhere to after the ceremony.

If, apart from perceived certainty, a life-world is also a scene of uncertainty (Racin and Schlesinger, 2022; Samimian-Darash and Rabinow, 2015), then grappling with perplexity, hesitation, fear, failure, disorientation and indecision is a key part of lived experience (described by Das (2014: 238) as 'fragility of action'), along with any preservation of order and balance, or management of risk or danger (Douglas, 2010; Murray, 2009; Parkin, 1985). How individuals make sense of and navigate their lives is not just about what they do, are encouraged or forced to do, but also about what they do not do, do not want to do, are advised not to do, and are prohibited from doing. There is thus a complex interrelationship between actions and counteractions, and it is important to focus analytically on, for example, avoidance or prudence. It is similarly important to understand how one may 'over(re)act' – that is, follow some rules in a highly restrictive way, emphasising absolute imperatives, both positive and negative ('musts' and 'mustn'ts', 'shoulds' and 'shouldn'ts') – or how one may ignore reacting to a circumstance and 'reasonably' respond passively. Anti-actions and non-actions illustrate how 'negative embodiment' shadows, yet also completes, its positive counterpart.

Spiritual life in Bandjalang Country was mediated through positive and negative forms of engagement with the spirit world. Avoiding a certain part of Country or not travelling to a nearby town after sunset were important matters of discussion, sense- and meaning-making. Similarly, Turkmen patients were so attentive and present to the prohibitions. In my applied work, strategic silence and disengagement have always been meaningful tactics in negotiating Indigenous land and cultural rights and interests. Applying trauma and healing-informed approaches to any social project also requires a careful attention to details which may or should not be verbalised. As ethnographers and social analysts, it is sometimes difficult to keep in mind that human agency encompasses and embraces passivity as well as activity, and positivity as well as negativity, and that both modes of engagement articulate practical options. Accordingly, silences, suspensions, ignorance and absence or sense of failure have analytical value in understanding people's worlds and conditions of being.

Counteractions and negative forms of engagement are fundamental in the formation of lived experience. People's process of reasoning is not merely influenced by and composed in the intertwinement of (re)actions but has roots in the invisible presence of counteractions. At one level this is about how anti- and non-actions are perceived, approached, interpreted and regenerated into action and counteraction and, on another level, how the *qualia* of 'negative engagement' feeds into the circulation of lived experience to and from knowledge, and how it influences and sustains the reproduction of a certain way of being in the world. In broader terms, this *qualia* is also featured in what I call ontology's double: non-ontology.

Ambiguity and ordinary pragmatism

In making sense of life, there are circles of knowledge that might not cover an event sufficiently to identify it, or information may arise which is not practical or directly related to lived experience. There might be actions which cannot be followed under particular conditions, or there may be moments when doing nothing is the preferred option. In fact, the relativity and flexibility of these situations represent an open space of improvisation, autonomy, will and negotiation. This suggests that a degree of ambiguity is fundamental in the circulation of knowledge to and from experience and regeneration of meaning and thoughts to perceive *reality* as a continuous narration of existence. The open space is where one finds revelation or perplexity, leading to various versions of decisional experience and risk management. Ordinary pragmatism as a practical, sensible and realistic response to the world reduces tension and creates cohesiveness in life. This can include both resolving and embracing ambiguity.

Being in the world and attending to life is a collage of prioritised, ignored or hybridised options and choices, contingencies and probabilities under the constant presence of ambiguity. There is an ongoing dynamism across certainty and uncertainty in ontology, and ambiguity is the moving force behind this dynamism. The dynamism of certainty and uncertainty is a process which keeps the two-way cycle of knowledge and experience alive. There is a certitude in this dynamism that at least one or some of the possibilities, options, outcomes or interpretations in any circumstance are fully or partially 'true' with a degree of tolerance for some 'reasonable' contradiction. As long as this is the case, knowledge and experience remain relevant and can explain the world. From the most ordinary to the most exceptional circumstances, ambiguity flows into life by forms of opacity, enigma, indetermination or unpredictability. Ambiguity in lived experience is the quality of engaging with opacity and enigma and dealing with a potential that none or all possibilities, contingencies or interpretations can be true or validated, even contradicting ones.

As taken up by Rosner (this volume), experience is always engaged in a chain of contingencies and consequences within a cycle of (re)actions which gives rise to a flow of events. In the Turkmen approach to health, the ambiguity in healing meant that for seeking cure and relief of affliction, one could choose among a series of options from visiting a medical or herbal medicine doctor to religious or traditional healer. These options are all accessible to Turkmen people, with one of the options fully or partially curing a malady probable. On the other hand, there is a potential that none of the options would work but there is always virtue in trying different options and living with hope and despair in search for improving health. Similarly, any Bandjalang spirit encounter was open to various interpretations from experiencing an illusion to being hunted randomly by a ghost, encountering a local spirit or nonhuman being or being visited by an ancestral being. Living the Bandjalang way meant that any of the above could be true, subject to the experience being shared with others and interpreted accordingly. There was also a chance that the process of meaning-making might remain unfinished and the spirit encounter become an unresolved issue. Nonetheless, there is always a virtue in settling in and being with perplexity in the spiritual lived experience.

Ambiguity's manifestations and projections like paradox and contradiction, or absence and deficiency, crack the walls of certitude and shape the existential dynamism across certainties and uncertainties. Nonetheless, a degree of balance is continuously rendered in this process amid the dynamics of certainty and uncertainty and maintaining the stability of a life-world regardless of paradoxes or contradictions. In other words, ontological ambiguities are filtered through pragmatism to create meaning and continuity. In the absence of equilibrium, if disruption and disjuncture in the spiral of epistemology and ontology reach an unrecoverable point, the inconsistencies may not be easily reconciled to create consistency and order. In such a case, *reality* may no longer make sense.

In the spectrum of being and becoming, or transitions and transformations, quotidian life is familiar with the occurrence of minor uncertainties as a multiplicity of interpretations or outcomes depending on one's living conditions. However, these are the 'atypical' events referred to by Kapferer (2015), and explored in the introductory chapter of this volume, which burst forth causing uncertainties. Sometimes events may cause fundamental interruptions and create a crisis of meaning or ethics and pose questions about openness and closed-mindedness (Rosner in this volume) or the logic and reasoning behind critical decisions (Marshall in this volume). This is where the ideal world may collapse in the face of crisis, realities may intertwine or confront one another, new visions may arise, or old ones may persist. On that front, both Bandjalang and Turkmen were responding to tensions and inconsistencies by accommodating alternative worldviews and expanding the spectrum of possibilities and options to keep the dynamic of certainty and uncertainty alive.

In light of the importance of negative forms of engagement[2] and balance within the dynamics of certainty and uncertainty, the attunement, entanglement or becoming, as being open to the world (Throop, 2018), is only fully analysed if it is considered in its relationship to being closed to the world or the world being closed to one. From dis-trust to dis-ability, from phobias to social panic, from vernacular taboos to suppressing rules of a political system, all can shape one's being-in-the-world in particular ways but not in others. Meaning, feeling, reflection and affect flow into life through both openness and 'un-openness' to the world, subject to circumstances and living conditions. This means that the relationship in the triangle of action, non-action and anti-action is ethnographically important in dealing with the human condition and dynamics of lived experience. Analysis of any circumstance or form of encounter is similarly based on what 'is' simply 'not present' and absent from the scene of action and sequence of events. In other words, lived experience emerges out of a nexus of potencies that is *accessible* to the individuals, but this pool of options and possibilities is regenerated in relation to limitation and constraints which can be manifested as negative engagement (counteractions) or a lack of presence (absence). The limitations often work as the point of reference to form opinion and to put things into perspective, evaluate self-experience, to engage with others and 'make sense' of the world and the known *reality*.

In fact, the critical force of negative engagement feeds into the knowledge and potency of facing the world. This is where I aim to bring in the idea of non-ontology as the shadow of ontology. Our perception of a 'possible' world extends back into our imagination of an impossible world (lost, forbidden or non-existent). Non-ontology defines the limitations or boundaries of pragmatism, potency and possibility. This may entail parallel or alternative ways of being which are non-conventional to the life-world of an ontology, and therefore are discredited, or classified as false or *unrealistic*. It could be all that won't be formalised or articulated according to the principles of one's existence and its associated conventional exceptions. It could be expanded to anything that is not recognised under certain paradigms as universals, like time or spatial being. It can also be things we believe we don't know, relying on future knowledge for demystification. Non-ontology is a complex construct and paradoxically it could be chaotic and random. It is composed of various conditions from ontological loss as a matter of voluntary or imposed change associated with time to the emergence of what is known and perceived as otherness or an otherwise. It involves exotica and phobia, or dream, fantasy and illusion (for example, see Cabrera Torrecilla, Piyarathne and Hizi in this volume). Non-ontology feeds into the reasoning process and vice versa. While ontology and its double are both infinite in their contingencies and probabilities, they are finite as being limited to one another, and to the continuum of dynamics between knowledge-potency and performance-experience.

In both Bandjalang and Turkmen worlds, spiritual and healing beliefs were under the influence of non-ontology. Absence and loss were critical in making sense of experience. A collective idea of highly performative Turkmen healing ceremonies of the past was in the mind of participants when attending the ceremony, completing their imagination of the healing experience. Also, a collectively perceived and referred to as the loss of Bandjalang knowledge and old ways of being continuously informed the interpretation of spiritual experience. Ideas or dreams of others' way of being in contrast or in association to the Turkmen or Bandjalang ways were highly influential in putting a situation into perspective and responding to it. The actual and possible worlds were received and perceived in entanglement with an 'otherwise'.

Humans do not make sense of their worlds by defining them against an infinite 'senseless world occasioned by purely undifferentiated existence' (Seligman and Weller, 2012: 22) but a sensible world occasioned by whatever is imaginable, thinkable but not liveable. The finitude of ordinary pragmatism and lived experience is crafted out of this complex. Significantly, when the dynamics of certainty and uncertainty, and the associated *reality* or familiar world, are disrupted, what is going to be replaced is not determined by non-ontology but is limited to the dynamics of ontology and its double. At the core of the dynamics between a possible (ontology) and an impossible (non-ontology) and becoming(s) there is the elementary force of ambiguity. From an ethnographic or methodological point of view, ambiguity may seem too abstract to be considered as a critical parameter in sociocultural or humanistic analysis, but in fact attending to ambiguity means paying attention to nuances and giving analytical credit to what is not observable from negative engagement, deficiency and absence to hope and despair, fear and courage, improvisation, hesitation or perplexity. The Zoroastrians' world in exile was as much the product of living in the current world as it was of what was left behind in the Iranian world and perceptions about what was carried to the new world or not. The touch of saffron story may be just a family joke about faith and knowledge contradiction or the fragility of meaning and perceptions. While there is an ambiguity in the 'truthiness' of the story, nonetheless this is a 'story' of being and sitting with ambiguity.

Conclusion

Reflecting on the touch of saffron story and Bandjalang and Turkmen lifeways, the question remains how it is possible to fully analyse human agency and social systems and processes without recognising that the constructed world is in constant association with its counterpart. The criticality of the interrelationship between two things (ontology and non-ontology) is not merely a matter of semiotic or hermeneutic analysis of existence and is not reducible to a binary or dichotomy. This is the matter of lived experience, of being in the world, as it is lived amid ambiguity. Any personal journey of hope and despair and any change and reform in sociocultural, political or knowledge systems are shaped by these dynamics.

Uncertainty is always definable in relation to what an individual or collective feels it knows and expects about the world. If the outcomes, consequences or flow of events are not in accordance with a prescribed order or recognisable familiarities and timespans, then incertitude emerges against and alongside certitude. There is an asymmetric, dependent relation between the two and between the possible world and the impossible world; where the meaning, ethics and sense of being in the world are continuously created. What is beyond is not just a blank canvas on which realities are constructed.

Ambiguity is both perceived through and created by paradox, contradiction, absence, and one's experience of time; and it is manifested or projected through features like improvisation, disengagement, silence or suspension and could be wrapped in hesitation, doubt, fear, hope, ignorance or anger. Nevertheless, ambiguity is found squarely within none of the above but is the vital force of constructing and deconstructing worlds, creating and destroying existence, and composing and decomposing realities, or truths. By its nature, ambiguity creates a field of openness, timelessness and plasticity in which the dynamics across knowledge and experience, certainty and uncertainty, and ontology and non-ontology emerges.

While this may seem analytically intangible it is in fact predominantly a shift in framing social enquiry to consider ambiguity and negative engagement systematically. This shift not only puts forward analytical themes such as equilibrium, paradox, perplexity, hesitation, avoidance and absence in relation to modes of action and being in the world, but it also looks at anti- and non-action as *qualia*, not merely as an absence of action.

Notes

1 The importance of performance and action has been at the centre of attention in phenomenological study of religious rituals (e.g. William Sax; Thomas Csordas), healing experience (e.g. Robert Desjarlais; Edward Schieffelin) and medical practices (e.g. Nancy Scheper-Hughes; Richard Selzer) as well as in performative studies (e.g. Bruce Kapferer; Richard Schechner; William O. Beeman) and the general treatments of practice and action as critical concepts in social theories (e.g. Sherry Ortner; Pierre Bourdieu).

2 It is worth mentioning that the analytical value of negative was explored in different ways by philosophers such as Derrida and Deleuze in their conceptualisation of difference which is referred to as Philosophy of Difference by François Laruelle. There has also been a long tradition of applying negation to worshipping practices by focusing on the attributes and qualities which are not applicable to the divine as a way to achieve transcendental experience. In the apophatic tradition, as the counterpart of cataphatic, one aims to perceive the divine (Truth) and the *presence* of the divine through modes of negativity and *absence*, stressing what the 'truth' is not.

References

Clifford, J. (1986) 'Partial truth', in James Clifford and George E. Marcus (eds), *Writing Cultures: The Poetics and Politics of Ethnography* (Berkeley: University of California Press).

Csordas, T.J. (1994a) *The Sacred Self: A Cultural Phenomenology of Charismatic Healing* (Berkeley and Los Angeles: University of California Press).

Csordas, T.J. (1994b) *Embodiment and Experience: The Existential Ground of Culture and Self* (Cambridge: Cambridge University Press).

Das, V. (2014) 'Action, Expression, and Everyday Life: Recounting Household Events', in Das, V., Jackson, M.D., Kleinman, A. and Singh, B. (eds), *The Ground*

Between: Anthropologists Engage Philosophy (Durham, NC: Duke University Press), 279–306.

Desjarlais, R. (1997) *Shelter Blues: Sanity and Selfhood among the Homeless* (Philadelphia: University of Pennsylvania Press).

Douglas, M. (2010) *Risk Acceptability According to the Social Sciences* (London: Routledge).

Foucault, M. (1980) *Power/Knowledge: Selected Interviews and Other Writings, 1972–1977*, ed. Colin Gordon (New York: Pantheon Books).

Howes, D. and Classen, C. (2014) *Ways of Sensing: Understanding the Senses in Society* (London and New York: Routledge).

Jackson, M. (2008) *Existential Anthropology: Events, Exigencies, and Effects* (New York: Berghahn Books).

Jackson, M. (1998) *Minima Ethnographica: Intersubjectivity and the Anthropological Project* (Chicago, IL: University of Chicago Press).

Jackson, M. (1996) 'Introduction', in Michael Jackson (ed.), *Things As They Are: New Directions in Phenomenological Anthropology* (Bloomington and Indianapolis: Indiana University Press).

Kapferer, B. (2015) 'Introduction', in L. Meinert and B. Kapferer (eds), *In the Event: Toward an Anthropology of Generic Moments* (New York: Berghahn).

Knibbe, K. and Versteeg, P. (2008) 'Assessing Phenomenology in Anthropology: Lessons from the study of religion and experience', *Critique of Anthropology,* 28:1, 47–62.

Korom, F.G., ed. (2013) *The Anthropology of Performance: A Reader* (Chichester: Wiley-Blackwell).

Laderman C. and Roseman, M., eds (1996) *The Performance of Healing* (New York: Routledge).

Leavitt, J. (1996) 'Meaning and feeling in the anthropology of emotions', *American Ethnologist,* 23:3, 514–39.

Leder, D. (1990) *The Absent Body* (Chicago, IL: University of Chicago Press).

Mattingly, C. (1998) *Healing Dramas and Clinical Plots: The Narrative Structure of Experience* (Cambridge: Cambridge University Press).

Murray, T. (2009) 'Reflections on the ethnography of fear', *Anthropologica,* 51:2, 363–6.

Parkin, D. (1985) 'Reason, emotion and the embodiment of power', in Joanna Overing (ed.), *Reason and Morality* (London; New York: Tavistock Publications).

Racin, C. and Schlesinger, E., eds (2022) '[In]certitude', *In Analysis,* 6:1, 1–120.

Rosaldo, M. (1984) 'Toward an anthropology of self and feeling', in Richard A. Shweder and Robert A. LeVine (eds), *Culture Theory: Essays on Mind, Self, and Emotion* (Cambridge: Cambridge University Press).

Samimian-Darash, L. and Rabinow, P. (2015) *Modes of Uncertainty: Anthropological Cases* (Chicago, IL: University of Chicago Press).

Schechner, R. (2003) *Performance Theory* (Oxford: Routledge).

Seligman, A. and Weller, R.P. (2012) *Rethinking Pluralism: Ritual, Experience, and Ambiguity* (New York: Oxford University Press).

Stein, E. (2009) *Potency and Act: Studies toward a Philosophy of Being*, ed. L. Gelber and Romaeus Leuven OCD, trans. W. Redmond (Washington, DC: ICS Publications).

Stoller, P. (1989) *The Taste of Ethnographic Things: The Senses in Anthropology* (Philadelphia: University of Pennsylvania Press).

Throop, C.J. (2018) 'Being open to the world', *HAU: Journal of Ethnographic Theory*, 8:1–2, 197–210.

Throop, C.J. (2009) 'Intermediary varieties of experience', *Ethnos*, 74:4, 535–58.

Throop, C.J. (2005) 'Hypocognition, a "sense of the uncanny," and the anthropology of ambiguity: Reflections on Robert I. Levy's contribution to theories of "experience" in anthropology', *Ethos*, 33:4, 499–511.

Throop, C.J. (2003a) 'Articulating experience', *Anthropological Theory*, 3:2, 219–41.

Throop, C.J. (2003b) 'Minding experience: An exploration of the concept of "experience" in the early French anthropology of Durkheim, Lévy-Bruhl and Lévi-Strauss', *Journal of the History of the Behavioral Sciences*, 39:4, 365–82.

Turner, V. (1987) *The Anthropology of Performance* (New York: PAJ Publications).

Turner, V. (1986) 'Dewey, Dilthey, and drama: An essay in the anthropology of experience', in Victor Turner and Edward M. Bruner (eds), *The Anthropology of Experience*, Urbana and Chicago: University of Illinois Press), 33–44.

Turner, V. (1985) *On the Edge of the Bush: Anthropology as Experience*, ed. Edith L. B. Turner (Tucson: University of Arizona Press).

Turner, V. and Bruner E.M., eds (1986) *The Anthropology of Experience* (Urbana and Chicago: University of Illinois Press).

2

Ambiguity and catastrophe: crises of understanding in the age of COVID-19

David J. Rosner

Introduction

This chapter has been written in the middle of the COVID-19 pandemic, a time in which a deep sense of fear and apprehension has entered collective consciousness. In the United States, the focus of this chapter, the pandemic posed significant threats to healthcare and social unity, leading to questions about how people ought to collectively respond and protect one another, but also how people should understand and make sense of disruptive events (Roitman, 2022). Over one million Americans died of COVID-19 between January 2020 and December 2022. On the financial front, March 2020 started with the three worst Dow Industrial Average point drops in US history: a 7.79 per cent drop of the Dow on 9 March 2020, a 9.99 per cent drop on 12 March 2020, and a 12.9 per cent drop on 16 March 2020 (see Frazier, 2021). For Americans, this cavalcade of large-scale death and ever worsening financial chaos suddenly revealed the world as profoundly uncertain, with no predictable end to this chaos in sight. Taking as its starting point the social, economic and health implications of the pandemic in the United States, this chapter examines the crisis of understanding (*aporia*) experienced as part of this multifaceted emergency and response.

The telos of the mind consists of making sense out of impossibly complex worlds. But often, as is the case with the pandemic, we are challenged to make sense out of the world *as it has suddenly revealed itself*, defined by a fundamental sense of uncertainty. This chapter is chiefly concerned with the knowledge practices and traditions that structure and support knowledge surety amid intense change. By examining how the particular culture of the United States has gone about this, we can better understand catastrophe and its disruptions in and of themselves and extrapolate this understanding beyond the present COVID-19 moment. The Manchester School of anthropology was concerned with notions of disruption and change, examined through the extended case study methodology. The pandemic represents the kind of fracturing of order and the threat of disorder that was at the heart of Mancunian anthropology. Indeed, in our time, many people are faced with continuous dynamics of disruption and unpredictability that were also characteristic of the postwar years of the twentieth century when anthropology was firmly becoming a discipline. Kapferer (2005: 87) reminds us how Gluckman's guiding methodology 'marks out the domains of the complexity and flux of social life and becomes the means for entering within them so that they reveal the forces that are engaged in the generation and production of such complexity and flux'. It is through understanding how complexity bears upon regularly practised life that disruption and its attendant changes can be understood and, following the work of Turner (1969), be potentially reconciled.

Practitioners of the Manchester School were quick to caution against 'denying structure while overdetermining the subject' with reference to modernist philosophical thought (Kapferer, 2004:151). I argue, however, that there is merit in exploring the philosophical underpinnings of the thinking subject in light of the upheavals that have been experienced with the pandemic, which have made knowledge of life and the future unclear. Ambiguity now appears to structure experience and characterise the mental grappling with what has come before and what will come next. Moreover, this chapter will also consult several modernist texts for inspiration and guidance. I believe it is valuable to consult these sources in this connection precisely because many such texts fundamentally defined modernity in the specific terms of radical change and contingency, basic features of what people have undergone during the pandemic. Through my exploration of modernist and contemporary texts about ambiguity, I argue that *open-endedness* ought to be part of attempts to understand ambiguity, demonstrating the role of contingency in daily life as people set about trying to reassemble their life-worlds after catastrophe. The chapter will discuss the interrelation and implications of the concepts of uncertainty, contingency and ambiguity – not only to help formulate a deeper appreciation of the crisis of understanding brought about by the pandemic, but to assist with the difficult task of finding a way out of catastrophe to a state of renewal, resilience and, hopefully, wisdom.

Uncertainty, contingency and ambiguity

This chapter is an exploration in philosophical anthropology (Jackson, 2012), which explicitly and directly explores the existential aspects of human life that all human beings must confront, regardless of time, place, gender, culture or ethnicity (e.g. what it means to be human in all its complexity). Uncertainty, contingency and ambiguity are among these conditions.

Of course, while these conditions are always present in the background of how people past and present understand and navigate the world, they are processed with reference to cultural specificity. Moreover, they move to the forefront of consciousness most forcefully during times of catastrophe, such as COVID-19. To grapple with these conditions, this chapter first provides a definitional framing of uncertainty, contingency and ambiguity to better understand these concepts in and of themselves. It then grounds these concepts in a discussion of the particular manner in which the pandemic was understood and responded to in the context of the United States.

Uncertainty, which has revealed itself in a number of ways during the pandemic, is defined as a condition in which key pieces of information are presently unknown or perhaps are even unknowable, leaving people not only unable to meaningfully interpret present events but also unable to anticipate outcomes in the future (Heffernan and Pawlak, 2020), thus hindering their ability to effectively solve problems (Hubbard, 2014). Regarding COVID-19, it was first thought the virus was spread by physical surface contact, and scientific authorities first stated that masks weren't of much efficacy against the virus. People were encouraged to wear gloves and disinfect surfaces, but it was confirmed later that COVID-19 spread through aerosols. As a result, masks were emphasised. At each turn, Dr Anthony Fauci, then Director of the US National Institute of Allergy and Infectious Diseases, highlighted the need for better protocols around virus response and control:

> The United States has been hit very severely by this [virus]. We just need to look at the numbers and see the number of infections … the number of deaths, [and] increasing hospitalizations. We need to get better control, we need to open up the country because staying shut has economic, employment, health and other negative consequences that are significant. We've got to have a delicate balance, carefully and prudently going towards normality. (C-Span, 2020)

The surety of knowledge in such instances, when reassessment and reconfiguration were needed, has been primarily thought of in terms of scientific knowledge. This knowledge has been in lockstep with the virus itself, meaning new developments in terms of how the virus has acted or mutated have led to new scientific pursuits. However, while scientific explanations are tentative and can be later superseded, as seen through revisions around masking, there are still far more unknowns than knowns, even at this late juncture. In fact, just as things were beginning to look more promising with the availability of vaccines, highly contagious variants of the virus later appeared (such as Delta), and still continue to appear, further reducing certainty.

The related notion of contingency is also important in our analysis. Contingency is a condition in which a state of affairs which currently exists could just as easily not exist, and/or could easily have turned out otherwise.

To illustrate this notion, the pandemic revealed how any number of situations could easily be otherwise if the conditions had been different. For example, some countries got under control the spread of COVID-19 relatively quickly, while others did not and suffered much worse death tolls over the course of the pandemic. The outcome could have been far different (and far less devastating) in many communities than it actually was, *if only* another leader had been in power with a different attitude towards the pandemic, *if different* bureaucratic structures had been in place, or *if different* religious or cultural attitudes were held by populations toward vaccinations (see Rorty, 1989; Geiger, 2019). We will see in this chapter how such factors specifically impacted the progression of the pandemic in the United States, and we will also discuss ways to develop alternative perspectives that could possibly help to improve outcomes regarding similar crises in the future.

Contingency is also an unsettling yet basic fact of life. Jackson (2012: 11) reasons the importance of 'recogniz[ing] and be[ing] reconciled to the painful truth that the human world constitutes our common ground, our shared heritage, not as a place of comfortably consistent unity but as a site of contingency, difference, and struggle'. Although there appear to be regularities in experience, we don't (and can't) ever fully know exactly what the day will bring. Suppose that I am stuck for hours in an unexpected traffic jam. Because of this traffic jam, I narrowly miss arriving at the airport on time and making my scheduled flight, which in the early days of the pandemic, actually turned out (unbeknownst to me) to be carrying many infected passengers, making this plane a key site of mass-infection – a 'super spreader' situation. Was my missing this ill-fated plane predetermined? Did it happen by necessity, a consequence of a seemingly infinite causal nexus that goes backwards through time? Or was it just plain old luck? The reality of contingency suggests that I wouldn't have missed the plane if I hadn't got caught in the terrible traffic jam. I could just as easily have decided to leave earlier, thus ending up on this particular plane that happened to be a dangerous site of mass-infection.

One of the most comprehensive illustrations of this phenomenon is to be found in Robert Musil's (1995) modernist novel *The Man Without Qualities*, a work that directly and repeatedly addresses how contingency characterises the basic fabric of life:

> Few people ... really know how they got to be what they are, how they came by their pastimes, their outlook, their wife, their character, profession, and successes ... but nowhere is a sufficient reason to be found why everything should have turned out the way it did; it could just as well have turned out differently; whatever happened was least of all their own doing but depended mostly on all sorts of circumstances, on moods, the life and death of quite different people; these events converged ... only at a given point in time. (1995: 136–7)

It follows that contingency has also shown itself relevant to the progress of COVID-19, since the plague's spread has in many ways been determined by factors subject to chance. In this way, catastrophe appears as it does because there are myriad alternative outcomes that *could have* radically changed the world we live in and our understanding of it.

In this context, existence and our cogent understanding of life are rendered as full of ambiguity: a condition in which a situation could reasonably be interpreted in multiple ways, and indeed the pandemic has revealed the ambiguity of life in that the meaning of a given situation is not always definite, singular or clear. Many situations could be interpreted in more than one way, depending upon the larger context in which they occur. But this is not all that is at stake in terms of defining ambiguity. In many situations, it is impossible to discern any criterion by which any one interpretation could be judged as more reasonable than another (see Chisholm, 1973). As elaborated by Alimardanian (this volume) ambiguity is thus also about impossibilities of understanding – i.e. there being perhaps no 'correct' interpretation at all, or that all interpretations could be true at once. In the case of COVID-19, the uncertainty confronted by the United States in attempts to interpret the source and impact of the pandemic revealed how 'sense-making' was not only about a multiplicity of interpretations and contingencies, but also the uncanny realisation of knowing that none or all of these interpretations could be found to be true. For Alimardanian, ambiguity highlights the curious notion of indeterminacy in our grappling with being in the world, as a grand number of possibilities and contingencies shape experience and our ability to cogently understand life in moments of certainty and uncertainty.

These terms (uncertainty, contingency and ambiguity) are distinguishable from one another, but they can also be seen to relate to each other in basic ways. If a situation is fundamentally uncertain, then we cannot act as if it is certain. If the outcomes of a given situation could easily have gone one way rather than another (and thus appear to be contingent rather than necessary), we cannot interpret these states of affairs as if they happened of necessity. Hence, we must be more tolerant of ambiguity in our processes of understanding and action (see also de Beauvoir, 1962), and understand that, although different groups of people may conceptualise and deal with the term and its implications differently, ambiguity constitutes a basic feature of the world. This insight, in turn, necessitates more of a sense of *open-endedness* regarding how people ought to understand an event or what course of action to take, and not to rigidly insist that the answers conform to a false dichotomy of 'black or white' formulations. Of course, intolerance of ambiguity is in many ways a natural psychological reaction to the overwhelming complexity of the world. This tendency towards rigidity in the face of ambiguity will be discussed later in this chapter in connection with the work of Arie Kruglanski in the field of social psychology. Jonathan Marshall (this volume) also discusses it in his chapter on the Australian government's response to climate change.

Ambiguity and COVID-19 in the USA

How must existing patterns of daily life now be reoriented (Roitman, 2016)? The fundamental uncertainty of the COVID-19 situation has revealed the considerable limitations of scientific knowledge (even in an advanced technological age) and also resulted in changes in assumptions about everyday life. There is fundamental uncertainty involved in the very notion of COVID-19 infection: living in the midst of a multitude of infected yet asymptomatic people who don't even know they are carrying the virus. Social life itself has also had to be rethought. 'Social distancing' for most people is unnatural. People need contact with other people in real (as opposed to virtual) space and time. But fear of contracting the virus (i.e. the fear of death) has proven itself an even more powerful counterforce to these natural social desires. So even major life events like weddings and funerals have shifted into virtual modalities, as human contact has been deemed too risky even for these weighty milestones. Agamben (2020) in a controversial article lamented the tragedy of a generation of very young children growing up in fear – not just fear of the virus, but fear of 'the other' in general, as all people are now seen primarily through a terrible lens as being potentially lethal carriers of death and disease.

Similarly destructive patterns have also bled into other spheres of activity. Consider the political arena and the current hyper-partisanship occurring in the United States. Such partisanship of course existed previously but has become more pronounced during COVID-19 (though it should be noted that some similar patterns have also occurred elsewhere). At the time of writing, liberals/Democrats and conservatives/Republicans in the United States seem hopelessly divided, at times teetering on the edge of violence. Why is such hyper-partisanship so pervasive today? Perhaps it reflects a need for certainty in one's beliefs amid catastrophe, a need to be 'right' in the face of complicated and contingent situations involving opposing and competing perspectives. We therefore feel the need to 'erase doubt' (McBrien, 2013: 252). When events are increasingly chaotic and our assumptions are upended, we seek order. When futures are uncertain, we seek certainty. The doubling down on pre-existing beliefs in the face of opposing views, and the inherent dislike of ambiguous realities shows a need to control the narrative of events. But so much about these events is simply out of people's control.

The pandemic has become a politically divisive issue in the United States to a disturbingly large degree, on a greater scale than has occurred in many other countries. From the left side of the American political spectrum, state governors issued mandates for strict lockdowns and prolonged school closings, citing the pandemic's obvious threat to public health. On the right, many reacted negatively to what they saw as authoritarian mandates and an overdetermined response to the pandemic, arguing that draconian lockdowns and mandates were already leading to economic, educational and social disorder, in some ways more destructive than the pandemic itself. Many on the right thus downplayed the seriousness of the pandemic, the left then berating them for being ignorant and selfish; conversely, politicians on the left were accused of being unnecessarily controlling, hypocritical, moralistic and authoritarian. This political division has raised larger philosophical questions in the United States about the nature and limits of rights and obligations, as well as what constitutes the proper relation between the individual and the state (for a discussion on this in the context of postcolonial Aotearoa New Zealand, see Clifford, this volume). This situation has also led to increasing levels of confirmation bias in US political discourse. Pieces of evidence confirming people's preconceived beliefs are accepted unquestioningly as valid, while any evidence offered against their preconceived ideas is ignored (see Cassam, 2019). People double down on their beliefs because they cannot tolerate ambiguity and doubt. They may need to convince *themselves* of the rightness of their position even more than they need to convince others. But when this need for certainty turns into intolerance of different beliefs, things can get dangerous. Can this tendency be harnessed in a more life-affirming direction? Can it be seen as an opportunity for positive change?

Let us examine this opportunity further through examples from everyday life in the context of the United States and its capitalist economy. In my own work, I see these issues unfolding in my teaching. I teach humanities and philosophy courses (as well as experiential learning modules) in a Business School in New York City. Many of the students have entrepreneurial aspirations. But in today's business environment in the prolonged aftermath of the pandemic on economics and society, entire industries and business models may suddenly need to be rethought. Restaurants, hotels, gyms, beauty salons, performance and sports venues, education, commercial real estate – these industries have all been dramatically altered due to lockdown and social distancing measures, and many working in these fields have lost their livelihoods and face economic and career disruption. Can these businesses return completely to 'normal' post-COVID-19, or have the business models for these industries been permanently changed? Can we find the creativity to configure new, sustainable business models in these industries, so businesspeople can adapt, survive, and even thrive in the face of this and future threats? What would be the thought process involved?

One approach to consider is that in difficult times we must understand that solutions cannot always be expected to be final or perfect. Some solutions might be the best we have, and the best we can hope for, given the insecure parameters of the present moment. Consider a soldier going into a battle. All the training exercises in the world might not have prepared the soldier for what actually is now occurring on the ground because all possible eventualities cannot be anticipated (see Engberg-Pedersen, 2018). So matters sometimes must be decided on a case-by-case basis, rather than based on hard and set rules. Rules and regulations may in some cases need to be put aside if they are in fact impeding progress. The best-laid plans may need to be altered considering unexpected facts on the ground. And sometimes a decision needs to be made right now, even if all the data is not at hand. These are some of the thought processes that become relevant when dealing with complicated situations. Of course, these thought processes are in most cases not merely an individual decision-making process. The soldier has been trained in a certain military context that is socially constructed and sanctioned (even in cases where the actor is on its own, and when he/she then integrates imaginary interlocutors into the decision-making process). But in any case, all of us often find ourselves in moments of having to navigate unfolding situations, trying to solve complicated problems and, what is perhaps most unsettling, doing this spontaneously, all in real, split-second time.

While these suggestions are easier said than done, they suggest that finding potentialities in paradoxes and opportunities for change may be more helpful than clinging to a rigid thought process that in many cases is no longer appropriate, given the fluid nature of crisis conditions. As Janet Roitman (2016: 19) suggests, it would be helpful to think more in terms of an experiential approach, as a 'consideration of the ways in which crisis can function as an enabling blind spot for the production of knowledge' – one which enables 'judgment about latencies, or errors or failures that must be eradicated and hopefully overcome'.

Sense-making and its challenges

The mind as a sense-making entity is hardwired to search for order and regularities, to make distinctions, and try to understand the complexities of the world. According to Emma Cohen (2010), anthropological accounts of the emergence and transformation of knowledge can be further advanced by 'joint engagement with relevant research in neighbouring disciplines';

hence neuroanthropology explores how individuals relate to sociocultural environments and how this is processed neuroscientifically to create meaning out of sense-perception (see Lende and Downey, 2012). A relevant issue here is that of 'plasticity of mind': the mind's ability to change, to reconfigure cognitive patterns, to stretch its capacities, to create new connections, and therefore to adapt as the result of new experiences. This concept was originally discussed in the nineteenth century by William James in *Principles of Psychology* and has been taken up as a research programme in contemporary experimental psychology and neuroscience (see James, 1950; Churchland, 1986). In social psychology, researchers have conducted empirical studies examining attitudes towards uncertainty, open-endedness and ambiguity. It is to these findings from social psychology that we will now turn.

There is evidence from theoretical psychology suggesting that our brains naturally seek closure in the face of ambiguity and open-endedness, and that 'redundancy in the system is absolutely necessary to resolve ambiguities that occur when different sensory challenges offer conflicting information' (Downey, 2012: 173). One example of this is Gestalt psychology, which shows through perceptual diagrams how the mind automatically seeks to close circles and similar shapes, in order to form wholes as opposed to leaving these shapes seemingly unfinished. In social psychology, Kruglanski's (2004) work analyses closed-mindedness as stemming from a need for 'closure' vis-à-vis ambiguity. Moreover, Kruglanski and Webster (1996: 265) conducted extensive research on ambiguity-tolerance and intolerance and analysed this thought pattern in terms of what they call a 'seize and freeze' perspective:

> The motivation toward cognitive closure may affect the way individuals process information en route to the formation, alteration, or dissolution of knowledge ... We posit two general tendencies that need for closure may instill: the urgency tendency and the permanence tendency. The urgency tendency refers to the inclination to 'seize' on closure quickly. People under a heightened need for closure may perceive that they desire closure immediately. Any further postponement of closure is experienced as bothersome, and the individual's overriding sense is that he or she simply cannot wait. The permanence tendency refers to the desire to perpetuate closure, giving rise to the dual inclination (a) to preserve, or 'freeze' on, past knowledge and (b) to safeguard future knowledge. Individuals under a heightened need for closure may thus desire an enduring closure and, in extreme cases, abhor losing closure ever again.

This psychological mechanism of ambiguity-intolerance is not only exemplified in individual behaviour but in that of institutions through a sort of 'collective intentionality'. Financial markets have traditionally shown themselves averse to uncertainty, as financial indicators on Wall Street

(Dow Industrial Averages, NASDAQ, etc.) often post losses when world events are left unresolved. Kruglanski and Webster (1996: 265) write how the need for closure can lead to heightened incidence of confirmation bias, a phenomenon that contains disturbing implications for epistemology and how we conduct our inquiries, attain knowledge and find 'truth':

> The abstract tendencies toward urgency and permanence may translate into a variety of concrete social psychological phenomena. Specifically, people under a heightened need for closure may seize on information appearing early in a sequence and freeze on it, becoming impervious to subsequent data.

Selective perception is a dangerous mindset to maintain as it can shut down inquiry and impede scientific progress (Cassam, 2019). If newly discovered ideas don't fit pre-existing theories, the theories themselves need to be rethought. Data can't be ignored or rationalised away just because it doesn't fit one's pre-existing narrative. However, as demonstrated across this volume, there is a tendency to *sit with* ambiguity or else to use it or deploy ambiguity to negotiate unclear social, political and economic trajectories. In light of the above problem, is there a better way for us to try to make sense out of the world, especially in times of crisis?

New ways of understanding

Simone de Beauvoir (1962) argued that attempts to dispense with ambiguity are not theoretically sound, and that *staying with* the threat posed by ambiguity, both theoretically and in the course of human life, is a more realistic project. Musil's literary work illustrates the futility of lamenting the loss of traditional ways of life, or of foundational ideals such as certainty, security and moral absolutism, a lament found in the ideas of many conservative thinkers of interwar Europe. According to McBride (2006: 16), Musil came to believe that accepting and embracing ambiguity, though difficult, could be seen to be 'emancipatory'. How can this be a helpful way to think during catastrophe? Facing ambiguity can free us up by 'clearing the slate' and sweeping away illusions about absolute certainty and truth, thus opening mental space to think broadly and creatively about solutions to problems. When our most basic assumptions about the world no longer hold true (see Kaufmann, 2002; Janoff-Bulman, 2002) how can we work to replace these assumptions, and thus discover new ways of thinking and being? Trying desperately to preserve pre-existing perspectives and presuppositions can often hinder progress. Sudden, radical change sometimes occurs as a basic aspect of reality, and flexibility is required to adapt along with it (see also Sattler, 2014). What might such adaptation look like?

In *The Man Without Qualities*, Musil (1995: 11) makes the following observation:

> But if there is a sense of reality ... then there must also be something we can call a sense of possibility. Whoever has it does not say, for instance: Here this or that has happened, will happen, must happen; but he invents: Here this or that might, could, or ought to happen. If he is told that something is the way it is, he will think: Well, it could probably just as well be otherwise.

We must therefore accept and even embrace the uncertainty and ambiguity in the human condition, and adjust our thinking accordingly:

> Every generation treats the life into which it is born as firmly established, except for those few things it is interested in changing. This is practical but it's wrong. The world can be changed in all directions at any moment, or at least in the direction it chooses; it is in the world's nature. (Musil, 1995: 295)

Such suggestions for living with ambiguity are not easy – perhaps they are even counterintuitive. In fact, I admit that many of the dynamics described by Kruglanski and Webster above have been present in my own thought processes. I myself have sometimes made large decisions prematurely to achieve a state of simplicity and closure. Because I could not tolerate living with an open-ended situation and I wanted it resolved quickly, I sometimes did not gather enough information, seek out other viewpoints, or let the situation play itself out enough to optimally inform myself and make the correct decision. And I have known many people who have stayed in exploitative jobs, unpleasant living arrangements, unfulfilling relationships, etc., rather than leaving them for the possibility of new ones, just because they were so change-averse or apprehensive of the unknown. Embracing ambiguity and open-endedness are difficult attitudes to achieve – they don't come naturally. Yet such a shift in mindset is sometimes necessary, as the world is complicated and fluid, not cut and dried. This has in many ways been absent from the social, political, economic and health response to the pandemic in the United States.

Ambiguity, humility and the opened mind

Earlier I mentioned the phenomenon of 'plasticity of mind'. Are there practical ways to increase the degree of this plasticity in our own minds in order to achieve positive results? Let us consider in this connection the philosopher Hilary Putnam's (2001: xi) insight in *Representation and Reality*:

> In this book I ... am thus, as I have done on more than one occasion, criticizing a view I myself earlier advanced. Strangely enough, there are philosophers who criticize me for doing this. The fact that I change my mind in philosophy has

been viewed as a character defect. When I am lighthearted, I retort that it might be that I change my mind because I make mistakes, and that other philosophers don't change their minds because they simply never make mistakes.

Putnam's perspective is important because it can be extrapolated beyond the realm of academic scholarship to larger arenas. It may offer a better understanding of catastrophes such as the current pandemic and help with more effectively confronting emergencies in the future. States of emergency can be seen as emancipatory for humankind, but only if we are open to opportunities for change, and only if we can learn how to cultivate the virtues of intellectual humility and flexibility in our efforts to understand and overcome the crises that inevitably will come our way. For example, it takes intellectual humility to admit that one is (or might have been) wrong. Many people find it difficult to do this. Needing to be 'right' all the time can shut us off from authentically engaging in further inquiry, and thus open-mindedness must allow for our sometimes miscalculating situations and misjudging events. But being able and willing to change one's mind is a positive trait, a sign of intellectual strength, confidence and openness, rather than a sign of weakness and indecision. Being unwilling to change one's mind (and being unable to entertain and accept contrary evidence and perspectives) is by contrast a sign of rigidity and insecurity in one's own beliefs. Humility also involves admitting that events are in many ways fundamentally ambiguous and therefore we don't possess certainty about the workings of the world, although we would like to believe we do. Catastrophes like COVID 'can thus serve an adaptive purpose in our lives'. According to Celinski and Gow (2012), catastrophes can

> force us to address undiscovered or ignored issues. Yet the process can only be adaptive if we are able to take an authentic stance – to face the truth about the situation, acknowledge the cognitive dissonance it has created, withstand the tension caused by this dissonance and gather the strength and insight to seek out the resources (cognitive, emotional, social, spiritual and material) to help put the experience in broader context and ultimately create new meaning in the catastrophe's aftermath.

This pandemic has revealed that none of us can readily know or comprehend all that much about the world and its mysteries; experience and knowledge are thus linked. Even given the advanced technology we have in the twenty-first century, there has been (and still is) considerable concern among scientists regarding specific predictions about the course and progress of the pandemic. In many cases, predictions turned out to be inaccurate, or things did not happen according to plan. It turned out that even multiple vaccines and booster shots could not and did not prevent people from ultimately contracting and spreading COVID-19, though they have been instrumental in drastically reducing rates of hospitalisation and death.

The complexity of the virus and its worldwide spread have also revealed so many multiple factors, moving parts, variables and variants that it has been challenging for even the smartest human beings on the planet to accurately pinpoint relevant causes and effects. Although different cultures have experienced and understood this in different ways, we as human beings are all trying our best to navigate an uncertain world and to make sense out of factors larger than we are, especially in a frightening time when many of these factors are deadly, and seemingly out of our control. It is vital now to think beyond the present moment. The intellectual virtues of open-mindedness and humility are what can best facilitate effective problem-solving and the envisioning of new solutions. This is the way out – and the only way things will eventually improve, not only with the COVID-19 catastrophe but with other impending catastrophes as well.

Conclusion

Ambiguity has been examined as the site of potential progress and change in the work of the Manchester School of anthropology. Practitioners of the Manchester School were quick to caution against 'denying structure while overdetermining the subject' with reference to modernist philosophical thought (Kapferer, 2004: 151). I argue, however, that there is merit in exploring the philosophical underpinnings of the thinking subject in light of the upheavals that have been experienced with the pandemic which have made knowledge of life and the future unclear. This chapter has applied this perspective on the phenomena of ambiguity, uncertainty and contingency, specifically to the culture of the United States during the ongoing COVID-19 catastrophe. The chapter has shown how the reaction to the pandemic in the United States has revealed the challenges of maintaining the intellectual virtues of humility and open-mindedness during times of crisis.

References

Agamben, G. (2020) 'The invention of an epidemic', www.quodlibet.it/giorgio-agamben-l-invenzione-di-un-epidemia (accessed 1 February 2022).

Cassam, Q. (2019) *Vices of the Mind: From the Intellectual to the Political* (Oxford: Oxford University Press).

Celinski, M. and Gow, K., eds. (2012) *Mass Trauma: Impact and Recovery* (Hauppauge, NY: Nova Scientific Publishers).

Chisholm, R.M. (1973) *The Problem of the Criterion* (Milwaukee, WI: Marquette University Press).

Churchland, P. (1986) *Scientific Realism and the Plasticity of Mind* (Cambridge: Cambridge University Press).

Cohen, E. (2010) 'Anthropology of Knowledge', *Journal of the Royal Anthropological Institute*, 16, s193–s202.

C-Span (2020) 'Dr Fauci Remarks on the Coronavirus Pandemic and Reopening the Economy', www.c-span.org/video/?473956–1/dr-fauci-remarks-coronavirus-pandemic-reopening-economy (accessed 15 June 2023).

de Beauvoir, S. (1962) *The Ethics of Ambiguity*, trans. B. Frechtman (Secaucus, NJ: Citadel Press).

Downey, G. (2012) 'Balancing between cultures: Equilibrium in Capoeira', in D.H. Lende and G. Downey (eds), *The Encultured Brain: An Introduction to Neuroanthropology* (Boston, MA: MIT Press), 169–94.

Engberg-Pedersen, A. (2018) 'War atmospheres', *Textual Practice*, 32:3, 437–53.

Frazier, L. (2021) 'The Coronavirus crash of 2020 and the investing lesson it taught us' (*Forbes Magazine*, 11 February).

Geiger, P. (2019) 'Swords of Damocles: An essay on catastrophe and globalization', in D.J. Rosner (ed.), *Catastrophe and Philosophy* (Lanham, MD: Lexington Books), 309–19.

Heffernan, T. and Pawlak, M. (2020) 'Crisis futures: The affects and temporalities of economic collapse in Iceland', *History and Anthropology*, 31:3, 314–30.

Hubbard, D.W. (2014) *How to Measure Anything: Finding the Value of Intangibles in Business* (Hoboken, NJ: Wiley)

Jackson, M.D. (2012) *Lifeworlds: Essays in Existential Anthropology* (Chicago, IL: University of Chicago Press).

James, W. (1950) *Principles of Psychology* (New York: Dover).

Janoff-Bulman, R. (2002) *Shattered Assumptions* (New York: Free Press).

Kapferer, B. (2004) 'Introduction: The social construction of reductionist thought and practice', *Social Analysis*, 48:3, 151–61.

Kapferer, B. (2005) 'Situations, crisis, and the anthropology of the concrete: The contribution of Max Gluckman's thought and practice', *Social Analysis*, 49:3, 85–121.

Kauffman, J., ed. (2002) *The Loss of the Assumptive World: A Theory of Trauma and Loss* (New York: Brunner-Routledge).

Kruglanski, A. (2004) *The Psychology of Closed Mindedness* (New York: Psychology Press).

Kruglanski, A. and Webster, D. (1996) 'Motivated closing of the mind: Seizing and freezing', *Psychological Review*, 103:2, 263–83.

Lende, D.H. and Downey, G. (2012) *The Encultured Brain: An Introduction to Neuroanthropology* (Boston, MA: MIT Press).

McBride, P. (2006) *The Void of Ethics: Robert Musil and the Experience of Modernity* (Evanston, IL: Northwestern University Press).

McBrien, J. (2013) 'Afterword: In the aftermath of doubt', in M. Pelkmans (ed.), *Ethnographies of Doubt: Faith and Uncertainty in Contemporary Societies* (London: Bloomsbury), 251–68.

Musil, R. (1995) *The Man Without Qualities*, trans. Sophie Wilkins and Burton Pike (New York: Knopf).

Putnam, H. (2001) *Representation and Reality* (Cambridge, MA: MIT Press).

Roitman, J. (2022) 'The ends of perpetual crisis', *Global Discourse*, 12:3–4, 692–6.

Roitman, J. (2016) 'The stakes of crisis', in Poul Kjaer and Niklas Olsen (eds), *Critical Theories of Crisis in Europe – From Weimar to the Euro* (Lanham, MD: Rowman and Littlefield), 17–34.

Rorty, R. (1989) *Contingency, Irony and Solidarity* (Cambridge: Cambridge University Press).

Sattler, B. (2014) 'Contingency and necessity: Human agency in Musil's *The Man Without Qualities*', *The Monist*, 97:1, 86–103.

Turner, V. (1969) *The Ritual Process: Structure and Anti-Structure* (Ithaca, NY: Cornell University Press).

3

Ambiguity and politics: the suppression of complexity in Australian governmental responses to climate change

Jonathan P. Marshall

Introduction

This chapter outlines the political response to climate change in Australia and the way it failed to deal with ambiguity or complexity.[1] Ambiguity constitutes the fundamental existential circumstances of human social, ethical and political action. This arises from the properties of 'complex systems', both natural and social, including economies, politics, climate, ecology, and so on, and secondarily through social information-processing systems which may not deal well with complexity, and can render even simple events unclear. Attempts to reduce ambiguity and complexity can become defence mechanisms that can diminish both problem-awareness and ethical concern. Recognition of these basic facts of life is vital to the anthropology of ambiguity and to studying the challenges of climate change, and social challenges in general.

As is recognised by several contributors to this volume (Steindl-Kopf, Hutchings and Hizi) Simone de Beauvoir's *The Ethics of Ambiguity* (1962) highlights the inevitable 'ambiguity-problems' of political and ethical action, suggesting that suppression of ambiguity is likely to be harmful. However, de Beauvoir downplays some challenges around both ambiguity and concern, and her work can be extended. A typology of concern, and its suppression, is introduced through the work of Martin Buber, while similarly criticising his retreat from ambiguity. This thinking enables us to observe that Australian climate and energy politics deals with challenges through suppressing ambiguity by compartmentalising (or effectively separating) different problems so they cannot appear to interact, even if their interaction is inevitable. This process sanctifies a vision of 'The Market' as an impersonal, unambiguous, beneficial, almost divine and certain force which governs life, must be protected and preserved, and which justifies ambiguous action on climate. Ambiguity is itself ambiguous; as acceptance of ambiguity can become a mode of engagement, involving openness and experiment while, at the same time, ambiguity can arise from giving different messages to different audiences, obscuring knowledge and hindering action.

Clarifying 'ambiguity' and 'complexity'

Ambiguity and complexity are related. Many chapters in this book take specific positions on ambiguity and its experience based on ethnographic observations of this phenomenon, but by using the *Oxford English Dictionary* a conservative but useful definition can be constructed to understand ambiguity in relation to complex systems and climate change. Ambiguity often arises when events, situations, beings or words have 'different possible meanings; [the] capacity for being interpreted in more than one way; [or] lack of specificity or exactness'. Ambiguity can be both an individual and sociocultural response which implies uncertainty, doubt, multiplicity or dispute, and it seems a natural reaction within complex systems. Ambiguity can also be constructed to hide problems for political purposes or deflect blame (see Heffernan, this volume). As Barth (1989) suggests (necessary) cultural ambiguities can drive social processes. Ambiguity is inherent in the idea of complex systems and processes and hence within the dynamic interactions in all living systems (including social and cultural systems).

Complex systems are systems in which the 'beings' in the system interact, and their behaviour is modified by, or in response to, other beings and the system itself. As Ladyman and Wiesner (2020: 1) remark, 'there is no agreement about the definition of "complexity" or "complex systems" nor even about whether a definition is possible or needed'. However, some properties of complexity seem generally agreed (see Prigogine, 1997; Fisher and Pruit, 2020). Complex systems are 'self-correcting' and 'self-ordering' under stable conditions, but are always in flux and can rapidly change process into previously unobserved states. Their dynamics is both multi-causal and non-linear, so small local changes can produce big changes in the system. Systems evolve and can be described as adaptive, but they may not adapt beneficially for humans, or other beings.

Borders between complex systems may be vague or 'fuzzy' (e.g. a culturally specified 'economy' is not separate from culturally specified 'ecologies' or vice versa). Trends can often be predicted, but there is only limited predictability for specific outcomes. For example, the weather will get more extreme if we keep adding to greenhouse gas emissions, but we cannot predict the exact weather next month. These factors mean unintended consequences and failure are the common outcomes of action. These factors add to uncertainty in life.

Complexity, climate and informational confusion

Climate forms a large-scale 'complex system' and contemporary climate change, largely produced by burning fossil fuels, is merged with other processes such as ecological destruction, economics or politics. It is non-local, with multiple causations that can't be directly observed in totality, and its components are interrelational. Emphasising that climate change is a *process* allows easier recognition that humans, as both fractious collectives and individuals, can be interrelated with these processes in complex multidirectional ways. Suppressing ambiguity or responding ambiguously to climate change adds further complexities to the situation.

While climate change may be conceivable, it resists being broken up into simple and discrete parts for societies to label and interact with. The magnitude and danger of climate processes similarly escapes complete conception, and does not allow a single place from which to observe and describe it. It is unprecedented and constantly fluxing and is impossible to describe in terms of statistical risk, as calculation of risk and danger depends on previous events. Likewise, because climate forms a complex system, and interacts with other complex systems such as ecologies, technologies and economies, we cannot predict its course with accuracy. People may predict rising sea levels, but not how fast, how high, nor when they will become a problem locally, even if some people have problems now. Similarly, we can predict that unusual or destructive weather events will occur more intensely, but not when and where they will happen. Ambiguity is an essential part of climate change and of how we engage with it. Being aware of ambiguity should help with our engagement and our analysis of response.

As many twentieth-century thinkers (Jung, Tillich, Voegelin, etc.) have argued, these types of huge, complex, ambiguous and shifting events tend to become represented *symbolically* and tied to existing systems which have previously helped express the inexpressible. One common way of deploying symbols to contain and downplay climate change is through the 'religion of The Market', in which a supposedly self-balancing and beneficial capitalist market subsumes ecology and the whole of life, rather than (more realistically) the ecology subsumes the market. If, in this symbolisation, The Market is supported, then climate change will be controlled, and no business can be blamed. This symbolisation rejects the inherent ambiguity of climate complexity, suggesting climate change is relatively minor, will sort itself out beneficially through existing market relations, and requires no economic or other sociocultural change.

Complexity, limited predictability and symbolic reference mean the effects of climate change are politically and culturally uncertain and, hence, easily caught in existing political or symbolic informational disputes (for example, 'left' versus 'right', as raised by Rosner, in this volume). Social attempts at resolving or removing ambiguity and complexity may involve suppressing important realisations and the struggles that are vital for facing challenges with some agreed ethics. The activities of corporately sponsored think tanks are long documented and add to confusion (Oreskes and Conway, 2011), such as bolstering the established economic order and fossil fuels by increasing the ambiguity of scientific information, or denying it through unambiguously championing The Market as a solution. Likewise, recognition of climate change may also function as an unintentional mode of suppressing awareness of more complex ecological collapse (for example, the decline of drinkable water, deforestation, de-oxygenation and acidification of the ocean, disruption of the phosphorus cycle, collapse of insect populations, and so on). While people may hope that renewable energy alone will counter these and other challenges, anthropologists describing the way societies face these challenges need awareness of harmful 'de-complexifying' processes.

Ethics of ambiguity

De Beauvoir clarifies some of these issues for both social theorists and actors in *The Ethics of Ambiguity* (1948), by showing the importance of recognising ambiguity for ethical and political action. However, there is an argument to be made that she did not press this far enough, and some points of her argument can be refined by looking at Buber's work on how we limit concern and turn people and ecologies into simple and manipulable *things*.

De Beauvoir (1948: 7–10) begins her argument with Jean-Paul Sartre's binary distinction between 'determined' and 'free', which for humans is ambiguous (and essential) because we live amidst what appear to be determined processes *and* we experience freedom of choice: '["Man"] asserts himself as a pure internality against which no external power can take hold, and he also experiences himself as a thing crushed by the dark weight of other things.' De Beauvoir points out that 'philosophers' often try to 'mask' or suppress ambiguity by reducing it to one side of a binary, such as determination *or* freedom, mind *or* matter, human *or* natural, and so on, and establishing a hierarchy whereby the favoured side is, or should be, more significant and dominating than the other (mind *over* matter). De Beauvoir (1948: 8) says, 'it has been a matter of eliminating the ambiguity by making oneself pure inwardness or pure externality, by escaping from the sensible world or by being engulfed in it, by yielding to eternity or enclosing oneself in the pure moment'. She hopes to retain awareness of these ambiguities which, as previously suggested, helps in dealing with complexity. However, her sharp distinction between freedom and determinism potentially sets up a binary, leading to *human* choice becoming valued over the supposedly determined and obstructive world. Rather than claiming humans make our 'being' through completely free choices, it seems more accurate to say our 'being' is made in *the interplay* between choices and processes. This more ambiguous approach might emphasise both the relationships between humans, and between humans and nonhumans (including ecosystems, climate and other complex systems), thus giving a more interconnected picture and a greater openness to current challenges, failures of choice and unintended consequences.

From her dominant valuing of freedom, de Beauvoir (1948: 24) argues that freedom requires that other humans be free, as freedom occurs (only?) in relationships between humans; freedom 'requires itself universally'. One must 'act to defend and develop the moral freedom of oneself *and* others' (de Beauvoir, 1948: 98). However, this produces further ambiguity, as promoting general freedom may limit someone's freedom to oppress others, which may be the social basis of their freedom: 'I am oppressed if I am thrown into prison, but not if I am kept from throwing my neighbor into prison' (de Beauvoir, 1948: 91). This sets up the 'paradox that no action can be generated for man without its being immediately generated against men' (de Beauvoir, 1948: 99). Likewise, restraining climate change means restraining freedom to pollute, which challenges The Market and the power relations that freedom to freeload and maximise profit exists within.

Although de Beauvoir (1948: 72) says 'I concern others and they concern me. There we have an irreducible truth', she appears to reduce concern for others to a concern about their freedom. De Beauvoir does not develop and extend concern, and recognition of interrelationship, to nonhumans, perhaps because she regards the nonhuman world as *determined*, unfree and hence without value. This position uses freedom to perpetuate suppression of the nonhuman. With climate change, recognising the right of nonhumans to exist *and* function may constrain human freedom while being essential to the existence of those human freedoms, which require functional ecologies.

De Beauvoir's writing evokes the suggestion that the bases of ethical positions are *already* ethical positions, open to denial by another ethical position (even her own), and are thus ambiguous themselves. For example, the utilitarian principle of the greatest good (or happiness) for the greatest number already assumes that benefiting most people is ethically important, while others could assume it is better for specific minorities to have privileges. Likewise, valuing freedom is already an ethical position, not a basis for an ethical position. De Beauvoir does not explore this ambiguity but tries to make the value of freedom obvious by making freedom and determinism opposites, ignoring the possibility of a continuum between free and determined, and reinforcing devaluation of the supposedly determined nonhuman.

Similarly, concern for others is an ethical value used to justify ethics, but can be denied. People could easily value freedom without valuing concern.

Concern itself can be a concern, as it might lead us to be concerned for particular people and not for others; *concern for all* might be ambiguous as we may have to choose some beings over others, as de Beauvoir (1948: 18–19) notes of revolutions.

Ethics arises within difficult problems; there 'is an ethics only if there is a problem to solve' and, we might add, disagreement on ways of solving or viewing the problem, as seems inevitable with complex processes like climate change. With general agreement, people might be unaware of these ethical and political concerns. Given general disputes, ethics is already political as it asks, 'what should we do in this situation?', which can further promote disputes and group struggles. Complexity adds to the problem as the results of actions are often unpredictable, and attempts at ethical action may generate unintended and unethical consequences, or fail in some other way; 'without failure, no ethics' (de Beauvoir, 1948: 10). Furthermore, 'the freedom of man is infinite, but his power is limited' (de Beauvoir, 1948: 28), particularly when dealing with a system that escapes complete control. Hence, it may be necessary to insist on openness and concern for others (human or not) and their complexity.

Furthermore, as complex situations are ambiguous, non-repeatable, and escape complete understanding, there are no guaranteed ethical formulas. 'Ethics does not furnish recipes any more than do science and art' (de Beauvoir, 1948: 134). 'The movement of the mind ... always starts up in the darkness ... at each particular moment we must ... manoeuvre in a state of doubt' (de Beauvoir, 1948: 123), recognising uncertainty and ignorance. Ethical actions should be experimental, as we don't know the ethical results until we have acted, and may need to change or refine our actions after observing those results, as elaborated by Rosner (this volume). It is the recognition of this ongoing ambiguity, struggle and the unfinished nature of action that makes ethical thought 'concerned'. This might also inculcate ethical modesty, and concern for unexpected effects.

Defence from ethical awareness of ambiguity

This inherent ambiguity and incompleteness have consequences for human behaviour and hence for those describing human behaviour, and de Beauvoir (1948: 42) devotes considerable space to the ways ambiguity causes a 'fundamental fear in the face of existence', with people fleeing their freedom, refusing to engage with others or to live with ambiguity. In this process, they seek to defend themselves from ethical problems through absolute rules, certainty and authority; or, by wishing to please everyone, remaining paralysed. Such a person embraces a social persona/role: 'no longer a man, but a father, a boss, a member of the Christian Church or the Communist Party' (de Beauvoir, 1948: 48). They may also seek to suppress awareness of ambiguity through the defence mechanisms of isolation or compartmentalisation, where contradictions, conflicting emotions or other ambiguous phenomena are kept separate and unrelated, and dealt with individually as if there were no ambiguity (Baumeister et al., 1998). A person can, through compartmentalisation, be opposed to climate change *and* be a good economic citizen by promoting fossil fuels. This defence against ambiguity seems normal in Australian climate politics.

These defence mechanisms make people 'deficient' in their ability to have concern for others *in general*, or to encounter ambiguity of ethical process. People cannot move beyond themselves into mutuality with the world and others. Buber adds usefully to de Beauvoir's ethics by exploring the nature of concern. Buber (1958) suggests that there are two main ways of relating: 'I-Thou' and 'I-It', recognising that a person's sense of self ('I') is created within these relationships: 'All real living is meeting' (Buber, 1958: 11). After a brief exposition of this argument, I suggest there is a third way of relating useful to understanding the failures of climate response.

The *I-Thou* relationship treats the other as an opening, a mystery, a being full of potential and value, which resists reduction to linguistic labels that can modify us and be modified by us, to whom we have responsibility and concern, offer respect to, and so on. In this complex meeting, we become open and vulnerable, so ethical relationship involves peril or hazard. While the relationship aims for mutuality, it remains ambiguous because of its unpredictable and transformative possibilities. This relationship with complexity may run less risk of assuming that 'I' know what is best for you based in *my* vision of *your* freedom. This ought to describe the relationship of meeting, being open to mystery and misunderstanding, and not rushing to closure.

In the *I-It* relationship, the other becomes an object to be manipulated, not another rich subject. Rendering something thus helps hide incomprehension while suppressing complexity. If others are its, there appears less need to explore their complexity, and more danger of unintended consequences, because of a lack of exploration. People tend to make their enemies 'its' to suppress concern. The 'I' itself may become impersonal when it treats another as an 'it'. However, much of modern life is easier if we treat some beings as 'its', as when we build Ikea furniture, fill a car with petrol, and so on. However, extending the I-It relationship to such situations removes concern and awareness. Similarly, the defence mechanisms discussed previously can reduce the world to simple and manipulable 'its', with harmful consequences.

Buber posits that I-Thou relationships are possible with the natural as well as the human world, although there might be differences. He wonders what kind of mutuality or reciprocity humans can have with nature. This question assumes that humans are separate from, or completely different from, nature rather than ambiguously interconnected with it. Buber struggles with this ambiguity, stating that animals are 'not twofold like man', able to relate as I-Thou or as I-It, but are at a 'threshold', implying liminality or ambiguity of action or interpretation, which he then pushes aside. When discussing plants, Buber is surprisingly more open: humans can indeed grant a tree the opportunity to manifest its 'living wholeness and unity' and 'now the tree that has being, manifests [that being]'. This suggests humans have the ability to choose (individually or collectively) an I-Thou relationship of concern and openness for the 'natural' other. Such mutuality and relationship are clearly recognised in many Indigenous cultures. The question, then, is can people more broadly be open to the mystery and depth of the complex ecologies we participate within (Buber, 1958: 126)? The suspended, open listening of I-Thou may help apprehend complex systems in general, as it avoids a rush to understanding, the removal of ambiguity, or the reduction of the world to utilisable 'its'.

There may be another relationship, not mentioned by Buber. That is the 'It-Authority' relationship, where the 'I' becomes an 'it' before authority, and there is no 'thou'. In contemporary life, the It-Authority relationship seems common in sites of neoliberal employment or social services, in which employees or clients become inconvenient cost centres to be controlled, restructured, punished or dismissed. No concern for others is shown: authority is diffuse but implacable and not a subject. The question is how to rebel without losing awareness of others' thou-ness, which depends on openness to their complexity.

Political responses to ecological crises often seem conditioned by both an It-Authority relationship to The Market and an I-It relationship to natural systems. This combination helps constitute the religion of The Market (Foltz, 2007; Bloomfield, 2019), in which the market is not recognised as constructed, but as a self-existent, holy, unyielding and beneficent force (Walker, 2016). In the religion of The Market, the Authority of The Market becomes unambiguous, superior to the ecology in which it is immersed, while ecology is stripped of complexities, capacities and ambiguities, becoming an 'it' to be endlessly exploited, sacrificed or dismissed; in this religion there is no ecological 'thou'. Recognition of harmful connections between The Market and the processes of climate change seems broken and compartmentalised in Australian climate politics, while The Market must be placated by helping those sanctified by market success, such as fossil fuel companies. Giving The Market Authority reduces the possibility of recognising markets as ambiguous, political and economic, or harmful and useful.

With Buber added to de Beauvoir, humans become free to be sensitised to the wider complex, or ecological context, rather than just 'free' to choose freedom. Sometimes this sensitisation may change what we think of as freedom, or what we demand of others. It opens concern to the world and makes each incidence of relating an ethical encounter. Together, the work of de Beauvoir and Buber emphasises that ethics is never complete, never totally avoids hazards or failures and, hence, that ethical action is experimental rather than pre-guaranteed. Ethics is not a set of formulas, but a way of relating in fullness. They suggest that repressing awareness of inevitable ambiguities can lead to tyranny over the processes of others (human and nonhuman), reducing relationships to 'I-It' or 'It-Authority' modes. This repression prevents concern from developing, especially concern for nonhuman processes. Without such concern and awareness, we may not be able to solve the challenges of climate change.

The Australian politics of climate and energy

Incoherence in climate and energy politics is not unique to Australia, but ambiguity within the Australian system has stretched over at least twenty years, even with increasing evidence of climate disruption (Chubb, 2014; Wilkinson, 2020). As part of a wider anthropological project studying energy transitions, I suggest that this incoherence arises from suppression of ambiguity, acceptance of an It-Authority relationship with The Market and an I-It relationship with ecologies. This allows people to suppress concern, compartmentalise contradictory policies, and apparently remain unaware of the contradictions. Both major parties (the Liberal/National Coalition on the 'Right', and the Australian Labor Party on the 'Left') yield to the authority of the market, with Labor suggesting that transition can lead to new jobs, as if The Market always provides. Neither party seems open to engagement with the complexities, ambiguities and 'thou-ness' of nonhumans, or the potential for unintended consequences to result from their own polices. In practical terms, hope of a constructive approach to climate and energy transition lies with Labor. However, since 2019 when they lost a national election to the Coalition, which kept the Liberal/Nationals in power for another term, further reducing action on climate change, Labor seems devoted to compartmentalising ambiguity. While claiming to act, Labor supports established markets and wealth by isolating them from the climate change they generate, perhaps fearing they will lose funding, suffer hostile campaigns, or be split through internal conflict.

However, polling repeatedly implies that Australians want action on climate. A poll by the Lowy Institute think tank (2021) reports 60 per cent think action should be taken 'even if this involves significant costs', and 55 per cent say the government should be reducing emissions, while 91 per cent support subsidies 'for the development of renewable energy technology'. Enthusiasm for renewables is also displayed in practice. 'More than two million, or 21 percent, of Australian households now have rooftop solar PV [photovoltaic systems] ... Installations continue to rise' (ARENA, 2021). However, support remains politically ambiguous. Labor, and many commentators, expected that climate would be decisive in the 2019 election, but the Coalition attracted a positive swing. Voters also appeared to make The Market primary.

Australian politics grew around Australian exports which, historically, have primarily consisted of unprocessed minerals, fossil fuels and agricultural products. The country is a leading coal, and now gas, exporter. Politically this appears to be a positive in the light of The Market. Both parties support mining coal and gas for export, separating out the effects of emissions on climate in Australia when minerals are burnt overseas, as if national boundaries constrained climate change. This is reinforced by emissions from exported fossil fuels not counting against Australia's official emissions, and hence having no 'visible' or 'measurable' consequence. Concentrated wealth follows, giving mining corporations considerable political power, which justifies exploitation and the freedom to pollute and destroy, as The Market is benevolent. While it is not known how much of that wealth reaches the general population, polls suggest that Australians think mining unambiguously contributes to their prosperity (Richardson and Dennis, 2011; Gittins, 2017). However, mining taxes and royalty payments seem low, while subsidies can be high (and hidden). Within Australia, attempts to redistribute wealth generated from extraction, or implement mechanisms to reduce impacts of mining on the environment, are heavily contested. The Minerals Council of Australia, for example, spent A$17.2 million over six weeks in 2010 to discredit a Prime Minister proposing a tax on mining 'super-profits'. They claimed the tax 'would have destroyed shareholder value, shelved projects and been a massive disincentive to future minerals industry investment' (Davis, 2011).

The Coalition Government's repeal of carbon prices in 2014 was symbolically important. Coalition claims about the effects of the price seem fictional ('A$100 lamb roasts', for example). It is difficult to give accurate reasons for this opposition, apart from financial support from mining companies, or general faith that carbon prices would affect The Market and curtail the freedom of polluters. The Coalition did not allow the carbon price to be ambiguous with possibly good and bad consequences;

it was turned into an evil, price-increasing tax, despite redistributing the proceeds to consumers. While the Coalition compartmentalises The Market from climate change to avoid awareness that The Market causes damage and threatens its order, the more environmentally concerned Labor also downplays this ambiguity. Their carbon price did not extend to oil, petrol or agriculture, for instance, and they further encouraged coal mining for export, with then Minister for Climate Change and Energy Efficiency, Greg Combet, predicting that the coal sector would double its output (Combet, 2011).

Labor seemed to suppose The Market could continue largely unchanged. There was no obvious struggle with the ambiguities of economic processes, or any open display of awareness that extractivism could cause problems, and there was little concern with the complexity and ambiguity of humanity's place in nature. The Market became the Authority, with the human and nonhuman reduced to 'its'. Climate and economy were separated, with economy made the dominant side of the binary.

The Coalition Government

After the massive bushfires of 2019–20, the Coalition became even more decisive in compartmentalising. They promoted a taxpayer-funded gas-led recovery, supported new coal and gas projects, funded new gas-power stations and refused finance for renewable projects, while claiming to reduce emissions. To reduce ambiguity, the government cultivated its own 'information group', avoiding information which could complexify their policies: 'representatives of the Climate Change Authority confirmed to a Senate estimate hearing earlier in the week that Angus Taylor [Minister for Emissions Reduction] has never asked the expert authority to provide [or model] a pathway to net-zero' (Mazengarb, 2021). You might expect a Minister for Emissions Reduction would want to model emissions reduction. Later, Minister Taylor (2020) clearly supported the established market: 'the Government backs the gas industry, backs Australians who use gas and it backs the 850,000 Australians who rely on gas for a job'. These job figures may be inaccurate (Thomas, 2021), but the religion of The Market reduces ambiguity; nothing is more important than the established market; ecologies and humans are ignorable 'its', unless reinforcing market Authority. However, even economics is bypassed, as Australia received less than $2 billion in gas royalties between 2016 and 2018, whereas Qatar, with similar sales, is estimated to have received $26 billion (Khadem, 2019). The importance of fossil fuels is emphasised by Taylor (2021): 'we're now saying to the big energy companies, if you don't invest in [fossil fuel] generation, we will do it ourselves'. Fossil fuels appear to symbolically stand for The Market and survival, even when subsidised by government. By being unambiguously declared good in economic terms, they must be good in every other way.

This declaration of absolute good means it is difficult to set emissions targets or reduce fossil fuel exports. When talking about Coalition plans, including the gas-led recovery, the Prime Minister said, 'our goal is to reach net zero emissions as soon as possible, and preferably by 2050'. This was to be achieved not by less fossil fuels, exports or targets but by imagined 'technology breakthroughs', such as carbon capture and storage (CCS), hydrogen and green steel (Morrison, 2021). There is no reason to expect that CCS will suddenly become useful despite its long-term history of failure in Australia and elsewhere (Marshall, 2016), while 'blue hydrogen' is made from methane with CO_2 emissions. Morrison emphasises his position by instancing non-breakthrough technology such as diesel storage facilities and more gas (Morrison, 2021), none of which diminish emissions. 'Breakthrough technology' does not have to arrive because we need it, when we need it, at a price we can afford, with no unexpected consequences, *unless The Market is divinely beneficent* and the ambiguities of 'breakthroughs' can be ignored.[2] These imagined technologies maintain The Market establishment and its It-Authority relationship to ecology and people. Any ambiguity or complexity of relation between climate safety, coherent social functioning and promoting fossil fuels remains unacknowledged. The absence of emissions targets reinforces hope in the unambiguous virtues of The Market, even while the government is 'interfering' in those markets by 'choosing winners' such as gas.

The new energy market

Capitalist markets and technologies exist with regulation and attempts at control. In practice The Market is political and only ambiguously settled. Australian energy ministers were to decide the new design for the National Electricity Market, based on Energy Security Board (ESB) advice. Implementation of the design intended to maintain reliability, stability and security. The advice thus far appears to assume fossil fuel electricity has these features while renewables and storage do not. There is no tolerance of ambiguity; one is completely adequate despite its capacity for disruption, one is not. Emissions reduction seems secondary to maintaining fossil fuel use.

Technology is often designed for particular ends, such as supporting (or challenging) power relations and established ways of organisation. Regulation forms part of this social background; it derives from struggles between competing social groups, and regulatory intentions may be undermined by unintended consequences. That the new energy market will arise through the conflicting social intentions of various groups, and interaction with reality, makes this claim clear, as well as suggesting The Market is a construction, not a natural force. The energy ministers deciding the future regulation/structure of the market meet as part of a 'National Cabinet' subcommittee. Participants are bound by strict Cabinet confidentiality rules; external parties are excluded from the meetings, and records are secret. Despite these information restrictions, ACT climate change minister Shane Rattenbury said, 'If the federal government doesn't want to talk about it, [the minister] just doesn't let it on the agenda' and others have reportedly complained that the government will not allow discussion of emissions reductions (Mazengarb, 2020). Information is disrupted, presumably to reduce ambiguity, prevent discussion, keep challenges and dissent hidden, and support established forms of The Market. Suppression by the minister limits options, prevents discussion, ignores complexity, acts to quash innovation and makes a particular politics appear normal.

The Labor Party conference and platform

Suppression of climate ambiguities was also visible at Labor's 2021 conference, where the Party supported lock-in for gas and removed emissions targets for 2030. Their provisional document makes ambiguous statements, which avoid complexities and challenge to The Market, such as:

> We will develop and implement practical, collaborative policies informed by the best science and consistent with the goals of the Paris Accord to realise Australia's huge renewable energy opportunities and ensure all Australians benefit not only through stronger economic growth but also access to more affordable energy. (ALP, 2021: 37)

But is economic growth unambiguously compatible with any decline in ecological destruction? This question is avoided, not by recognising ambiguity, but by ambiguous messaging. Labor does recognise that, despite the virtue of transition, harms can arise for workers 'which requires a just transition of the workforce and the creation of decent work and quality jobs in accordance with nationally defined development priorities' (ALP, 2021: 39). But again, harm is phrased in terms of economic effects and not through concern for ecologies or climate.

Like the government, they support imagined technology to preserve gas use, such as CCS (ALP, 2021: 39), and when previously in government they provided large amounts of money for CCS. However, fossil fuel industries were largely uninterested in carrying out research. It is still unclear whether the risks of CCS (such as undetectable leakage, poisoning water supplies, or massively expensive infrastructure) are balanced by usefulness, ease or practicality. It seems doubtful that CCS will ever be more than a tool for delaying fossil fuel reduction (Marshall, 2016). The ambiguity of CCS's possibility serves its function of delay, without it being implemented; it puts concern for the freedom of polluters ahead of concern for ecology. Labor follow in supporting 'the critical role that gas plays in the Australian economy ... This includes support for new gas projects and associated infrastructure ... Labor will ensure access to affordable gas to support Australian households, power generation and industry' (ALP, 2021: 40–1). The platform does not say Labor will ensure access to affordable renewable energy to support households, power generation and industry, and there seems no discussion of whether new gas is needed, or of the consequences of extra emissions. Non-economic harms are bypassed.

Approaching ambiguity?

Independent, but largely conservative, MP Zali Steggall has come closest to recognising ambiguity, in a private member's bill, 'Climate Change (National Framework for Adaptation and Mitigation)', put to parliament. The bill avoids prioritising the economy and its It-Authority relationship, placing the market on a level with national security, health and environment (Steggall, 2020a). The bill acknowledges climate change is a problem 'with immediate and deepening risks to our natural environment, economy and way of life' (Steggall, 2020b) and is intended to provide a *framework* for action, rather than *specify* actions in advance. By so doing, it appears to open up the process to deliberation, dispute, data gathering, targets, independent monitoring of results and experiment, while supporting employment and equity, and providing investment security. The bill received support from the Business Council of Australia, prominent NGOs and the Greens, and is not hostile to Labor, which is a potential breakthrough (Morton, 2021), but it was rejected by the Coalition and Labor.

Conclusion

De Beauvoir demonstrates that existence, meaning and action are fundamentally ambiguous for humans. This is important for anthropologists studying complex socio-political systems and their challenges. Ethical and political action must also recognise ambiguity to cope with reality and to be creative. This is particularly the case when dealing with complex processes such as climate change, which appear informationally ambiguous to begin with. Climate crosses over into other complex systems such as economics and politics, cannot be represented with ease, and is caught by attempts to preserve other existing symbolic justifications like The Market. The problem, in Australia, seems intensified by social defence mechanisms which compartmentalise concern, separate out ambiguities into unconnected and 'simple' issues, and reduce both nonhuman and human to 'its' in the face of The Market's authority. There seems little regard as to whether the market system is self-disruptive, disordering its own ability to survive and function, or whether economic processes which were once producers of 'goods' now are producers of harm. For successful action The Market may need de-sacralisation, and the nonhuman, non-economic world to be recognised as self-acting, or free-acting, 'thous' to help better awareness of challenges and the consequences of actions. The apparent conflict of life-in-general with the religion of The Market may need recognising, so that the conflict, and its ambiguities, can be processed.

Rather than pursue compartmentalisation and the reduction of the world to determined and passive 'its', we may need to explore living reality, its ambiguities, and 'thou-ness' as best we can, being aware of the limits of prediction and the possibility of unintended consequences. We could recognise that fossil fuels and their emissions have to go, but consider the complexities and harmful consequences that might result. Politicians could recognise that fossil fuels are not an unambiguous good, or that burning them overseas still harms Australia. Australian politicians could accept that some of their favoured 'breakthrough technologies' won't protect fossil fuels and are unlikely to diminish the climate challenges; investing taxpayers' money in already working technology could be better. People should be allowed to protest if emissions reduction cannot be discussed in energy market policy. Market action should not be isolated from care and concern for environments and harm. People should be able to admit they do not know exactly how to solve the problem, and that The Market is not God, always delivering the best possible result. With these simple recognitions, ethics and politics can become open and experimental, recognising information as imperfect and inadequate, and that even the most concerned doctrine can lead to unexpected results.

Ambiguity arises necessarily because the world is made up of complex systems. Complex systems have properties and must be embraced rather than replaced with false certainties, or increased by policies which attempt suppression. Anthropologists can become more sensitive to the ways that ambiguities and complexities are suppressed and have the means to discover how different societies deal with these complex challenges in more constructive ways than Australian politics does, and therefore help to illuminate the dynamics of that problem-solving.

Notes

1 This research was sponsored by an Australian Research Council Future Fellowship Grant FT160100301: 'Society and climate change: a social analysis of disruptive technology'. The views expressed may not be those of the ARC.
2 The NSW Coalition, by comparison, is less reluctant than its national counterpart to promote renewable energy, setting up renewable energy zones, and supporting new gas and coal fields.

References

ALP (2021) ALP National Platform: As adopted at the 2021 special platform conference. Australian Labor Party, https://alp.org.au/media/2594/2021-alp-national-platform-final-endorsed-platform.pdf (accessed 3 January 2024).

ARENA (2021) Solar Energy. Australian Renewable Energy Agency, https://arena.gov.au/renewable-energy/solar/ (accessed 15 February 2022).

Barth, F. (1989) 'The analysis of culture in complex societies', *Ethnos*, 34, 120–42.

Baumeister, R.F., Dale, K. and Sommer, K.L. (1998) 'Freudian defense mechanisms and empirical findings in modern social psychology: Reaction formation, projection, displacement, undoing, isolation, sublimation, and denial', *Journal of Personality*, 66:6, 1081–124.

Bloomfield, E.F. (2019) 'The Rhetoric of Energy Darwinism: Neoliberal piety and market autonomy in economic discourse', *Rhetoric Society Quarterly*, 49:4, 320–41.

Buber, M. (1958) *I and Thou*, 2nd edn (Edinburgh: T&T Clark).

Chubb, P. (2014) *Power Failure: The Inside Story of Climate Politics under Rudd and Gillard* (Collingwood: Black Ink).

Combet, G. (2011) 'Abbott absurdities on climate change: Bulletin no.8', Government Press Release, 22 July, https://parlinfo.aph.gov.au/parlInfo/download/media/pressrel/1120577/upload_binary/1120577.pdf (accessed 3 January 2024).

Davis, M. (2011) 'A snip at $22m to get rid of PM', *Sydney Morning Herald*, 2 February, https://www.smh.com.au/business/a-snip-at-22m-to-get-rid-of-pm-20110201-1acgj.html (accessed 3 January 2024).

De Beauvoir, S. (1948) *The Ethics of Ambiguity*, trans. B. Frechtman (New York: Philosophical Library).

Fisher, D.N. and Pruitt, J.N. (2020) 'Insights from the study of complex systems for the ecology and evolution of animal populations', *Current Zoology*, 66:1, 1–14.

Foltz, R. (2007) 'The Religion of the Market: Reflections on a decade of discussion', *Worldviews*, 11, 135–54.

Gittins, R. (2017) 'Mining's economic contribution not as big as you might think', *Sydney Morning Herald*, 4 February, https://www.smh.com.au/business/minings-economic-contribution-not-as-big-as-you-might-think-20170203-gu4r5l.html (accessed 3 January 2024).

Khadem, N. (2019) 'Tax credits for oil and gas giants rise to $324 billion', *ABC News*, 1 April, https://www.abc.net.au/news/2019-04-01/tax-credits-for-oil-and-gas-giants-rise-to-324-billion/10959236 (accessed 3 January 2024).

Ladyman, J. and Wiesner, K. (2020) *What is a Complex System?* (New Haven, NJ: Yale University Press).

Lowy Institute (2021) Climate Poll 2021. Lowy Institute, 26 May, https://www.lowyinstitute.org/publications/climate-poll-2021 (accessed 3 January 2024).

Marshall, J. (2016) 'Disordering fantasies of coal and technology: Carbon capture and storage in Australia', *Energy Policy*, 99, 288–98.

Mazengarb, M. (2020) ' "Angus doesn't let it on the agenda:" State energy ministers slam federal policy', RenewEconomy, 5 August, https://reneweconomy.com.au/angus-doesnt-let-it-on-the-agenda-state-energy-ministers-slam-federal-policy-94278/ (accessed 3 January 2024).

Mazengarb, M. (2021) 'Taylor requests yet another review of future grid needs, to deal with "intermittents" '. RenewEconomy, 25 March, https://reneweconomy.com.au/taylor-requests-yet-another-review-of-future-grid-needs-to-deal-with-intermittents/ (accessed 3 January 2024).

Morrison, S. (2021) 'Address – National Press Club Barton ACT', 1 February, https://pmtranscripts.pmc.gov.au/release/transcript-43214 (accessed 3 January 2024).

Morton, A. (2021) 'Business Council of Australia backs Zali Steggall's climate change bill for 2050 net zero target', *The Guardian*, 26 January, https://www.theguardian.com/australia-news/2021/jan/26/business-council-of-australia-backs-zali-steggalls-climate-change-bill-for-2050-net-zero-target (accessed 3 January 2024).

Oreskes, N. and Conway, E.M. (2011) *Merchants of Doubt: How a Handful of Scientists Obscured the Truth on Issues from Tobacco Smoke to Global Warming* (New York: Bloomsbury).

Prigogine, I. (1997) *The End of Certainty* (New York: Free Press).

Richardson, D. and Dennis, R. (2011) Mining the Truth: The Rhetoric and Reality of the Commodities Boom (Australia Institute), https://australiainstitute.org.au/wp-content/uploads/2020/12/Mining-the-truth-IP7_4.pdf (accessed 3 January 2024).

Steggall, Z. (2020a) 'Climate Act Now', https://web.archive.org/web/20210531125804/https://climateactnow.com.au/ (accessed 3 January 2024).

Steggall, Z. (2020b) 'Climate Change (National Framework for Adaptation and Mitigation) Bill 2020: Explanatory Memorandum and statement of compatibility with human rights', Parliamentary Library, Canberra, 9 November, https://parlinfo.aph.gov.au/parlInfo/download/legislation/ems/r6780_ems_db1f5677-78d1-4f14-af88-b794d55109aa/upload_pdf/21131b01EM%20Steggall.pdf (accessed 3 January 2024).

Taylor, A. (2020) 'Australia's energy future', 29 October, speech, www.minister.industry.gov.au/ministers/taylor/speeches/australias-energy-future (accessed 3 January 2024).

Taylor, A. (2021) Interview with Luke Grant, 2GB, 5 January, https://www.minister.industry.gov.au/ministers/taylor/transcripts/interview-luke-grant-2gb (accessed 3 January 2024).

Thomas, S. (2021) 'Former Trump adviser Andrew Liveris admits "incorrect" jobs claim from natural gas on Q+A', RMIT ABC Fact Check, 28 May, https://www.abc.net.au/news/2021-05-26/andrew-liveris-incorrect-claim-feedstock-natural-gas-fact-check/100160172 (accessed 3 January 2024).

Walker, J. (2016) 'Bringing liquidity to life: Markets for ecosystem services and the new political economy of extinction', in K Kohli and M Menon (eds), *Business Interests and the Environmental Crisis* (New Delhi: SAGE), 3–27.

Wilkinson, M. (2020) *The Carbon Club: How a Network of Influential Climate Sceptics, Politicians and Business Leaders Fought to Control Australia's Climate Policy* (Crows Nest: Allen & Unwin).

Part II

Navigating temporal disruption

4

Queering the crisis–recovery nexus: personhood and societal transformation after economic collapse in Iceland

Timothy Heffernan

Introduction

This chapter examines the nexus between crisis and recovery by exploring the ambiguity that many communities experience in transitioning out of collective crisis. Such transitions are often glossed over a priori in anthropological studies of adversity. In earlier scholarship, however, crisis was a central concept of inquiry, especially in the Manchester School's extended case analysis. A guiding premise was that the social realities of crisis should 'reveal the forces and processes of [societal] formation' (Kapferer, 2005: 87), but this has since given way to 'reductionist' descriptions of the realities of a society under strain (Kapferer, 2015). A focus on crisis, therefore, takes precedence over sustained engagements with transformation, meaning the contemporary crisis–recovery nexus remains underexplored. This is concerning for three reasons. Firstly, due to the presence of *compounding* local and global crises. Secondly, rarely are such crises experienced uniformly, with many groups facing increased, yet uneven, vulnerability. Thirdly, the liberalisation and privatisation of services under neoliberal policy have hampered the nation-state's ability to provide crisis support, ushering in new relations between citizens and authorities.[1] This chapter explores the crisis–recovery nexus by examining individual and societal transformations after severe disruption, examined here with reference to the global financial crisis (GFC, 2008–11), an event that affected much of the Global North socially and economically. Throughout this chapter, ambiguity is shown to be embedded in crisis as people set about contending with what is knowable and what is not-knowable.

The 'friction' of global capitalism under crisis in Europe was felt through the shift from *shared prosperity* to *individualised crisis* amid the nation-state's reduced capacity to protect against global fluctuations (Tsing, 2005). During the GFC, institutional stability was prioritised by governments, resulting in networks of citizens rallying together, even revolting against elites (Loftsdóttir et al., 2018). Here, I explore crisis and recovery in Iceland, a country whose entire banking system collapsed in October 2008, with Icelanders protesting what they saw as an inadequate crisis-response and need for reform. The effects of crisis on the coherence of the nation form and the development of the person in cultural terms (i.e. personhood) are central to my analysis. Sudden disruptions produce feelings of knowledge deficit, what Rosner (this volume) explores as mental perplexity (*aporia*). Questions of 'What happened?' and 'What next?' (Roitman, 2014) bring about a thirst for knowledge. But access to knowledge is not always guaranteed given the political and institutional tendency during crises to harness ignorance to deflect, obscure or conceal information, thus 'increas[ing] the scope of what remains unintelligible' (McGoey, 2012: 1). I use affect and queer theory to explore sense-making practices as forms of resistance, which I studied in Iceland through ethnographic fieldwork (2016–18).[2] I argue ambiguity emerges through the tension of *knowing* and *not knowing*, or the capacity (or incapacity) to embrace dominant epistemes amid crisis. This produces 'affective atmospheres' seen in shifting public moods from optimism to despair, and in novel acts of world-building across time and space (Stewart, 2011).[3]

Affective atmospheres are not confined to the crisis–recovery nexus, however. They are perceptible outside of calamity via ethnographic attempts to understand how collective moods build up, slacken or even dissipate, revealing how meaning is produced, acted upon, denied or used to support or critique the conditions of collective life (Stewart, 2011). Under capitalism, knowledge and meaning are produced through calculating, tracking and reporting, with rationality, stability and growth being markers of success (Muir, 2021). However, instances of miscalculation and failure are not necessarily oppositional to this, with capitalism's boom/bust dynamic showing that failure is common. A focus on affective atmospheres is important for showing how, in the Mancunian sense, forces and processes reveal something about society, and thus the pathways people can take towards recovering. Miscalculation can surely spell trouble, but failure can be illuminating for how people get by and reconcile with unrealised futures. Queer theory, which takes up this mantle, is premised on scholarship examining 'hegemonic ideologies of gender and sexuality' (Weston, 1993: 348), including how the latter structure knowledge (Weiss, 2022). Since its inception, queer theory has paid attention to affective forces (e.g. desires, pleasures, fantasies and 'the otherwise') to critique the dominance of modernist developments (e.g. the nation-state, family and economy) as well as heteronormative stances (e.g. on 'proper' social reproduction and life 'success'; Berlant, 2011). Affect and queer theory posit that understanding can be gleaned through the sensory and affective world, not only challenging conventional knowledge production but calling attention to modes of thinking, acting and being 'otherwise' (Povinelli, 2022).

What kinds of futures might be invoked when questions of 'What happened?' and 'What next?' are uttered? In Iceland, crisis led to new projects such as searching for a new personal ethics after hyper-consumption and rewriting the nation's constitution to recast the collective moral landscape. Through analysis of these projects, I focus on failure by government, economists and individuals amid efforts to understand and rebuild life post-crisis. I first explore the affective atmospheres prior to the banking collapse, locating crisis and recovery in the ways that *affects are drawn into form* (Berlant and Stewart, 2019). I then explore how this bears upon notions of trust, personhood and future-making. I use the example of two men from Iceland's queer community, Hörður and Jóhannes, involved in individual and collectivist recovery projects. I use interviews and timelining exercises to explicate the crisis–recovery nexus. The chapter concludes with a discussion of trust, ethics and world-building in Iceland's transition from crisis, noting how anthropologists can innovate ethnographic methods to make 'thick descriptions' of ambiguity.

The nation-state in crisis: diminishing trust in Icelandic society

The thud of Hörður's hand on the café table in downtown Reykjavik took me by surprise, bringing me back into the room we sat in together as he recounted the severity of the collapse nine years previously. I had been introduced to Hörður through Reykjavik's queer scene and was promised a lively and informative interview about the banking collapse. A well-known musician, Hörður Torfason had garnered national attention as a singer. In the 1970s he came out as gay in what was then still a socially conservative Iceland. Growing up in the postwar decades and after Iceland's independence from Denmark (in 1944), Hörður was rebuked for coming out while one of the country's biggest popstars. This led him down a path of social justice and advocacy work, establishing Iceland's gay and lesbian organisation in 1978, and organising local demonstrations against social and political injustices abroad. Following Iceland's 2008 economic collapse, Hörður used his connections to start The People's Voice, a collective that held mass anti-government protests over a three-month period, gaining widespread appeal among a public that felt blindsided by the crisis.

> It was so sad when the crash came and I talked to people and they had obviously lost their dreams of life … They got back on their feet financially, but it took a long time. And all because some people – the managers of the banks – wanted to make more money. Our parliamentarians played along. They gave the banks permission to behave this way. They should have kept an eye on things and said, 'No,' [thud] 'this isn't allowed!' But they failed.

Unequivocal in his summation of the antecedents of the banking collapse, Hörður highlighted the systemic failure and negligence of Iceland's political and economic leaders, and invoked the democratic premise that elected officials should work in the interests of the populace. An adherence to, and safeguarding of, democracy and the welfare state came to be important in post-independence Iceland, with government seen as the protector of today's national 'family' of 370,000 people. In Iceland's proud social democratic tradition, the nation-state is charged with securing individual rights, economic security, equality and emancipation (Anderson and Björkman, 2018). However, amid crisis, the state was shown to be faced with its own limits, a view that was very different to the nationalistic pride experienced prior to the banking collapse.

In the early 2000s, the country's banks were privatised and expanded abroad as part of neoliberal restructuring in an affective atmosphere of economic growth, consumption and upward mobility. This was a wholly new mood in Iceland. Within a few years, Iceland's banks had grown to the point of becoming emerging players in international finance, creating new jobs and industries in the country's traditional agricultural, fishing and tourism economy, and leading to increased availability of cheap credit. Many Icelanders used credit to pay for luxury vehicles, renovations and travel as part of what Mixa (2009) calls the 'manic millennium', a far cry from the economically impoverished, former Danish dependency Hörður was born into. At the turn of the Millennium, Iceland was experiencing an 'economic miracle' and had finally 'made it' on the international stage, the atmosphere likened to that of the roaring 1920s in the United States (Mixa, 2009). However, with the collapse of the international banking sector, many Icelanders were unable to meet their debt obligations, causing increased stratification in a country that prides itself on equality.[4]

Initially, the banks' hasty expansion was made palatable by politicians referencing core traits of nationhood, including the country's proud Viking history and the 'purity' of its nature; reinterpreting these as Iceland's natural climb on the world stage, led by a group of 'business Vikings' going abroad to expand business operations to build the country's wealth (Loftsdóttir, 2019). Discourse such as this shows how nationalist sentiment connects the state, its operations (including the economy) and the culture of citizens (Harvey, 2013). It shows how people invest affectively in what Berlant (2011) calls the good-life fantasy, which Hörður refers to in his summation of people's 'lost dreams' (see also Cabrera Torrecilla, this volume). Icelandic anthropologist Kristín Loftsdóttir (2014: 175) remarks that in this context the public was 'encouraged to spend as if there was no tomorrow', with signs of growing affluence and consumption becoming pronounced. Indeed, what was used by elites to lend credibility and stoke attachments to fantasies of upward mobility decisively ended with the crisis. In turn, the attitudes that provided discursive consistency and meaning for the public came under scrutiny.

In this sense, crisis in Iceland became a 'multivocal sign' connoting many things simultaneously, after the work of Victor Turner (1967), which Loftsdóttir (2019: 130) highlights as 'important in mobilizing different sensibilities and emotions on key questions in the crisis years: the future of democracy, the viability of the economy, the boom year's destructiveness and Iceland's international position'. Trust connotes the social intimacies between people and the 'glue' behind democracy and civility (Broch-Due and Ystanes, 2016). Crisis erodes this trust at the precise time it is needed; it also calls forth important questions about collective identity, belonging and security. This context establishes the state's role in managing and negotiating crisis but also shows the disparate narratives of crisis often held by state (elites) and society (citizens) as each tries to contend with the effects of sudden disruption.

For anthropologist and affect theorist Kathleen Stewart (2011: 445), an analytic attention to 'charged atmospheres' is useful for understanding how public 'forces are generated as atmospheres per se, how they spawn worlds, animate forms of attachment and detachment, and become the live background of living in and living through things'. In early 2009, the government caved to public demands at protests organised by The People's Voice, and they resigned. During these demonstrations the protest site 'was an exciting location to meet with people and enjoy "magical" moments of affective solidarity' (Bernburg, 2016: 15). Attendance at protests was social, with friends and family travelling to the protest site together. This affective space renewed optimism and hope, often expressed through signage that called for a renewed politics after government failure and questioned the political justification of Iceland's prosperity bubble. Of course, the 'economy of appearances' (Tsing, 2000), seen through Iceland heralded as a new node in international banking, could never have lasted, showing how atmospheres of elite greed cut short people's dreams for securing the 'good life'.

Some of the first people I worked with as part of fieldwork were social activists and members of progressive political parties who attended these demonstrations. This included Jóhannes, who had taken out a large mortgage before the crisis with his now ex-boyfriend, which he was still struggling to pay off. Jóhannes studied environmental science abroad before returning to Iceland to study ethics, which he frequently discussed among leftist groups who had a desire to reform politics. This group of like-minded individuals was pushing for the new constitution to be legislated that had been crowd-sourced and written by select members of the public in the years after the crisis. Ultimately, however, the new document was shelved when a conservative government returned to power in 2013. What continued to bring this group together even nine years later was a desire for a new moral framework. Steindl-Kopf (this volume) has charted a similar desire among activists in Serbia, noting that such a desire often stems from collective aspirations to overcome the 'moral decay' of elite impropriety. For many Icelandic activists, this search for a new framework was spurred on by the feeling that a disjuncture had occurred 'where there are overlapping but still floating pieces that do not seem to fit together in the same way as they did before, i.e. not creating an apparently coherent ideological landscape' (Loftsdóttir, 2014: 169). Indeed, collective sentiment was *in crisis*.

While, as Hörður suggested, people 'got back on their feet financially', the crisis had also come to be part of personal biography. In the next section, I explore how crisis and recovery were narrated by Jóhannes through strategies to make ends meet, desperate searches for secure work, reflections on personal growth and relationship breakdown. I use queer theory to critique modernist developments at the centre of politicians' narratives of crisis and recovery (e.g. the centrality of the nation-state, family and economy) and heteronormative stances (e.g. social reproduction and the strictures of life success and failure). The sexual identity of my participants is secondary to my focus on queer life and theorisations of non-heteronormative orientations. This focus provides the basis for 'queering' the crisis–recovery nexus. To this end, queer theory opens a space to observe, firstly, individual and collective worldmaking projects as part of the transformation from crisis towards an 'otherwise' state. Secondly, queer theory and criticism are capable of shedding light on the plasticity of ambiguity to demonstrate how ignorance is feigned normatively to justify the systemic failures of globalised capitalism.

Failure, growth and ignorance in competing logics of crisis narration

Failure is a curious notion, whether it occurs in an individual's life or in the context of an organisation, society, or at the level of the nation-state and beyond. The GFC was an extraordinary *failure* of the global economic order that pervaded individual and societal experience. This was especially so across Europe, where private and consumer debt quickly rose and became immediately payable with the international collapse of many banks. When banks did not hold or have access to enough liquid assets to cover debt obligations and maintain stability, governments became the lender of last resort, leading to the introduction of harsh austerity measures. This was felt acutely through housing and asset repossession and sudden changes to the tenure and nature of employment. Given the mathematical and analytical operations underpinning (inter)national economics, the GFC has been labelled a crisis of knowledge as much as finance (Loftsdóttir et al.,

2018), raising the question of whether economists adequately *understood* the risks being taken. Demonstrating that neoliberal economics is driven by specialised knowledge and valuing systems, Davies and McGoey (2012: 65) reason that crisis is all too often deemed unforeseeable and, therefore, *less* knowable. It is 'through the partial and limited nature' of each individual's knowledge that mishaps are justified and economists are excused from blame, showing how system-knowledge and outcome-ignorance work within an economic framework of rationality (Davies and McGoey, 2012: 65).

Given the focus here on affective atmospheres, the sensors are useful in understanding how system-knowledge and outcome-ignorance are employed. In countries where deep recessions were experienced, economists' miscalculations were attributed to decisions based on prior performance, perceived market stability, and speculative calculation. What comes into view is the relationship between knowledge as known and rational, and knowledge as sensed and speculated about. In social science, the senses connote the embodied, intimate experiences, knowledges, perceptions and practices borne of participating in and exerting agency over one's environment (Pink, 2015). Sensory ethnographers posit that the senses can guide and elicit information about how people endure and respond to adversity. Yet part of the expansion of sensory research at the turn of this century came through the suggestion that scholars focused too narrowly on textual and verbal cues, stressing the senses also shed light on the materiality of culturally constituted processes of sense-making (Porcello et al., 2010). Not only does this apply to understanding interlocutors' experiences, but also the wider socio-political and economic context within which people live, work and build their lives day-to-day.

Thrift (2004: 583), for example, argues that risk and opportunity calculation is part of contemporary life, ranging from 'listing and numbering and counting through to various kinds of analytical and transformative operations'. Such operations are employed in financial systems used by governments, central banks and financial service providers to weigh up decisions for generating and protecting profit and wealth. This calculative background highlights a shared social experience of time: an electronic time-space mediated by calculation that produces new knowledges and relationships (Thrift, 2004). Indeed, analytical operations connote a sensory form of engagement, whereby 'because of massive increases in computing power, [calculation] has become a means of making qualitative judgements and working with ambiguity. In other words, what we are seeing is *a new form of seeing*, one which tracks and can cope with uncertainty in ways previously unknown' (emphasis added; Thrift, 2004: 584).[5] People without this specialised knowledge, but who trust in the power of such calculation, become deeply embedded in this manner of thinking and sensing, as seen through public moods of economic excess and optimism. Participating in the affective atmospheres that result can court failure: if we want something enough, we pursue it, in spite of the costs that such a pursuit might entail.

Failure is not necessarily the binary opposite of success, however; nor is it one end of a success–failure continuum, as evidenced by my discussions with Jóhannes about how he managed his affairs post-crisis. Failure, rather, is deeply embedded within a cultural logic that has axiological purchase, with cultural notions of order being stressed as needing to prevail over disorder, in spite of failure being a common occurrence under capitalism. Hizi (this volume) highlights the connection between cultural notions of order and person-making in neoliberal spaces of urban China. In anthropological studies of personhood what is stressed in the making of the person is 'the collection of traits and qualities that constitute the nature of human beings among a certain social group' (Bielo, 2007: 323). In Iceland, this is premised on self-efficacy and self-reliance, particularly due to the need for Icelanders to brave the island's harsh climate and topography; personhood is realised through the notion of the self within the natural world and in connection with a network of family linked to a 'national' family in terms of the country's populace. During our discussions, failure was the unfortunate outcome of Jóhannes' pursuit of 'the good life', as he took out a mortgage as the economic crisis hit in 2008:

> I started a relationship with a guy I met overseas who ended up moving to Iceland. I was studying [environmental ethics] and was trying to keep costs low by living with family. The deal was I helped my uncle and his wife, who had a degenerative disease. When my partner moved to Iceland, we rented a flat and then bought. This was spring 2008 when everybody had access to cheap loans, meaning everyone was heavily affected by the crash.

As shown by the Euro-American housing crises (2007–11) as part of the GFC, home ownership in the 2000s was assisted by liberalised lending practices to unsound mortgagees. Having only recently moved back to Iceland after studying abroad, Jóhannes never had the chance to save up a deposit, instead taking out a loan using his grandmother's property as collateral. Home ownership signifies economic independence in Iceland, a step in becoming a full person through culturally prescribed ideas about individuation that is achieved through saving money, navigating the property market, and buying. This is expected in many capitalist societies, with home ownership a significant step in the life course that resembles a 'landmark event', providing one with economic security as much as with shelter (Sabaté, 2016). A landmark is something noticeable from multiple points used to *judge* a position relative to one's surroundings, signifying movement across the life course and across cultural ideas of maturity.

Crisis therefore bears upon personhood in capitalist societies: failure is experienced through the inability to meet mortgage repayments and the threat of asset repossession and financial ruin. It further calls attention to the direction and pace of one's life movement: of staying the course, going off course, or necessitating a new course altogether. As fate would have it, the pressure of growing mortgage repayments contributed to the end of Jóhannes' relationship, leading to a 'debt-sentence' of paying off the home while living alone. If the life course is archetypically viewed in modernist terms as forward-oriented, Jóhannes' experience was oblique, feeling 'betwixt and between' (Turner, 1969) as he tried to carve out a sense of normalcy. His grandmother provided financial support and he slept on several close friends' couches while he rented out his house to pay the mortgage. This didn't feel becoming for his age, with the majority of his peers aspiring to live close to the city centre ('Reykjavik 101').

> I mean, it's fine when you're happy and you don't need to make your own nest, but it's absolutely ridiculous to do this. I think I lived in eight different friends' places. ... I couldn't get a place because the rental market wasn't working well ... I lived on a farm that used to belong to my relatives, and then [a new partner and I] moved to Iceland's east.

Jóhannes' sizeable mortgage was taken out during pre-crisis optimism, when people felt guided by the calculations of politicians and economists. With the collapse, however, the recent past and anticipated future were no longer stable markers with which to guide one's journey. In our interview, Jóhannes mentioned that this sense of not knowing or not understanding life's path was something he'd thought about before: 'I'm a very late bloomer, even when it came to understanding my sexual orientation [laughs] ... I honestly didn't understand it or realise it earlier. It's not that I was hiding from anyone. I still have [heterosexual] friends who don't understand this. But finally, I realised and came to terms with it.' Coming out, whether transitioning out of crisis or pursuing new orientations in one's sexuality, is a messy and uncharted path. Phases of pre-announcement, exploration, announcement, relationship development, and identity integration commonly characterise identity formation. Here, the known and the unknown collide, highlighting the betwixt-and-betweenness of one's journey.

Indeed, 'queer embraces the instability of identity and encourages a fluid movement "betwixt and between" bodily possibilities and manifestations' (LeMaster, 2011: 106). In so doing, queer theory draws attention to the fact that 'virtually any aspect of modern Western culture, must be, not merely incomplete, but damaged in its central substance to the degree that it does not incorporate a critical analysis of modern homo/heterosexual definition' (Sedgwick, 2008: 1). As such, theorisations about queer life advocate:

> that individual identities and differences are constantly being (re)constructed and that such liminal instability is socially productive. Accordingly, a queer

criticism embraces what has been abandoned as unimportant or as socially absent; it looks just beyond and beneath the location of normalcy ... to locate those instances that are subjugated to the margins of social imagination. Once located, a queer criticism unpacks the social significance of absent phenomena and forwards possibilities as to why ... they have been rendered moot. (LeMaster, 2011: 106)

This postulation provides an alternative to thinking about the crisis–recovery nexus that goes beyond Turner and the Manchester School's reliance on van Gennep's rites of passage. Such passages 'accompany every change of place, state, social position and age', particularly instances defined by 'immoderacy', 'paradox', 'absurdity', physiological or economic 'distress' (Turner, 1969: 44–5). I extend this to include failure brought about by such changes, but query how reformatory practices are sustained when a community operates under sustained socio-political tension (i.e. highlighting the unresolved quality of disruption within the nation form and personhood). Key to this transformation is the 'proper' interpretation and enactment of cultural practice that involves individual and collective projects that are premised on worldmaking practices that reveal the factors that are important to the crisis–recovery nexus.

Creating alternative narratives, building new worlds

Anthropologists have shown how citizens' responses to hardship and adversity employ divergent social and political realities (Povinelli, 2022). In doing so, 'queer' chastises hegemonic space-times and notions of personhood. Jóhannes' move 'east', to the other side of the country, became part of his journey along the pathway toward recovery: 'I started working there to just build a career in nature conservation. I needed to change, and I needed to do something else. So, it's just made me the kind of person I am.' In *Uprootings/Regroundings: Questions of Home and Migration* (2003: 1), Ahmed and colleagues posit that 'being grounded is not necessarily about being fixed; being mobile is not necessarily about being detached'. For them, the dynamic between 'uprooting' and 'regrounding' is a frame to contemplate fixity and mobility 'beyond oppositions such as stasis versus transformation, or presence versus absence' (Ahmed et al., 2003: 1). Indeed, such a dynamic can be a kind of sense-making. Similar to the dynamic of pursuing certainty amid uncertainty, uprooting and regrounding incorporate life calculations that are intertwined with an embodied sense of being in the world, based on ideas of self-cultivation, duty, convenience, and gestures towards future-affirming actions. 'It's not that I couldn't live in the house – I *couldn't* live in the house – but it was not the worst thing to move,' Jóhannes noted. 'Perhaps also it helped with looking at things in new ways. Because I couldn't pay the mortgage, I rented it out. I wasn't able to deal with the house. I had to move out of it to make life easier.'

Queer and affective literatures show how worlds are made and remade through world-building, developing the person as they undertake particular pathways. Scholars have long stressed the ability of queer life-worlds to challenge – and often to completely dismantle – the binary in terms of sex and gender but also the heteronormative aspects of life as it is conceived in the mainstream (Boellstorff, 2007). In capitalist societies, queer studies seek to understand life beyond the straight, progressive and positive niche of life lived 'right', in order to consider the messy, uneven and faltering agency of lifeways and ways of being outside the mainstream. In this way, failure has much to offer and teach: 'while failure certainly comes accompanied by a host of negative affects, such as disappointment, disillusionment, and despair, it also provides the opportunity to use these negative affects to poke holes in the toxic positivity of contemporary life' (Halberstam, 2011: 3). In my discussion with Jóhannes, I used timelining, a form of graphic elicitation in the context of interviews (for a description, see Sheridan et al., 2011), to understand how he thought about and reconciled with an unrealised future. The pairing of interviewing with timelining uncovered important ideas about sense-making during economic hardship and the competing logics used to narrate the trajectories of crisis and recovery.

Timelines comprised a large sheet of paper with a single horizontal line and no start or end dates. The hope was participants would compile their experiences. Sitting down with Jóhannes, however, the straight line proved to be confusing, and threw up several barriers. The temporality of crisis is never straightforward or linear, much like the life course. Metaphorically, the straight line appeared to go against a queer imagining of life. Queer theory has always played a critical role in exploring ambiguity through 'destabilising what hegemonic culture takes to be stable' (LeMaster, 2011: 105). This allows for a thick description about failure and success, but also of knowledge and ignorance. Eventually, Jóhannes filled out the timeline, drawing all over the page in a way that adhered to calendrical time but which didn't rely so heavily on landmarks and points of 'success' to recapitulate the crisis years, but rather that unfurled the relative failures he endured: relationship breakdown, being a burden on his family, moving between friend's houses and to different parts of Iceland, searches for stable employment, government decisions he viewed negatively, and so on (Figure 4.1).

The timeline comprised memories, feelings and events that punctuated his experience, culminating in a graphic that went beyond crisis alone, to

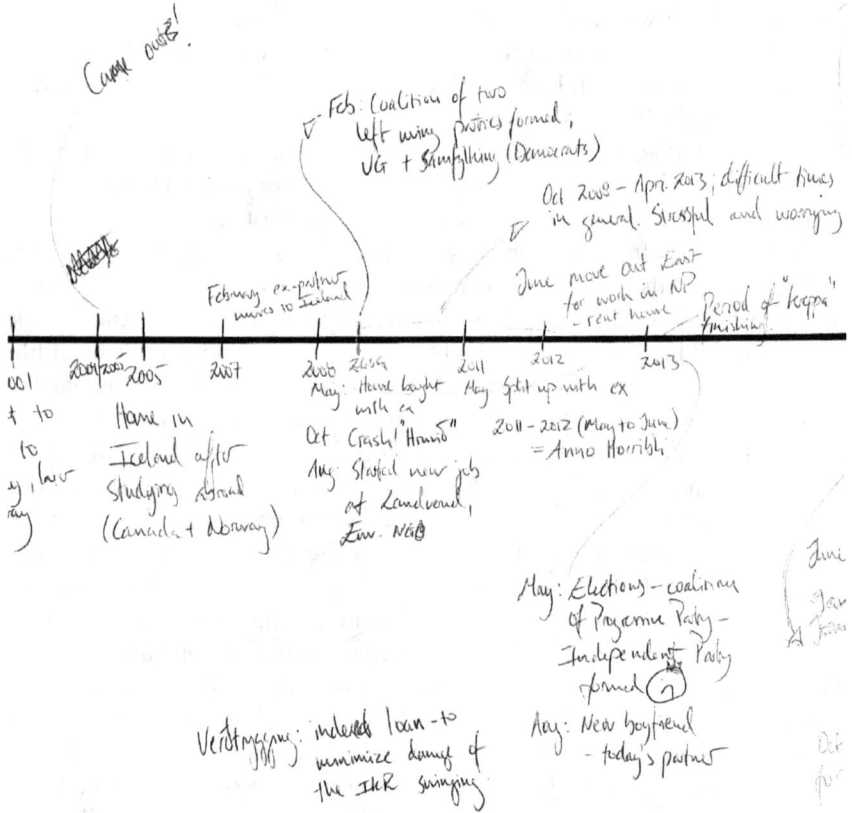

Figure 4.1 Part of Jóhannes' timeline detailing his crisis–recovery experience

also canvas recovery. This activity paired verbal and graphic elicitation techniques to understand Jóhannes' thinking, sensing and being in the world amid crisis, as not just an historical event in temporal terms, but a cultural and individual one, too. While in the good-life fantasy people become caught up within an optimistic moment that can avoid thinking and behaving in ways that engage directly with the consequences of their actions, timelining provides a participant-constructed view of crisis and recovery. Jóhannes reflected on what he had endured over the last nine years, taking to the open-endedness of the timeline by making jottings, crossing things out, and including emotional signifiers through drawings. This was a reflexive moment for calculating the experience of crisis and recovery. As Halberstam (2011: 2–3) notes, 'failing, losing, forgetting, unmaking, undoing, unbecoming, not knowing may in fact offer more creative, more cooperative, more surprising ways of being in the world'.

The activity prompted my interlocutor to engage with the future through a discussion of what kind of life is worth pursuing, given the setbacks he had experienced, and, based on his tertiary studies, what kinds of ethics should guide this pathway.

The project that Jóhannes envisaged for himself and Iceland sought to confront the *ignorance* central to dominant economic thinking (premised on opacification and esoteric knowledge). So, too, he challenged the tendency for people to obfuscate individualised risk, characteristic of the 'manic millennium' years, amid participation in atmospheres defined by capitalist accumulation. Ignorance can be very convenient politically and economically, promoting sentiments of *not* knowing (McGoey, 2012). But knowledge is important for reformation, and can be a vital tool for recasting shared cultural values. 'There's a lot of ignorance in our systems and in people themselves,' he lamented. 'The banking crash was a shock, and many people didn't realise just how ridiculous things had become. We had one of the biggest ecological footprints … we didn't understand the impact of our consumerist way of thinking.' Knowledge is paired here with ridicule, noting how failure has an inherent potential for reformation. This challenge is mounted through what he and Hörður engage as a mode of thinking, doing and being beyond the atmospheres of the pre-crisis years. For both, this is found through legislating the new constitution. As Jóhannes stated:

> I'm quite fond of the society that has nurtured me and made me the kind of person I am; given me the chance to go abroad and study and rely on the healthcare system, et cetera. It's a small society, sometimes too small. But when you belong to a minority group [the queer community], it's even smaller. So, I've always been very interested in politics and what sort of society we are actively building, and how we can build it to change it for the better … The constitution is a voice … to promote mutual understanding of what's going on and having the right to challenge what's going on [i.e. economic and political immorality]. What I would like us to be able to do is legislate the new constitution, finish the good work we started.

During fieldwork, several weekend protests were organised by Hörður ahead of parliamentary elections in 2017. At these events, the constitution was held up as important for the nation's future to reinvigorate politics and deliver reform. Meeting each weekend outside parliament, attendees discussed the virtues of the new constitution, highlighting that it is in effect dedicated to the future of the country, and seeks to dismantle power imbalances in which power is concentrated in the hands of prominent economic and political players (see Heffernan, 2020). For Hörður, these demonstrations provided an opportunity to develop notions of trust and reciprocity by concentrating on open and transparent communication and tactics of listening and engaging, thereby eschewing notions of secrecy and ignorance through not knowing. Hörður relied upon the tools of performance and storytelling to communicate, and upon attuned listening to understand people's concerns: 'I talk to a lot of people before I do something,' he stated; 'I ask, "what do you think about this?" … I see my job as telling stories, singing and getting a response.' During the final demonstration, protesters formed a large circle and held hands as they collectively yelled out their hopes for the future (Figure 4.2).

In times of disruption, Pink (2021: 196) asks how 'anticipatory concepts, such as trust, hope, and anxiety might become engaged to understand both actions in the present and feelings about possible futures', as worlds are made and remade in response to critical events. Further, Pink (2021: 196) notes that it is through an engagement with the senses that trust, much like hope, 'can be thought of as a feeling, or category of feeling, which describes anticipatory sensations' in connection with local worlds and programmes for world-building. Continuing, Pink (2021: 196) reflects on connections between the senses and knowing during periods of ambiguity:

> [T]rust is experienced when things 'feel right,' a sensation often achieved through the accomplishment of mundane everyday routines. Thus, trust is associated with the ongoing and incremental modes of knowing that we accumulate as life is lived, whereby the concept of knowing (instead of knowledge) implies the unfinishedness of what we purport to know.

Figure 4.2 Attendees in favour of legislating Iceland's draft constitution gather at an anti-Government demonstration (2017)

Knowing and sense-making are in this way firmly oriented toward the future and are capable of engaging experiences and understandings of the (un)known, the possible and the imagined (Pink and Salazar, 2017). However, this temporal orientation is different from the aforementioned electronic time-space produced through technologically mediated rationality/ignorance derived from technical calculation. To this end, a sensory approach to thinking about the future amid ambiguity operationalises in sensory terms the unknown, the possible and the imagined, and pairs these with culturally sanctioned ideas for contending with ever-changing local worlds.

Conclusion

In an era of cascading, unequally experienced crises affecting communities the world over, anthropological examinations need to go beyond looking at crisis alone, in order to understand recovery and transformation in sociocultural terms. The ethnography presented in this chapter on the crisis–recovery nexus benefited from a dual stance of looking back over nine years and looking forward towards the aspired future by engaging with social actors intent on reforming society and politics. An affective, queer reading of crisis and recovery provides two things. It demonstrates how affect is drawn into form to become atmospheres per se (i.e. 'manic millennia' and yearnings for 'moral' reform). Further, it disrupts the crisis–recovery nexus temporally and analytically to understand how affective atmospheres highlight sense-making patterns, including states of knowing and not knowing that eschew their usual positive and negative valences. Instead, the focus pursued here shows how system-knowledge and outcome-ignorance operate within an economic framework of rationality, while also subverting pessimistic views of personal failure to highlight its generative and creative potentials for individual and societal change. In turn, this chapter has explored personhood and showed the processes by which people are shaped in sociocultural terms, especially in relation to critical events that disrupt the life course.

Crisis, as a critical disruption, has been shown to be 'a cluster of factors that looks solid only at a certain distance' (Berlant, 2011: 103). Interviews and timelining pull apart these factors to uncover strands and threads of sensoria and experience that reveal the pathways people take towards recovery. This allows the crisis–recovery nexus to become more intelligible amid the ambiguity of crisis for the communities ethnographers work with, and during the task of conducting and writing ethnography. Kapferer (2015: 2) notes that crisis, 'as a singularity of forces', can show the 'critical dimensions of socio-cultural existence [to] reveal new potentials of the ongoing formation of socio-cultural realities'. This moves beyond event 'as representational of the social or of society and, instead, as a moment or moments of immanence and the affirmation and realization of potential' (Kapferer, 2015: 2). Moreover, it shows how anthropologists can study ambiguity without reducing the quality of this phenomenon or separating themselves from the reality of what it means to endure it. Further work is required to deconstruct the private/public split on failure, as failure on the part of the state has very real effects on social relationships and the materiality of the good life.

Notes

1 The state is called into action amid crisis, mobilising government responses, and strengthening its legitimacy (if their response is seen as adequate; Loftsdóttir et al., 2018).
2 This research was supported by an Australian Government Research Training Program scholarship and UNSW Arts and Social Sciences research funding.
3 The anthropological literature on affective states after crisis is now vast; see Knight (2015).
4 Equality and class are hotly debated, but contested, terms in Iceland; see Oddsson (2016).
5 Arguably, this perception or calculation has existed since the emergence of 'insurance' with Western modernity, colonisation and the development of globalised trade (see Zinn, 2008).

References

Ahmed, S., Castaneda, C., Fortier, A-M. et al. (2003) 'Introduction', in S. Ahmed, C. Castada, A-M. Fortier and M. Sheller (eds), *Uprootings/Regroundings: Questions of Home and Migration* (London: Bloomsbury), 1–19.
Anderson, L. and Björkman, T. (2018) *The Nordic Secret: A European Story of Beauty and Freedom* (Stockholm: Fri Tanke).
Berlant, L. (2011) *Cruel Optimism* (Durham, NC: Duke University Press).
Berlant, L. and Stewart, K. (2019) *The Hundreds* (Durham, NC: Duke University Press).
Bernburg, J.G. (2016) *Economic Crisis and Mass Protest: The Pots and Pans Revolution in Iceland* (London: Taylor and Francis).
Bielo, J.S. (2007) ' "The mind of Christ": Financial success, born-again personhood, and the anthropology of Christianity', *Ethnos,* 72:3, 316–38.
Boellstorff, T. (2007) 'Queer studies in the house of anthropology', *Annual Review of Anthropology*, 36:1, 17–35.
Broch-Due, V. and Ystanes, M., eds (2016) *Trusting and its Tribulations: Interdisciplinary Engagements with Intimacy, Sociality and Trust* (Oxford: Berghahn).
Davies, W. and McGoey, L. (2012) 'Rationalities of ignorance: On financial crisis and the ambivalence of neo-liberal epistemology', *Economy and Society*, 41:1, 64–83.

Halberstam, J. (2011) *The Queer Art of Failure* (Durham, NC: Duke University Press).

Harvey, P. (2013) *Hybrids of Modernity: Anthropology, the Nation State and the Universal Exhibition* (London: Routledge).

Heffernan, T. (2020) '"Where is the new constitution?": Public protest and community-building in post-economic collapse Iceland', *Conflict and Society*, 6:1, 236–54.

Kapferer, B. (2005) 'Situations, crisis, and the anthropology of the concrete: The contribution of Max Gluckman', *Social Analysis*, 49:3, 85–122.

Kapferer, B. (2015) 'Introduction', in L Meinert and B Kapferer (eds), *In the Event – Toward an Anthropology of Generic Moments* (Oxford: Berghahn), 1–28.

Knight, D.M. (2015) *History, Time, and Economic Crisis in Central Greece* (New York: Palgrave Macmillan).

LeMaster, B. (2011) 'Queer imag(in)ing: Liminality as resistance in Lindqvist's *Let the Right One In*', *Communication and Critical/Cultural Studies*, 8:2, 103–23.

Loftsdóttir, K. (2014) '"The enemy outside and within": The crisis and imagining the global in Iceland', in K. Loftsdóttir and L. Jensen (eds), *Crisis in the Nordic Nations and Beyond: At the Intersection of Environment, Finance and Multiculturalism* (London: Ashgate), 161–80.

Loftsdóttir, K. (2019) *Crisis and Coloniality at Europe's Margins: Creating Exotic Iceland* (Oxford: Routledge).

Loftsdóttir, K., Smith, A.L. and Hipfl, B., eds. (2018) *Messy Europe: Crisis, Race, and Nation-State in a Postcolonial World* (Oxford: Berghahn).

McGoey, L. (2012) 'Strategic unknowns: Towards a sociology of ignorance', *Economy and Society*, 41:1, 1–16.

Mixa, M.W. (2009) 'Once in khaki suits: Socioeconomical features of the Icelandic collapse', in I. Hannibalsson (ed.), *Rannsóknir í Félagsvísindum X: Hagfræðideild og Viðskiptafræðideild* (Reykjavik: Félagsvísindastofnun HÍ), 435–47.

Muir, S. (2021) *Routine Crisis: An Ethnography of Disillusion* (Chicago, IL: University of Chicago Press).

Oddsson, G. (2016) 'Neoliberal globalization and heightened perceptions of class division in Iceland', *Sociological Quarterly*, 57:3, 462–90.

Pink, S. (2015) *Doing Sensory Ethnography*, 2nd edn (London: SAGE Publications).

Pink, S. (2021) 'Sensuous futures: Re-thinking the concept of trust in design anthropology', *The Senses and Society*, 16:2, 193–202.

Pink, S. and Salazar, J.F. (2017) 'Anthropologies and futures: Setting the agenda', in J.F. Salazar, S. Pink, A. Irving and J. Sjöberg (eds), *Anthropologies and Futures: Researching Emerging and Uncertain Worlds* (London: Bloomsbury Academic), 3–22.

Porcello, T., Meintjes, L, Ochoa, A.M. and Samuels, D.W. (2010) 'The reorganization of the sensory world', *Annual Review of Anthropology*, 39:1, 51–66.

Povinelli, E. (2022) *Routes/Worlds* (Cambridge, MA: MIT Press).

Roitman, J. (2014) *Anti-Crisis* (Durham, NC: Duke University Press).

Sabaté, I. (2016) 'The Spanish mortgage crisis and the re-emergence of moral economies in uncertain times', *History and Anthropology*, 27:1 (2016), 107–20.

Sedgwick, E.K. (2008) *Epistemology of the Closet*, 2nd edn (Berkeley, CA: University of California Press).

Sheridan, J., Chamberlain, K. and Dupuis, A. (2011) 'Timelining: Visualizing experience', *Qualitative Research*, 11:5, 552–69.

Stewart, K. (2011) 'Atmospheric attunements', *Environment and Planning D: Society and Space*, 29:3, 445–53.

Thrift, N. (2004) 'Movement-space: The changing domain of thinking resulting from the development of new kinds of spatial awareness', *Economy and Society*, 33:4, 582–604.

Tsing, A. (2000) 'Inside the economy of appearances', *Public Culture*, 12:1, 115–44.

Tsing, A. (2005) *Friction: An Ethnography of Global Connection* (Princeton, NJ: Princeton University Press).

Turner, V. (1967) *The Forest of Symbols: Aspects of Ndembu Ritual* (Ithaca, NY: Cornell University Press).

Turner, V. (1969) *The Ritual Process: Structure and Anti-Structure* (London: Routledge).

Weiss, M. (2022) 'Queer theory from elsewhere and the im/proper objects of queer anthropology,' *Feminist Anthropology*, 3:2, 315–35.

Weston, K. (1993) 'Lesbian/gay studies in the house of anthropology', *Annual Review of Anthropology*, 22:1, 339–67.

Zinn, J.O. (2008) 'Introduction: The contribution of sociology to the discourse on risk and uncertainty', in J.O. Zinn (ed.), *Social Theories of Risk and Uncertainty: An Introduction* (London: Ashgate), 1–17.

5

Accommodating care through strategic ignorance: the ambiguities of kidney disease amongst Yolŋu renal patients in Australia's Northern Territory

Stefanie Puszka

Introduction

Chronic health conditions blur distinctions between states of health and illness. Conditions such as kidney disease, diabetes, hypertension and cancer are long-term, often incurable, and can cause fluctuating symptoms (WHO, 2018), reconfiguring the temporal dimensions of being unwell. Sometimes referred to as 'silent killers', chronic conditions may not be evident until a crisis point is reached and may rupture the way that people understand and experience their own corporeality (Anderson, 1995). As this chapter shows through ethnographic enquiry in collaboration with Yolŋu, an Australian Indigenous people,[1] diagnosis of chronic conditions does not necessarily create a sense of certainty, subjecting people to regimes of surveillance and further risk assessment to prevent disease progression and complications. As Heffernan and Cabrera Torrecilla (both this volume) demonstrate, perceptions of crisis, rupture and liminality can disturb temporal experience. Here I show how the uncertainties of chronic conditions shape temporality and bring about new social and spatial imaginaries of centre and periphery, health and illness, and closeness and distance experienced through care.

I consider the uncertainties of Yolŋu renal patients' bodies and lives and of dialysis treatment, as bodily or affective sensations and knowledge formations. Uncertainty is understood here as a lived experience that emerges from senses of confusion, absences of clarity, of instability and liminality, of unboundedness. Acknowledging the impossibility of certain knowledge in any absolute sense, and that any sensation of certainty is likely to be fleeting or contingent, both certainty and its binary opposite are also understood as normative categories attributed to particular modes of knowing and being. I consider how Yolŋu and other actors in healthcare systems attempt to transform or exploit uncertainties understood to exist in patients' bodies, lives and modes of treatment. As the editors discuss in this volume's Introduction, ambiguity can be conceptualised as a dynamic interaction between certain and uncertain knowledge formations and modes of experience. Ambiguity is not only an experience or social condition, but also a means of *generating* action and meaning. Drawing on this understanding of ambiguity, I foreground the temporalities that emerge from the interplay between states of uncertainty and its opposite, to illustrate the ways in which ambiguity and its temporalities can be invoked in governing health in epistemically open ways.

The uncertainties of kidney disease and dialysis treatment for Indigenous patients

Internationally, Indigenous peoples contend with an epidemic of chronic conditions, including kidney disease, which is attributable to colonial conditions of subjugation and rapid social and dietary change (The NCD Alliance, 2012). Despite this, access to dialysis treatment, essential to sustain the life of people with end-stage kidney disease in the absence of a kidney transplant, remains poor, particularly in remote areas. In Australia's Northern Territory, approximately 85 per cent of all dialysis patients are Indigenous people who have been displaced from remote Indigenous communities to the urban centres of Darwin and Alice Springs in order to access treatment (Gorham et al., 2019). For Yolŋu, poor access to treatment in their communities can result in permanent displacement to Darwin. Yolŋu Country comprises the northeast region of Arnhem Land in Australia's Northern Territory (Figure 5.1), including the major communities of Miliŋimbi, Ramingining, Galiwin'ku, Gapuwiyak, Gunyaŋara and Yirrkala. For Yolŋu patients, displacement to Darwin for treatment requires a physical journey of around 500–1,000 km or more, complicated by the prohibitive cost of air travel and poor-quality roads that are often inaccessible during the wet season.

Dialysis treatment, like end-stage kidney disease, blurs boundaries, straddling healthcare systems' categories of specialist and primary healthcare, leading to disputed and unstable governance. In remote areas of Australia, poor access to dialysis treatment is the corollary of historical disputes over responsibility between federal and state and territory governments for renal patients' care. Dialysis facilities in remote Indigenous communities have often been funded in unconventional and, at times, questionable ways, including through the sale of Indigenous art, mining royalties and mining land use agreements and, in one case, in exchange for the relinquishing of a land rights claim (Gorham et al., 2005).[2] While a 2018 policy shift resulted

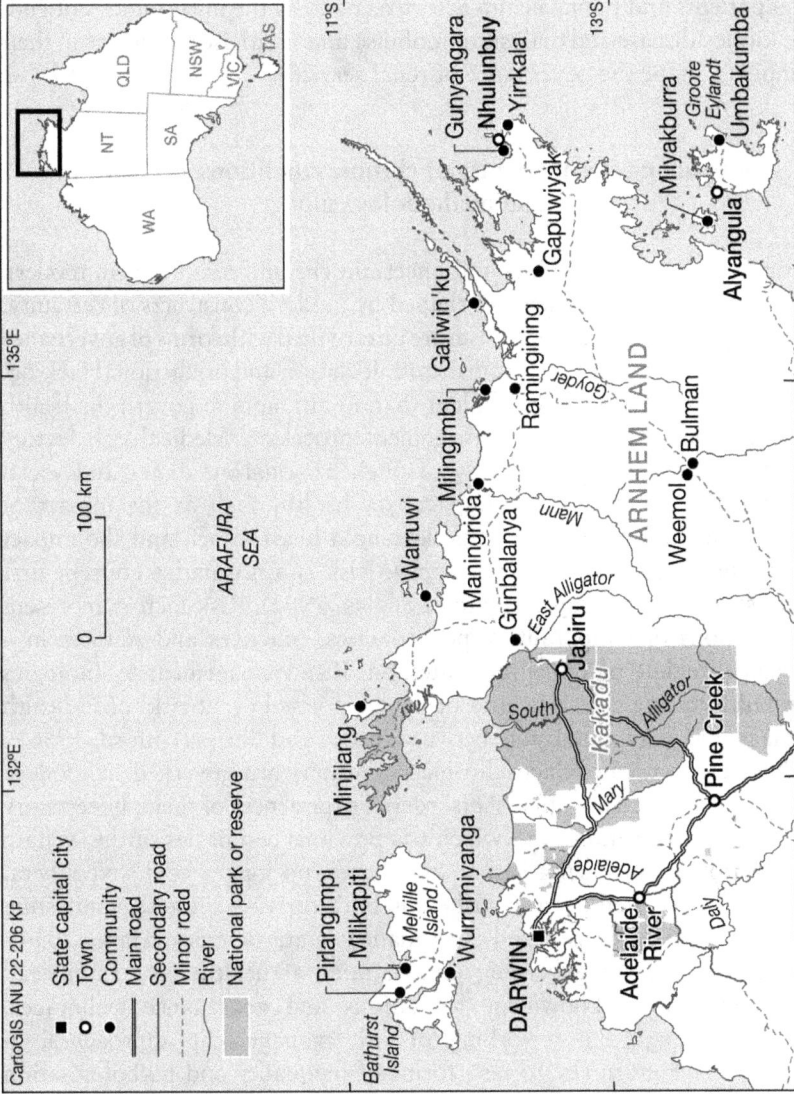

Figure 5.1 Study sites in the Top End of the Northern Territory of Australia

in new funding for remote dialysis services, Northern Territory renal services continue to prevent patients defined as 'high risk' from receiving treatment in remote areas, a category that remains undefined in medical protocols (Puszka, 2021). In this chapter I consider the multiple ways that Yolŋu patients and public health actors respond to the uncertainties of end-stage kidney disease and dialysis to mobilise and politicise ambiguity in their attempts to shape the governance of renal services.

Approaching the ambiguity of chronic conditions analytically and methodologically

Attempts to govern unsettling and uncertain chronic conditions in modern states and healthcare services are shaped by modern constructs of certainty. Modernity and industrial capitalism are intertwined with forms of governance that shape the future through statistical calculation and prediction (Hacking, 1990). Nowhere is this more evident than in attempts to govern the health of populations through risk management processes. Medical risk factors describe the statistical probability of one's personal attributes and social practices leading to negative impacts on health, such as the impact of smoking on the likelihood of experiencing a heart attack and the impact of Indigenous status on life expectancy. Risk is a normative concept that defines states of safety and danger (Douglas, 1992). Risk factors represent configurations of temporalities, potentialities, practices and statuses in a biomedical regime of value and valuation. Risk management technologies often fail to create certainty, and being categorised as 'at risk' of ill health can place one in a liminal state between health and illness (Gifford, 1986).

While the ways in which chronic conditions are governed in modern states are implicated in patients' disordered experiences of them, uncertainty is central to neoliberalism, in which the previous certainties of the welfare state, including universal access to healthcare, no longer hold.[3] Neoliberal governance has often been described as both thriving on and manifesting in conditions of precarity and a permanent state of crisis (Hage, 2014). Neoliberal modes of governing uncertainties of health have manifested in new biomedical knowledge formations and governance techniques, including through the reworking of risk management approaches, in ways that have given rise to new forms of inequality and pathologisation (Samimian-Darash, 2013; Kidron, 2015). In response to the uncertainties of the COVID-19 pandemic, states have redoubled the use of national health infrastructures, population surveillance and behavioural interventions in approaches to managing risk, in what some are denoting as post-neoliberal governance (Davies and Gane, 2021).

Analysis of the particular uncertainties of kidney disease and dialysis, and the ways in which these inform contested ways of knowing and governing Indigenous renal patients' health, has the potential to contribute a new vantage point on the productive power of ambiguity. This chapter illustrates how contending policy responses emerge from attempts to govern the embodied, social and temporal uncertainties of kidney disease. It foregrounds the non-linear temporal dimensions of renal patients' health, and the open-ended sociality of health, or the social conditions and relationships that make one well and make one the person one is, drawing on Yolŋu conceptualisations of personal vitality and time. I show how Yolŋu and public health actors seek to navigate, resolve or exploit the interplay between certainty and uncertainty in patients' bodies and lives and in healthcare systems. While risk management and attempts to eliminate uncertainty constitute the predominant response to the uncertainties of kidney disease in Northern Territory healthcare systems, I also show how practices of strategic ignorance amongst some public health actors, and relations of care between patients and health professionals, emerge as alternative modes of governing renal care, in ways that deploy its ambiguities. Through not-knowing, public health actors do not seek to resolve uncertainties in renal patients' health and care. As illustrated by Heffernan (this volume), practices of not-knowing within state institutions can deploy ignorance to deflect blame. Here, I argue that public health actors' practices of not-knowing deploy ambiguity to move beyond conflicts between biomedical and Yolŋu imaginaries of health to enable moments of co-existence and practices of care.

My analysis of the ambiguities of renal care is informed by F.G. Bailey's approach to the manipulation of ambiguity in social and political institutions. An acolyte of the Manchester School, Bailey's political anthropology was concerned with processes of social change through the dynamic interplay between social and political institutions and social action (Barrett, 2020). In *Tribe, Caste, and Nation* (1960) Bailey analysed the interaction between Indigenous socio-political institutions of tribe and caste with institutions of the modern state in postcolonial India. He developed the concept of 'bridge-actions' to denote, according to Barrett (2020), Bailey's student, 'the manner in which individuals pursued their interests by mobilising support across competing political structures'. Bridge-actions capture the tactics of political actors who exploit and manipulate conflicts and contradictions in ways that can at once bring heterogeneous institutions together and further actors' own political objectives.

While the interplay between structure and agency has since become a central concern of anthropological inquiry, Bailey's early approach continues to have contemporary relevance. Subsequent to Bailey, the enormously influential practice theory of Bourdieu, Giddens, Ortner and others considered dynamic interactions between human agency and social structures; however, a frequently cited critique centres their inability to explain how structures can produce social action that ultimately transforms them (Ahern, 2001). The poststructural approaches of theorists such as Deleuze, Latour and Haraway, meanwhile, disperse agency among human and nonhuman actors and, in place of a concern with social structures, consider the networks or assemblages of actors, objects, discourses, events and social worlds that cohere in distinct spatial and temporal settings (Greenough, 2011). In this chapter I approach knowledge formations and social practices associated with renal patients' health as not necessarily entirely determined or bounded by socio-political institutions such as healthcare systems and Yolŋu kinship; however, these organising systems nevertheless remain pertinent to an account of how ambiguity in renal patients' health emerges and is instrumentalised. Drawing on Bailey, I consider the conflicts, contradictions and tensions that arise within biomedicine and its intersection with Yolŋu practices of kinship and health in renal services. I foreground the manoeuvres and tactics of actors in navigating and exploiting the uncertainties of kidney disease and dialysis treatment, as processes holding the potential for social change.

I undertook an ethnography of Yolŋu renal patients' care, through collaboration with Yolŋu families, health service managers, Department of Health bureaucrats and evaluators over sixteen months (2017–19), drawing on an extended case study approach (Kempny, 2005). This approach led me to examine the divergent and overlapping narratives of health and health threats articulated by patients and other actors in healthcare systems; and also what was left unsaid. While working with a single group of interlocutors might have enabled me to attend to the particularity of their narratives in more depth, this approach enabled me to consider the interaction between Yolŋu and public health narratives and practices, and how meaning and action may emerge from ambiguity through experiences of marginalisation, and through relations of care.

My fieldwork was conducted in Darwin, where most Yolŋu patients receive treatment, and also in the community of Galiwin'ku on Elcho Island, in northeast Arnhem Land (Figure 5.1). This included fieldwork conducted during a pilot of dialysis at Galiwin'ku, in which some patients from the community who had been receiving treatment in Darwin were given the opportunity to return and undertake treatment there for two-week periods. Two Yolŋu co-researchers, the late Mr Muŋulpurr[4] and the late Miriam Dhurrkay, advised on the conduct of fieldwork and assisted with brokering relationships with renal patients within their social networks. They also shared their own narratives of end-stage kidney disease with me. Additionally, I conducted semi-structured interviews with thirty-five Northern Territory public health actors in Darwin and northeast Arnhem Land.

The risks of dialysis in remote Indigenous communities

Biomedical processes of risk assessment show that renal patients are at elevated risk of cardiac arrest (Zachariah et al., 2015). This was a possibility that caused apprehension among many public health actors I interviewed. For public health actors, the risks presented by the uncertain bodies of renal patients were heightened by their presence in remote communities. The absence of hospitals and specialist health services, in concert with the risks seen to inhere in patient sociality, were argued to pose dangers for remote patients. The potential for exposure to infectious disease presented by crowded housing conditions and intergenerational households was described as presenting a threat to patients who had compromised immunity. Several interlocutors were also concerned about poor food security in communities known for their material poverty. Public health actors located medical risk in patients' bodies, communities and in their modes of sociality.

Discourses amongst public health actors that located medical risk in the social geographies of remote communities invoked particular disease explanatory models. Public health actors' narratives often foregrounded the poverty and marginality of Indigenous peoples living in remote communities and drew on the concept of the 'social determinants of health'. Attributing population-based health inequalities to material and structural factors, the 'social determinants of health' concept has been popularised in Australian healthcare, and particularly in Indigenous health (Kowal, 2015). One public health actor, for example, described the high rates of end-stage kidney disease as the 'end game' of an onslaught of low birth weight, crowded housing, smoking, poverty, food insecurity, racial discrimination, poor education, chronic stress and inflammation. In such narratives, through heartfelt concern, a panorama of remote Indigenous communities emerges as places of disadvantage and as places in which biomedical health is difficult to govern. Notably, a social determinants explanatory model does not blame either patients or healthcare providers for these conditions. However, as I have argued elsewhere, in these narratives, residence in a remote community itself becomes a risk factor (Puszka, 2021).

The risky social geographies that public health actors attributed to patients forged a means of governing dialysis treatment in the Northern Territory. Renal patients are triaged through medical protocols that prohibit those considered to be 'medically unstable' from receiving treatment in remote areas. 'Medical instability', undefined in medical protocols, invokes clinical judgement in concert with a particular way of knowing remote Indigenous communities as inherently possessing risk. Health professionals also at times advised patients against returning to their communities for short visits between dialysis treatments or for ceremonies. As Elizabeth

Povinelli (2011) has elucidated, chronic conditions lack the eventfulness of more immediate crises. Probabilistic calculation and risk management are approaches that can transform chronic conditions into 'quasi-events', making them governable threats.

In Northern Territory renal services, the uncertain bodies and lives of Indigenous renal patients are rendered knowable and governable through discourses of (potential) events. Medical risk, as a mode of ambiguity, transforms the abiding, non-linear temporality of chronic conditions into a prescriptive set of future threats to be averted at all costs. The possibility that some patients might accept the biomedical risks of receiving treatment in remote areas in order to remain on Country did not appear to be canvassed among public health actors.

The health of Yolŋu patients on Country and the threats of urban displacement

As my collaborator, Mr Muŋulpurr, explained to me, kinship is the 'foundation' of Yolŋu society. Yolŋu interlocutors described the quality of one's relations with kin and one's presence on Country as shaping personal vitality, foregrounding social and experiential dimensions of health and illness. Another patient, Dianne, described the Yolŋu notion of *märr* as denoting one's 'inner strength, spirituality, fullness, inner activity'. When replenished, according to Dianne, *märr* nurtured an embodied state in which 'the body, mind, soul are one'. The sense of inner vitality and unity of being full of *märr* enabled Yolŋu to 'think the right way, go along the right path', thus helping to constitute agency and moral subjectivities. As Tamisari (2014) illustrates, *märr* becomes embodied in people through co-presence and sensory experience. Interlocutors described *märr* as constituted among Yolŋu socially and temporally through the rhythms of everyday life, through activities such as sitting with family and caring for children within their communities. Through *märr*, Yolŋu embody the kincentric moral ecology described by Amanda Kearney (2017), in which states of health and illness are intersubjective experiences shared among kin, who may be people, land or waterways.

While my Yolŋu interlocutors did not reject biomedical treatment, they made sense of their uncertain health in ways that diverged from the temporalities and threats of risk discourse. Interlocutors often attributed the emergence of kidney disease to colonisation and associated changes in customary foodways. Dialysis treatment that removed pain and discomfort, and that did not cause the social pain of displacement, however, could be assimilated into Yolŋu narratives of health. Mr Muŋulpurr reflected on his experiences of the Galiwin'ku pilot, describing the feelings and sensations of being in the presence of kin as improving biomedical metrics of his health:

> When I miss renal (dialysis) in Darwin I feel sick, but not back in Galiwin'ku. [In Darwin] I have pain, I don't feel like eating, I don't feel like walking. [In Galiwin'ku] that's because you're home and you can feel the atmosphere and feel the voice of the wind talking to you and saying 'I'm here', and you say to yourself 'I should be back here with my great great great ancestors because the spirit is talking to me ... [when patients return to Galiwin'ku] the sand, the sea will laugh for us and we'll talk to them and everything will be run smooth, no high blood pressure, no salt, no sugar. They'll laugh every day.

Yolŋu described renal services in their communities, complemented by care for patients by kin, ancestors and Country, as improving the health of individual and social bodies.

Patients appeared to be more physically active on Elcho Island during the pilot than when residing in Darwin. An older participant in the Galiwin'ku pilot, who appeared frail in Darwin and didn't often go out, walked from Galiwin'ku to a homeland with which she was connected and back, a journey of approximately 10 kilometres. Yolŋu undertaking treatment on Country attributed their renewed vitality to the ways in which physical and social geographies were experienced.

While Yolŋu readily assimilated dialysis treatment on Country into their own explanatory models, receiving dialysis treatment through urban displacement was said to minimally sustain patients without inducing a full state of health. Patients described displacement to Darwin as eliciting a deep sense of loss and despair, displacing them from the social relations, Country and hunted and gathered foods that sustained them. The loss of personal substance of displaced renal patients could present an existential threat. When I asked one patient, Wapiriny, about what happened to patients without close relatives in Darwin, he replied that those patients had 'already gone' – ending their treatment and leaving Darwin to return to their homelands, and departing from this life. Displacement for dialysis, and the loss of personal substance it caused, according to my interlocutors, could make one's life no longer worth living.

The displacement of renal patients to Darwin could also hazard broader threats to Yolŋu society. Mr Muŋulpurr suggested that displacement could dispossess Yolŋu societies of knowledge and leadership, as well as patients of social status. He lamented to me,

> When we get this sickness we feel like we nobody. That's how we feel. Like we bin let down. We lose everything. We lose family, we lose the good time, we lose friends, we lose future. That's what this sickness does ... I look at myself, I say I was not like this before. I was huge big man. I used to work for community

police for four years. I used to go hunting every day, on the weekend fishing, spearing, but this sickness bin slow me down. I used to be a tribal leader for the Djambarrpuyŋu clan, I used to lead them but not anymore, because this sickness shut down my future. Shut down the main transfer.

While interlocutors all agreed that those diagnosed with end-stage kidney disease required dialysis treatment, many felt that a return to customary foodways held the prospect of addressing the epidemic of kidney disease more broadly.

Yolŋu made sense of the uncertain health of renal patients through intersubjective bodily sensations, emotions and relationships; and through experiential modes of knowledge. Such conceptualisations lacked the specificity and eventfulness of risk discourse. Williams and Mununggurr (1989) describe how time is experienced by Yolŋu as cyclical and synchronous, marked by seasons and lifecycles, and by the simultaneous occurrence of specific events and conditions. For Yolŋu, health was the outcome of an abiding and recursive set of kincentric relationships to one's ancestors and Country, and present and future kin. When articulating what made renal patients well, interlocutors invoked the everyday rhythms of life in their communities involved in fulfilling social roles and procuring sustenance. The ambiguous sociality of Yolŋu health is not knowable through biomedical knowledge grounded in a positivist epistemology, liberal assumptions about autonomous individual personhood and methods of statistical analysis. The existential threat posed by urban displacement similarly lacked eventfulness and was not comprehensible through biomedical epistemologies and ways of knowing remote communities as inherently possessing risk. The existential threat of displacement could not be subjected to risk management procedures in Northern Territory healthcare systems. Medical risk functions as a means of transforming patients' uncertain health into governable bodies, places and time horizons through the denial of social and experiential dimensions of health and illness.

Care and shared objectives through strategic ignorance

While the ambiguities of chronic conditions could be invoked in risk management processes, they could also enable divergent narratives in public health to flourish. Yolŋu experiences of the health of renal patients undertaking dialysis on Country were paralleled by the narratives and also particular silences of some public health actors. Evaluations of remote dialysis services report that patients undertaking treatment in their home communities have comparable or better adherence to treatment and biomedical health markers, and fewer hospital admissions, compared to those receiving dialysis in hospitals and urban renal units (Gorham, 2000; Marley et al., 2010). In these studies, end-stage kidney disease is once again made eventful, but through a more opaque reduction rather than amplification of possible future threats. These studies generally attribute the success of remote dialysis services to improved 'quality of life' and 'satisfaction' among patients, with little further elaboration (Gorham, 2000; Marley et al., 2010). The authors decline to discuss what patient quality-of-life might entail, and the causal links between quality-of-life and health. Despite the growing volume of public health literature on the health of Indigenous renal patients, the particular phenomena that make patients receiving dialysis in remote areas well have been left peculiarly unexamined.

Some health professionals involved in administering dialysis in remote areas likewise observed dramatic improvements in patients' health when patients returned to their communities. One health professional recounted second-hand another nurse's observation of her patients during another stage of the Galiwin'ku pilot: 'She said that the change in these two gentlemen, one is particular ... the changes in him and his actual physical health while he was there was incredible. She said his blood pressure went down and she had to take him off his meds.' These interlocutors similarly offered little speculation about the precise factors in remote communities that led to improvements in renal patients' health, in contrast to risk management approaches.

It was not uncommon for public health actors to make broad statements about their lack of knowledge of Indigenous social structures, beliefs and healing practices, despite in some cases having worked in the same communities over long periods of time. In interviews I conducted with public health actors, interlocutors tended to refrain from discussing specific values and practices of the Indigenous peoples they worked with, and when such topics arose interlocutors instead tended to describe the improvisational strategies they adopted in their attempts to provide care in ways that did not offend patients. Despite an increasing emphasis on cultural safety in healthcare policy, which was generally embraced by interlocutors, understanding Indigenous beliefs and practices associated with health was curiously considered to be tangential to their professional practice. Public health actors' statements of not-knowing Indigenous sociality may have represented genuine ignorance. However, their openly articulated claims of not-knowing were also strategic interventions that marked the limits of biomedical epistemologies. Some public health actors cast patients as 'experts' of social and experiential dimensions of their health, according patients and their kin a technical expertise and status of partners in therapeutic relationships.

Public health actors' practices of strategic ignorance were deployed in attempts to construct shared objectives with patients premised on divergent imaginaries and uncertain conditions of health. Strategic ignorance offers a counterpoint to frequent critiques of biomedicine's 'immodest claims of causality' (Farmer, 1999). It emerged in response to the contradiction between explanatory models grounded in medical risk, the concept of the social determinants of health and the outcomes of remote dialysis services. Strategic ignorance constituted a bridge-action by enabling public health actors to advocate for the expansion of remote dialysis services on the grounds of improvements to patients' biomedical health, despite the absence of biomedical explanatory models for such outcomes.

Partnerships between public health actors and patients, forged through shared objectives and divergent epistemologies, were fragile and not always harmonious. During the Galiwin'ku trial, one of my Yolŋu interlocutors was reminded by a renal nurse to maintain personal hygiene in the community. Although the nurse was a supporter of dialysis on Country and had been contending with the opposing views of colleagues, my interlocutor complained that the nurse expected or assumed Yolŋu would 'live like Balanda (non-Indigenous peoples)'. Crowded housing conditions in the community, in which bathrooms were often shared by a large number of residents, could pose an impediment to regular showering and handwashing. Nevertheless, public health actors' strategic ignorance, in overlooking blindspots in biomedical knowledge and posing limits to its applicability, opened the possibility of alliances with patients.

The temporality and sociality of kidney disease and dialysis provided the conditions of possibility for such alliances to emerge. Haemodialysis, the most common form of dialysis, is usually performed three times a week, for four to five hours per treatment, for the remainder of patients' lives. The temporalities of kidney disease and dialysis, like the sociality of Yolŋu health, were cyclical and synchronous, marked by dialysis schedules, the continual accumulation and elimination of fluid and waste in patients' bodies, other medical appointments and patients' fluctuating vitality. The long hours of contact between patients and health professionals provided the grounds of possibility for healthcare to take the form of what Annemarie Mol (2008) describes as a logic of care, constituted through ongoing collaborative relationships rather than single transactions of treatment. Some health professionals described renal wards and units in Darwin as 'a community', and patients as 'like family'. Patients also understood such relations of care through the idiom of kinship, in some cases adopting health professionals as kin. One renal nurse working in a remote area saw herself as forging ties between communities and health bureaucracies, telling me 'we nurses you know, we are going-betweeners'. Practices of kinship and care in healthcare, as further bridge-actions, forged through ambiguities in narratives of renal patients' health, opened up further possibilities for new visions and practices in biomedicine.

The productive power of ambiguity
in Northern Territory renal services

While medical risk is a construct that is instrumentalised in Northern Territory renal services in attempts to define states and sites of health and illness to eliminate uncertainty, as I have illustrated, it does not always succeed in these objectives and can lead to particular modes of ambiguity. As Beck argued (1992), the consequences of risk management may lead to the proliferation of ever more threats over which no one can be held accountable. The concept of medical risk rendered renal services incapable of recognising and allocating responsibilities for the existential threat that urban displacement poses to Yolŋu. Dialysis treatment provided through urban displacement also had the potential to result in poor patient health in biomedical terms. Renal patients in the Northern Territory, who are overwhelmingly Indigenous people displaced from remote communities to urban centres for treatment, have low rates of survival on dialysis, at six years on average (Northern Territory Government, 2017). Low survival rates are partially attributable to the conditions of life in which patients receive treatment. In addition to the existential threats of displacement described by my interlocutors, patients receiving treatment in Darwin experienced food insecurity and were subject to housing precarity, and in some cases homelessness due to inadequate social support (Puszka, 2022). Here, ambiguity leaks out of attempts to manage risks. Social and material dimensions of end-stage kidney disease escape the definitional boundaries it imposes around health and danger.

The way in which medical risk is deployed to govern the health of patients in Northern Territory renal services works to institutionalise rather than eradicate uncertainty. Through the undefined category of 'medical instability', the indeterminate nature of patients' health itself provided justification for treatment in urban hospitals and for generating the existential threats of displacement. Ambiguity emerges here, in part, through contending temporalities. The lack of eventfulness of the threats of displacement, in comparison to the potential for a heart attack, and the inability of healthcare systems to govern and accept responsibility for social conditions, obscures the visibility of the threats of displacement in risk management processes. In making health eventful, medical risk provides a means of governing health through the transformation of the temporal dimensions of illness in ways that conflict with the sociality of health.

The generative power of ambiguity emerges from the responses of Yolŋu patients and alternative public health to patients' uncertain health. Renal care, while invoking risk management responses, could also foreground underlying conflicts in the liberalism of public health, between values of patient autonomy and choice, and the supremacy accorded to biomedical rationalities of health and illness, and their intersection with Yolŋu beliefs, values and practices. Alternative means of governing renal patients' health emerge through the bridge-actions that patients and public health actors deployed to navigate these fissures, in ways that do not necessarily foreclose meaning or explanation, or resolve contradiction or contention. Practices of strategic ignorance and of care spring from interplays of certainty and uncertainty in kidney disease to provide new ways of governing renal patients' health.

Strategic ignorance is a mode of ambiguity mobilised by some public health actors who remained silent on dimensions of patient health which were unexplainable in a biomedical paradigm. Strategic ignorance offers no explanation of how people from communities with some of the poorest population health in Australia in biomedical terms, and with poor access to healthcare services, improved their biomedical health by returning to the same communities. It offers no explicit critique of risk management approaches, yet provides grounds for other interpretations of the threats to patients' health to emerge and be granted legitimacy. Strategic ignorance is counter to the positivist epistemology of biomedicine and at first glance appears to be contrary to the commonsense notion that knowledge is power. However, by eliding explanation, strategic ignorance differs from the denial of social and experiential dimensions of illness through risk management approaches, and provides an avenue for acknowledging and responding to the limits of biomedicine. It affords space beyond the margins of biomedicine for ways of knowing and governing illness that foreground the social and experiential, and constructs an uneasy co-existence between biomedicine and Indigenous imaginaries of health. Strategic ignorance of the sociality of health also contrasts with the construct of the social determinants of health by imposing limits to biomedical knowledge and governance rather than seeking to subsume and transform the inevitably uncertain and open-ended social into the medical.

The 'bridge-actions' of public health actors and patients instrumentalised ambiguity in the pursuit of their objectives, yet these moves did not destabilise the institutions of biomedicine and kinship, and on the contrary, worked to strengthen them at their frontiers. Patients' relationships with health professionals provided a means of 'Indigenising' healthcare (Sahlins, 1999) by incorporating staff within the reciprocities and responsibilities of kinship, extending the sociality of health to the sociality of healthcare. As illustrated by Carsten (2019) in her ethnography of blood work in Malaysian healthcare, biomedicine operates through social relations between patients and staff. The insertion of needles into patients' fistulas, their regular attendance at treatment, and their ability to manage dialysis side-effects required collaborative relationships. Public health actors, through strategic ignorance, sought to expand access to dialysis on Country and accord legitimacy to Indigenous social practices and imaginaries of health. Dialysis on Country could enable the integration of medical advice into Yolŋu life-worlds and the generation of *märr* needed to adhere to treatment, and could also improve patients' health in biomedical terms. The ambiguities of kidney disease could inform conditions of possibility for moments of convergence and co-existence between Yolŋu and biomedical interests and objectives, and to some extent, possibilities of subverting risk management approaches that continue to displace patients. By strategically deploying social and temporal ambiguities of kidney disease, rather than seeking to transform them in a quest for certainty, the bridge-actions of patients and public health actors create space for relations of care.

Bailey developed the notion of bridge-actions (1960) to denote the active playbooks of political actors in exploiting institutional uncertainties and conflicts. I suggest that bridge-actions may also encompass strategic silences, omissions and evasions and other practices of 'care' (or 'negative engagements'; see Alimardanian, this volume) at the intersection of heterogeneous institutions that pave the way for the realisation of particular interests or objectives. As contemporary scholarship on human agency has illustrated, agency can take many forms which may include declining to act and conforming with social norms (Mahmood, 2001; Saethre, 2013). In this formulation, bridge-actions may not necessarily perform the work of synthesis of the disparate purposes and practices of socio-political institutions, but have the potential to construct fragile co-existences and alliances by leaving uncertainties and conflicts unresolved.

Conclusion

In Northern Territory renal services, ambiguity is not a counterpoint to stable governance, as risk management approaches illustrate. The false promise of certainty offered by medical risk can come into conflict with the irregular temporality of chronic conditions and with the open-endedness of the sociality of health and of care. The sociality of health exists in a non-linear time-space. It is inevitably opaque and unknowable through a biomedical paradigm, informing little prospect of bodily stability or durable approaches to treatment and its governance. While chronic conditions can be deeply unsettling for people with a diagnosis and for healthcare systems, we must ask what is at stake in our quest for bodily certainty.

Although Indigenous imaginaries of health represent a radically different way of understanding bodily states of being to biomedicine, the limited capacity of biomedicine to understand and govern the sociality of health extends beyond that of Indigenous populations. The COVID-19 pandemic and the social and economic malaise it has caused, during which this chapter was written, further illustrates how our sociality at once poses threats of viral contagion and sustains us in social and material ways. The threats of kidney disease and heart attack, as conventionally understood noncommunicable diseases, differ from those of coronavirus. Nevertheless, growing non-compliance with quarantine and social isolation directives and an outbreak of distress, anxiety and other psychosocial conditions during the pandemic further demonstrate that governing biomedical health requires healthcare to engage with the social in epistemically open ways, and in ways that do not seek to subsume the social within the biomedical.

Notes

1 I am indebted to Yolŋu renal patients and families who welcomed me into their lives during this research and shared their experiences and perspectives of kidney disease with me, and especially to two Yolŋu co-researchers who advised me and worked alongside me, the late Mr Muŋulpurr and the late Miriam Dhurrkay. As Mr Muŋulpurr's family wanted him to be remembered, Muŋulpurr ŋarra dhuwal, ga bulu ŋarra dhuwal dhayinhu, dhabanba. I am grateful to the families of Yolŋu interlocutors no longer with us for providing permission for me to publish this data. I would also like to thank health professionals and policymakers with whom I conducted interviews. This chapter is immeasurably improved thanks to comments and suggestions from Mahnaz Alimardanian, Tim Heffernan, Yasmine Musharbash, Katie Curchin, Paul Lawton, Alex D'Aloia and Frances Morphy. The included map was prepared by CartoGIS Services, The Australian National University. This work was supported by a National Health and Medical Research Council postgraduate scholarship, a National Health and Medical Research Council project grant and a Barbara Hale Fellowship.

2 Land rights comprise a grant of freehold or perpetual lease title by Australian Governments to Indigenous Australians.

3 In the Northern Territory, however, it is a questionable proposition that Indigenous people ever received the full benefits of the welfare state, and poor access to health and social services in remote Indigenous communities represents historical continuities in structural racism.

4 Interlocutors and their families have chosen the ways in which they have been identified in this chapter. The narratives of Yolŋu interlocutors who have passed away are included in this chapter with the consent of their families. Public health actors, interviewed on the basis of their professional roles, have been de-identified.

References

Ahern, L. (2001) 'Language and agency', *Annual Review of Anthropology*, 30, 109–37.

Anderson, I. (1995) 'Bodies, disease and the problem of Foucault', *Social Analysis*, 37, 67–81.

Bailey, F.G. (1960) *Tribe, Caste, and Nation: A Study of Political Activity and Political Change in Highland Orissa* (Manchester: Manchester University Press).

Barrett, S. (2020) 'Politics as theatrical performance and backstage pragmatism: Work and legacy of F. G. Bailey', BEROSE – International Encyclopedia of the Histories of Anthropology, www.berose.fr/?lang=fr (accessed 10 February 2022).

Beck, U. (1992) *Risk Society: Towards a New Modernity* (London: Sage).

Carsten, J. (2019) *Blood Work: Life and Laboratories in Penang* (Durham, NC: Duke University Press).

Davies, W. and Gane, N. (2021) 'Post-neoliberalism? An introduction', *Theory, Culture & Society*, 38:6, 3–28.

Douglas, M. (1992) *Risk and Blame: Essays in Cultural Theory* (London: Routledge).

Farmer, P. (1999) *Infections and Inequalities: The Modern Plagues* (Berkeley, CA; University of California Press).

Gifford, S. (1986) 'The meaning of lumps: A case study of the ambiguities of risk', in C. Janes (ed.), *Anthropology and Epidemiology: Interdisciplinary Approaches to the Study of Health and Disease* (Dordrecht: D. Reidel Publishing), 213–46.

Gorham, G. (2000) 'Tiwi dialysis centre: The economic and social repercussions of client relocation', a report (Darwin: Nightcliff Renal Unit).

Gorham, G., Howard, K., Zhao, Y. et al. (2019) 'Cost of dialysis therapies in rural and remote Australia – A micro-costing analysis', *BMC Nephrology*, 20:1, 231.

Gorham, G., Wagner, L. and Jose, M. (2005) 'The Northern Territory's remote and community-based Haemodialysis program: Interesting times', *Renal Society of Australasia Journal*, 1:2, 59–63.

Greenough, B. (2011) 'Assembling an island laboratory', *Area*, 43:2, 134–8.

Hacking, I. (1990) *The Taming of Chance* (Cambridge: University of Cambridge Press).

Hage, G. (2014) *Alter-Politics: Critical Anthropology and the Radical Imagination* (Melbourne: Melbourne University Press).

Kearney, A. (2017) *Violence in Place, Cultural and Environmental Wounding* (New York: Routledge).

Kempny, M. (2005) 'History of the Manchester "school" and the extended-case method', *Social Analysis*, 49:3, 144–65.

Kidron, C. (2015) 'Global humanitarian interventions: Managing uncertain trajectories of Cambodian mental health', in L. Samimian-Darash and P. Rabinow (eds), *Modes of Uncertainty: Anthropological Cases* (Chicago, IL: University of Chicago Press), 105–22.

Kowal, E. (2015) *Trapped in the Gap: Doing Good in Indigenous Australia* (New York: Berghahn).

Mahmood, S. (2001) 'Feminist theory, embodiment, and the docile agent: Some reflections on the Egyptian Islamic revival', *Cultural Anthropology*, 16:2, 202–36.

Marley, J., Dent, H., Wearne, M. et al. (2010) 'Haemodialysis outcomes of Aboriginal and Torres Strait Islander patients of remote Kimberley region origin', *Medical Journal of Australia*, 193:9, 516–20.

Mol, A. (2008) *The Logic of Care: Health and the Problem of Patient Choice* (London: Routledge).

Northern Territory Government (2017) 'Northern Territory renal services strategy 2017–2021', a report (Darwin: Northern Territory Department of Health).

Povinelli, E. (2011) *Economies of Abandonment: Social Belonging and Endurance in Late Liberalism* (Durham, NC: Duke University Press).

Puszka, S. (2022) 'A politics of care in urban public housing: Housing precarity amongst Yolŋu renal patients in Darwin', *Housing Studies*, 37:5, 769–88.

Puszka, S. (2021) 'The 'dirty work' of risk in Northern Territory renal services', *Australian Journal of Anthropology*, 32:1, 54–65.

Saethre, E. (2013) *Illness is a Weapon: Indigenous Identity and Enduring Afflictions* (Nashville, TN: Vanderbilt University Press).

Sahlins, M. (1999) 'What is anthropological enlightenment? Some lessons of the twentieth century', *Annual Review of Anthropology*, 28, i–xxiii.

Samimian-Darash, L. (2013) 'Governing future potential biothreats: Toward an anthropology of uncertainty', *Current Anthropology*, 54:1, 1–22.

Tamisari, F. (2014) 'Feeling, motion, and attention in the display of emotions in Yolngu law, song, and dance performance', *Journal for the Anthropological Study of Human Movement*, 21:2, 1–24.

The NCD Alliance (2012) 'Health inequalities and Indigenous people', a report (Geneva: The NCD Alliance).

Williams, N. and Mununggurr, D. (1989) 'Understanding Yolngu signs of the past', in R. Layton (ed.), *Who Needs the Past? Indigenous Values and Archaeology* (London: Unwin Hyman), 72–83.

Zachariah, D., Kalra, P. and Roberts, P. (2015) 'Sudden cardiac death in end stage renal disease: Unlocking the mystery', *Journal of Nephrology*, 28:2, 133–41.

6

Charting fields of uncertainty: disaster, displacement and resilience in Bangladeshi *char* villages

Mohammad Altaf Hossain

Introduction

While extreme weather, geologic and climatic events continue to affect the resiliency of communities, it is the regional poor who are most vulnerable to natural hazards as they cannot always readily afford access to safer places or the resources to carve out stable livelihoods. Indeed, many are in constant fear of losing their land, homes, community and employment due to disasters. Researchers argue that extreme events such as floods and cyclones are not only responsible for people's vulnerability; rather social and economic structures place certain groups in precarious conditions (Wisner et al., 2004; Oliver-Smith, 2009). This is particularly the case in Bangladesh where seasonal floods, riverbank erosion, cyclones, drought and salinity intrusion frequently intersect with structural disadvantage, which affects people's lives and livelihoods, as seen for example during the Bhola Cyclone in 1970, devastating floods in 1988, Cyclone Sidr in 2007, Cyclone Aila in 2009 and Cyclone Amphan in 2020.

This chapter explores uncertainty in the lives of people living on Onishchit *Char*, located in Gaibandha District, Bangladesh. *Char* is a Bengali term for an unstable river island that is formed through accretion of sand and mud, which traditionally remain for decades but which are now depleting with climate change and disaster. Although *char*s are characteristically hazardous, many people, particularly the poor and landless, find them relatively cheaper places for making a living (Baqee, 1998; Lahiri-Dutt and Samanta, 2013). Both *certainty* and *uncertainty* coexist which produces a double bind: certainty in that agricultural lands on *char*s are naturally fertile and good for farming compared with the mainland, and uncertainty in that such landscapes do not last long due to riverbank erosion.

These characteristics leave people in an ambiguous situation: should they live on or in fact leave these hazardous islands? Ambiguity is expressed in the common saying 'We are king today, beggar tomorrow' by locals, amid rapid changes to their socioeconomic conditions. The terms 'king' and 'beggar', it is worth noting, denote 'good' and 'bad' economic conditions, respectively. Flooding and erosion leave the landless and smallholders in seasonal income insecurity. By contrast, agricultural plots become more fertile when flood waters decline. In turn, people eagerly await the post-flood season when they can invest time and labour in agriculture that temporarily makes them 'king'. Agricultural land on *chars* can be seen as a 'social field' with multiple livelihood practices employed by different social actors across time and space as they contend with a changing environment, which greatly leads them to building resilience for survival. Such practices are set against the interventionist strategies of NGOs premised on increasing climate change knowledge and adaptation practices locally, as well as against the state system, which has proven to respond slowly to threats posed by climate change.

Throughout this chapter, ambiguity is taken as the effects of the uncertain socioeconomic conditions *char* community members face. Precarity leaves them with limited choices – that is to say, they have to reside in hazardous island villages, vulnerable to the devastating consequences of disasters. Annual flooding and frequent erosion – two devastating forces – affect every aspect of *char* dwellers' lives. For example, disasters cause displacement, which leads to searches for higher, unflooded or stable *chars*. While moving from *char* to *char* is not new, disasters make living with such uncertainty a common predicament. Recently, government and NGOs have jointly implemented development programmes to increase *char* people's disaster resilience to provide more livelihood certainty. This chapter explores people's understandings of disaster, experiences of displacement, aspirations of building resilience, and struggles to reduce hazard risk, conceptualised, after Bourdieu, as 'fields' of uncertainty, through challenging prevailing structures and relying on social capital to receive assistance from state and non-state actors.

Bourdieu's ideas are expanded upon using social theory to demonstrate the ways social practices buffer against external disruption. It is important to understand that the long-standing precarity of *char* dwellers and *char* ecology needs to be considered as one of national crisis that hinders socioeconomic development. The first section describes *char* dwellers' understandings of disaster and climate change. The second section deals with experiences of displacement. The final section portrays islanders' aspiration in relation to increasing disaster resilience.

Char dwellers' understanding of climate change and hazards

The geographic profile of Bangladesh is dominated by natural hazards and this comes to shape *char* dwellers' understanding of climatic disasters and their continued negotiation with place. The country is located in the Bengal Delta, which is formed by deposits of silt carried by three major rivers: the Ganges, the Brahmaputra and the Meghna. These rivers drain their waters into the Bay of Bengal that is situated in the south of the country. Bangladesh's rural economy is mainly based on agriculture – crop production, fishing and raising of livestock. Numerous songs of different genres (e.g. folksongs) reflect emotional attachment to rivers. Yet river flooding and sea-level rise frequently leave millions of rural Bangladeshis at the whim of natural forces, seen repeatedly through hurricanes and storm surges. Added to this are the impacts of climate change, which researchers argue have become exacerbated and more unpredictable due to global warming (e.g. Rashid and Paul, 2014). The unpredictability experienced in everyday life has led to low crop production and food insecurity.

The physical disconnection of villages from the mainland accelerates the effects of climate change on islanders' lives as they experience continual displacement and contend with shifting water, land and economic systems. *Chars* are also administratively disconnected. For example, on Onishchit *Char*, there is no government infrastructure except for two primary schools. There is no postal service to deliver letters because the people do not have a precise address. They can only be contacted by arriving physically at their door. Mobile phones have become a popular way of maintaining necessary and social communication, however. I got to know this reality during sixteen months of fieldwork, beginning in 2015. I participated in *char* dwellers' lives by travelling with them on boats, harvesting crops, hanging out at public places, praying in the mosque, and attending local festivals, noting how these shifting systems were experienced and negotiated.

On a hot day in March, I met Nurul, a key informant, who remarked: 'We don't even have a graveyard.' His family used to live in a *char* village that was thought to be on stable, higher land. Here, stability is configured as opposed to the ambiguous realities of shifting lower lands, and yet this shifting quality of *char* lands means ambiguity of place and formalised infrastructure is brought into everyday life. Kearney (2017) notes the harm inflicted on place and, by extension, cultural life-worlds through the effects of human-induced climate change and power differentials stemming from global industrialisation. Nurul's father died on 'stable lands' while living on the *char*. His father's body was buried next to a mosque and Nurul hoped to make a concrete boundary around the grave. Along with the settlement, the burial ground was washed away due to floods in 2012, showing the challenge of maintaining place relations and commemorating the life and death of kin amid the worsening effects of climate-induced disaster (Kearney, 2017: 110). Nurul said sadly: 'Disaster washes away not only our land but also our relatives' graves. It washes away our memories of our beloved family members.' *Char* inhabitants' practices of placemaking are therefore at risk. Place is never fully removed from human life and cultural significance; space is imbued with meaning to become place (see Cabrera Torrecilla, this volume). Placemaking is a social process through which people shape their behaviours and construct memories in relation to where they live (Basso, 1996: 6–7).

Given river island sustainability is always shifting, no big infrastructure such as emergency shelters, medical facilities, high schools or colleges are built by government. In their absence, however, NGOs have built primary schools to provide youth with education. *Char* villages, then, have become sites managed by NGOs amid a lack of governmental support and the unpredictability of river erosion. In this context, the state is found to be lacking in service provision. Through implementing a series of development activities (e.g. income-generating programmes), NGOs have been powerful non-state actors in rural areas, showing how it is that civil society plays an important – but no less powerful – role in administering services when the state is found wanting. This demonstrates how infrastructure development and placemaking connote discrete fields that involve multiple actors. This includes local and international NGOs whose work is based on poverty reduction, women's empowerment, and disaster resilience. This field is observed most noticeably in how knowledge is produced and acted upon by various actors.

A small number of *char* dwellers, particularly poor and landless peasants, are aware of recent climate change discourses through disaster risk reduction programmes. Local NGOs frequently arrange meetings to disseminate information about climate change and its consequences. NGOs invite locals, including influential individuals such as public representatives, headmen (*matbar*), wealthy farmers, freedom fighters, schoolteachers, and development volunteers. Saida, a middle-aged woman, was elected as a public representative at village level. She participated in several meetings regarding climate change, stating: 'The NGOs have trained us in how to adapt to hazard risks; say, how to store dry food and candles; how to protect children and elderly people, and how to move belongings to a safer place.' Here vulnerability is paired with disaster and unpredictability to establish a semblance of order and control. Other than interactions with NGOs, daily newspapers are the relevant sources that familiarise *char* dwellers, particularly a few college-going young adults, with climate change issues. *Char* dwellers have no access to electronic media – there is no electricity. The tea stalls at boat terminals are the only places for watching television. *Char* dwellers I spoke with frequently come across news on climate change while taking tea. Most of them find the news content difficult to understand. An elderly farmer said, 'It is hard to understand what the TV [news] says;

we only know that floods come every year.' It is worth noting that floods are expected, particularly on the dry river islands, as they facilitate fertile silt deposits on the agricultural plots when floodwaters flow. Local people expect seasonal floods, as long as they don't stay for longer and erode houses and agricultural plots.

Following the development of international discourse and awareness of the term, NGOs in Bangladesh popularised the term *jolbayu paribartan* (climate change) on many *char*s through disaster resilience projects, presented through colourful posters and billboards. The term has become an everyday topic for young people, particularly those paid NGO workers or volunteers on the islands, demonstrating how discourse on significant topics can dominate a community's knowledge of, and their responses to, climate change (Ford and Norgaard, 2020). The local terms *durgati* (wretchedness), *durjog* (disaster) and *sarbanasha* (catastrophe) are used interchangeably to explain climatic disasters by both *char* dwellers and NGOs. This produces a localised vocabulary that works to educate and thereby ameliorate the effects of climate change-induced disaster. Noting the multiple actors invested in raising disaster awareness, there is a unique field of practice (Bourdieu, 1985) among actors such as NGOs, *char* dwellers and other agricultural workers, which is further animated through the interaction of social positions amid the displacement and re-emplacement experienced through climate-induced disasters.

Char dwellers have observed that the duration of the seasons has shortened compared to the past. For example, winter comes late, and its usual duration is shortened. *Char* dwellers can explain in local terms how the climate is changing, because they have been living with some inevitable changes relating to losing their home and agricultural livelihoods over generations. People's knowledge of weather and climate transmits to the next generation through their folktales and weather-related proverbs and is supplemented by formal education (Strauss, 2003). Meanings are shared and, therefore, produced in social worlds. Bourdieu (1985: 734) argues, 'The social world is, to a larger extent, what the agents make of it, at each moment; but they have no chance of un-making and re-making it except on the basis of realistic knowledge of what it is and what they can do with it to form the position they occupy within it.' The social field at play, therefore, is one produced by agents contending with the onset of shifting weather and climate conditions. Diverse knowledge and strategies are relied upon by different groups, but these introduce new power dynamics and complicate social positions. The presence of disaster, then, complicates taken-for-granted social fields, the likes of which are often theorised in anthropological literature as operating with relative stability. When the idea of social fields is paired with the Manchester School's focus on change and continuity (Gluckman, 1963; Turner, 1968, 1975) a deeper understanding of networked, place-based socialities becomes visible.

Turner (1975) argued that social action takes on its form through metaphors, or cultural scripts. Climate change entails a process that does not simply imply the change to environment but also human and nonhuman relations (see also Marshall, this volume). For Turner (1975: 13) metaphors are used to guide typical and atypical processes, the sequence of which can generate new metaphors within a broader sociocultural field (1975: 14). For *char* dwellers, the period of flooding and riverbank erosion has become unpredictable. Momen, a *char* dweller, observed many *char*s that existed for one to two decades; rapid change has meant *char*s now only last for a few years on average: 'In the past, floodwater used to remain for a shorter period, say, two or three weeks. Whereas, in the recent years, floods come slowly and stay for a longer time.' In 2015, it took around three months for floodwaters to decline. Like other elderly *char* dwellers, Momen stated that the annual joining of the Tista River with the Brahmaputra River had accelerated the intensity of riverbank erosion. Consequently, erosion has transformed the bigger *char*s into smaller ones, with the latter being more vulnerable to these extremes. In the past, when *boro banna* (long-staying floods) arrived, floodwater remained for a few weeks, and the *char*s had more months to grow crops. In contrast, lingering floodwaters mean farmers now have fewer months in which to grow crops. Moreover, in the past, the river used to erode the *char*s only during the rainy seasons, whereas nowadays it happens almost every month. Previous floods occurred in the middle of the year (June–July), but now floods continue into August and September. The tacit knowledge via scripts (through which flooding has always been understood) has now been disrupted, since the dynamics linking knowledge and experience are no longer compatible with the on-the-ground reality of what it means to live on the *char*s (see Alimardanian, this volume).

In turn, islanders' knowledge and anticipation of seasonal change no longer apply, leading to the adoption of new understandings of climate and weather. A development researcher, who has been working for a local NGO, *Gana Unnayan Kendra* (GUK), observes that the flood-affected used to follow the organisation's disaster calendar, a sort of rough calculation for forecasting floods: 'I have been working for the *char* people more than a decade,' the researcher mentioned. 'I saw that elderly people could predict flooding periods and duration. Now their prediction does not work anymore.' Following the calendar, they used to anticipate agricultural and lean periods, where new land would appear, and where to relocate to. Traditionally, they used to follow ants' movements – they move in groups toward higher places when they anticipate that the torrential rains will destroy their nests. As such, the local people used to receive a warning message from ants' mobility. Ants build nests in groups. They live where food is available. When *char* dwellers see ants moving away from their nests, they anticipate a major change in weather. They fear heavy rain or flood could destroy their homes and sources of food. The ants have no better option than to move elsewhere. It is similar in the life of *char* dwellers, the sudden movement of the ants suggesting that they too must move to higher ground. Local practices, though disrupted, remain, and yet new ones have emerged to contend with change through the activities of NGOs and government bodies. Organised workshops and community meetings held by NGOs and government disseminate scientific discourses on climate change and its impacts on local lives and placemaking for *char* people.

Amid shifting scripts and social positions as *char* islands shift and change and, with them, their inhabitants, multiple narratives arise, forming different understandings of this field. Many *char* dwellers believe hazards are an act of God. For Momen 'only Allah knows well why hazards are taking place on the *char*s. We human beings can only guess about it, but Allah knows everything.' Hazards, according to Momen, especially floods, not only cause 'helplessness', but also produce 'opportunities', showing how it is that ambiguity can present as both confusion and as generating new horizons of expectation, opportunity and stability. He said, 'Allah gives us floods, we can get fertile land after declining floodwater.' Another informant, Shafik, a young man, felt similarly that God intentionally commands flooding and cyclones to test people and their faith in him in such precarious circumstances. Chayna, who goes to a college and works as a midwife for an NGO, believes in the supernatural power that causes riverbank erosion: 'There is, of course, something under the river, but we do not exactly know what it is.' Experiencing the precarious consequences of floods and riverbank erosion, they find *char* lands provide both instability (displacement) and opportunity (crop production).

In essence, everyday adjustments mean *char* dwellers have developed unique adaptive strategies in the face of climatic hazards, shifting social fields and temporary development intervention. Optimistic tendencies and expedient use of resources are practical responses to unprecedented change from disasters and social vulnerabilities (Cliggett et al., 2007).

Disaster, displacement and livelihoods

Sobuz, one of my acquaintances, who used to teach at a primary school on a *char*, stated, 'You will hardly find fat men or women on the *char*s. They all look physically fit. They work hard from early morning till going to bed.' He explains that there is no transport on the islands, and they walk for hours on the dry riverbed, earning a living from manual jobs. Mainlanders informally, sometimes jokingly, call *char* dwellers '*vatia*', a widely used slang word in Gaibandha. The local term *vati* is a formal Bangla word meaning downstream or lower ground along a river, the opposite of upstream (*ujan*). *Choura* refers to those who live on the *chars*. The terms *vatia* and *choura* are used interchangeably. It is believed that the *char* dwellers are somewhat of a *choura* subculture, which is seen as different from the mainland (Zaman, 1989: 197). Mainland communities think that *char* inhabitants are illiterate and uncultured. *Vatia* refers not only to the remote geographical location, as noted above, but also to the disconnection from sophisticated tastes, education and a 'good' lifestyle compared to the mainlanders. However, many mainlanders acknowledge that *char* dwellers are naturally very 'brave' and 'hardworking', compared to mainlanders, as they must contend with disasters and precarious livelihoods in their everyday lives, and yet their reputations precede them.

As the *char* people's livelihoods are based on exploiting the land, it is an important asset or capital. Agricultural land is inextricably linked with other forms of capital – social and cultural – which are converted into material capital. As Bourdieu (2004: 241) argues, 'capital is accumulated labour', which empowers agents or groups of agents 'to appropriate social energy in the form of reified or living labour'. In the context of Onishchit *Char*, land property is a vital form of capital, even though the existence of the land and its quality (fertility) are subject to floods and riverbank erosion. Both the labour and land are temporally specific, but they have learnt from past experience that the duration of their being and temporality ranges from a year to several years. In addition, it repeats. Nothing happens to the ownership, when lands are submerged. When their lands resurface, they reclaim their ownership. It is worth noting that the cultural practices of reclaiming lands often lead to quarrels and fighting. Hence, land is the most important capital or resource they need in order to struggle against rapid vulnerability. Above all, the uncertainty has become a constant for them. Bourdieu's field theory, then, works as a toolkit for analysing *char* dwellers' uncertainty and their struggles in securing livelihoods.

For Bourdieu (2005), a field is a micro social world where social agents interact with each other, and every field is relatively autonomous, governed by the respective laws. A field comprises 'forces within which the agents occupy positions' that shape the positions they take in the field, 'these position-takings being aimed either at conserving or transforming structure of relations of forces' that is a constituent element of the field (Bourdieu, 2005: 39). In *char* villages, the agricultural *social field* or *social space* consists of various social agents such as tenant peasants, day labourers, landowning classes, moneylenders and petty traders. To secure a livelihood in the agricultural field, peasants strategically maintain good connections (*valo samparka*) with landlords and moneylenders, who are the dominant agents, to rent land and borrow capital, respectively. Bourdieu's idea of social practices, in analysing livelihoods, is 'able to capture in a more realistic way the dynamic and multi-dimensional nature of the way in which people make their living' (Sakdapolrak, 2014: 23). Not only are *char* lands seen as unpredictable, this unpredictability is harnessed by peasants to carve out a life and livelihood. With the presence of climate-induced disasters, new actors, discourses and ways of understanding the world begin to emerge and are exploited within a shifting field of production.

Debates on land boundaries, land grabbing, and falsification of land documents have been everyday issues. The dominant actors – wealthy farmers, community leaders and kin persons of large lineages – establish their dominance in the field of the agrarian structure. It does not necessarily mean that relatively less dominant actors, such as landless peasants, are passive or external actors in the arrangement, however. Sometimes, they capitalise on the power held by the dominant actors by maintaining strategic 'good connections' with them; living in the same neighbourhood with the dominant actors; moving to the same higher ground with them; frequently renting their land and supporting them in local government elections. As Wacquant (1989: 40) argues, after Bourdieu: 'As a space of potential and active forces, the field is also a *field of struggles* aimed at preserving or transforming the configuration of these forces.' Thus, controlling land can be viewed as the conversion of immaterial social capital (large lineage) and cultural capital (knowledge in relation to complex land documents). Large lineages dominate, in that such groups control newly resurfaced land or state-owned land. In addition to the material importance of assets, there are non-material aspects – for example, domination and prestige. Thus, acquiring domination fuels conflict and violence between the *char* villagers.

When water submerges houses and agricultural plots, there are three options: a) moving to another *char* not inundated; b) taking shelter at the boat terminal; or c) temporarily moving to a second home on the mainland. The first two options are practised by those who are poor and landless. In contrast, relatively well-off families, who are very few in number, can afford to build their second homes on the mainland.[1] Moving and resettling requires day-long labour of a group of people. Culturally, relatives and neighbours help each other without expecting wages for this type of social support. In such cases, the house owners offer cigarettes and betel leaves to the helpers or volunteers, and if possible, a meal. In the absence of institutional services, social capital has been considered a significant way of surviving in *char* villages. Ashley and colleagues' (2000) study of livelihood practices on *char*s in Kurigram in Bangladesh suggests that social capital is a key resource to which most of the *char* dwellers have the greatest access.

All *char* dwellers put value on *char* lands. The value and meaning of *char* lands go beyond materialism. Unstable landscapes embody symbolic value. Value is the medium through which actors produce the importance of their actions (Graeber, 2005). For example, owning agricultural lands and growing crops on them are the ways in which farmers make their identity as *krishok*s (farmers). They praise themselves, emphasising that it is they who produce their own food as well as for others. For *char* farmers, owning land is the key for boosting their self-esteem as farmers. In this way, they gain *success* as farmers in their lives within and through their material and emotional attachment to *char*s (Hossain, 2021). In addition to influencing the ways climate change and disaster risk reduction are understood by *char* people, the government and international aid agencies have jointly implemented several projects for livelihood development to build resilience to disaster vulnerability. The following section focuses on the interactions between the *char* dwellers' agency, their field of production, and the recent development programmes run by two NGOs, named GUK and Friendship.

Disaster resilience of char dwellers

Broadly speaking, resilience refers to people's adaptive capacity during and after an adverse event. It implies the quality of flexibility in unpredictable and predictable consequences of extreme events. It refers to 'the capacity of a society to withstand impact and recover with little disruption of normal function' (Fiske et al., 2014: 12). The terms 'adaptation' and 'resilience' encapsulate human potential and tendencies of responding to environmental changes, building on the idea that *char* dwellers have developed adaptive capacities. People's actions in the context of disruptions are depicted by the idea of *resilience* (developed in psychology, ecological sciences and social sciences since the 1970s). Holling's (1973: 14) idea of resilience is a way of thinking about the continuity of systems and their competency to withstand hardships and maintain the interactions between different peoples and socio-ecological situations. Anthropologists have been dealing with interrelations between the associated issues of adaptation, vulnerability and resilience in the context of climate change (Nelson, 2011; Oliver-Smith, 2016). The resilience framework broadens the expansion of adaptation, as well as providing space for human agency.

It is when a concept such as resilience is viewed broadly within the field of production already sketched that additional forces and actors come to resonate in how ambiguity is experienced and understood. To date, the *Char*

Livelihood Programmes (CLP) represent a massive livelihood development project for islanders to increase their resilience.[2] At first, the CLP started to improve *char* dwellers' livelihood through 'asset transfers', whereby assets would be distributed from donors to local people via local NGOs. In most cases, the CLP provided a heifer to the recipient families. It also provided cattle feed for nearly two years. The recipients were guided by trained veterinarians to take care of the animals until maturity. CLP also played roles in social development, building financial capital and distributing relief during floods and cold spells. However, as I go on to show, notions of gender and identity were also mobilised.

Char dwellers' own understanding of 'development' and the narratives promulgated by NGOs have amalgamated on the ground through their engagement with projects such as that of CLP. It is hard to separate the local population's own understandings from the mainstream connotations of development because of the ubiquitous presence of discourses of development, including 'investment in the productive sector', 'education for all', 'women's empowerment', 'reducing poverty' and so on. Some common phrases are found in local discourses, such as going from 'low to high income', 'illiterate to literate' and experiencing greater certainty amid the uncertainty of shifting weather and climatic regimes. Marshall (this volume) has remarked on the ability of different actors to influence engagement with climate change, noting the Australian government's suppression of ambiguity and system 'complexity'. This demonstrates the ways that narratives and actions can be infiltrated. Among *char* dwellers, NGOs' development initiatives have contributed to social change, and yet some individuals use the terms 'development' and 'improvement' interchangeably, demonstrating how human agency, capital and disaster resilience come to overlap. Thus, while purportedly attending to *char* economic and social development through acts that dominate and control responses to climate change, development actors influence the ways livelihood ambiguity is thought about and addressed, further establishing their dominance within this social field.

However, practices of human agency and disaster resilience can be seen, for example, through Asma's story, a woman living on Onishchit *Char*: 'NGO development projects are not making us rich. But, unlike the past, we have been able to escape from the *monga* [seasonal food insecurity].' She has actively involved herself with the NGOs' income-generating project and has been able to change her household's economic condition. However, her 'success' does not necessarily mean development projects have changed household socioeconomic conditions evenly. *Char* women are motivated by different CLP actors, such as programme managers, field-level development workers, local volunteers and public representatives at village level. The actors include international aid agencies, national and non-state bodies, local government, civil society, and community leaders. For them, 'development constitutes a resource, a profession, a market, a stake or strategy', as in other contexts (Oliver de Sardan, 2005: 11). This can have very real effects on the tenor of local politics and customary thinking.

Indeed, the role of NGOs in mobility and economic empowerment created another local shift, in traditional gender relations in *char* villages. It can be observed that many men criticise NGOs' interventions and women's participation in these activities. They find development programmes to be the catalyst for breaking down traditional family values: men for earning and women for managing the household. Income-generating programmes of the CLP and other social development projects cause changes in traditional male-controlled settings. Such interventions have influenced the ways through which women are able to boost agency to change their socioeconomic conditions. That is to say, women's participation in community meetings, forming a cooperative society, raising cattle, and gender awareness mean they agitate and negotiate with the traditional patriarchal structure of society, as well as the household.

In addition to gender, social instability appears in *char* dwellers' participation in the development projects implemented by NGOs: local people receive resources and services, yet there is fear in the minds of many that they might be asked to convert to Christianity, as most of the NGOs operate development programmes with the support of Western and religious donors. I found no such cases of this fear. Maybe the main reason behind this fear of religious conversion is the history of marginalised Indigenous communities. For example, Santal, Indigenous (*adivasi*) communities living in northern Bangladesh, have gone through Christianisation and other external forces, such as marketisation and the ideas of modern education and health treatment through missionary activities (e.g. Brandt, 2011; Debnath, 2010). The power of Christianisation is locally negotiated as the missionaries' activities provide the ways in which the Indigenous communities can reduce poverty and disconnection from the mainstream societies.

Participants in development projects are the main witnesses to the implementation of the projects on the ground; they see the effects of social and climatic disruptions as they occur. Seeing the process of implementation in their community, they contemplate 'in times of [economic and social] changes who wins and who loses?' (Gardner and Lewis, 2015: 110). Many people criticise the unfair selection of target populations. For example, there was a rumour that NGO workers picked potential recipients according to the suggestions of influential local individuals. Many of the 'actual poor' people were excluded, whereas some wealthy families were included. What does this say about the 'adaptive' capacity (resilience) of island dwellers, whereby, in a field of uncertain spatiotemporal and social relations, social capital is as powerful as economic capital? Researchers argue that vulnerability of char dwellers needs to be understood holistically. Development programmes need decentralised, bottom-up governance that can include multiple actors, such as NGOs, administrators and local leaders and islanders (Zaman and Alam, 2021: 435). This would add to building local nuance around resilience and disaster risk reduction and further enable the landless poor on *char* islands.

Conclusion

Understanding *char* inhabitants' perceptions of disaster vulnerability needs to take into account their everyday experiences. Besides, religious belief remains an important factor that influences their viewpoints concerning the causes of disaster: they think that invisible forces as well as their fate are responsible for their livelihood uncertainty. Recent discourses of global climate change barely reach inhabitants of remote *char* islands. Remoteness disconnects them not only from administration and public supports but also from discourses of environmental changes, which are frequently discussed and displayed in the mainland's public sphere. However, some *char* dwellers are invited by NGOs to participate in workshops in relation to environmental changes and disaster resilience. Yet it can be stated that both NGOs and development professionals of the organisations have become dominant actors in the local socioeconomic arrangements. Bourdieu's and Turner's work on 'fields' has been used to understand the power relations and sociocultural transformation of dominant social scripts brought about by such changes.

Disaster-induced displacement and precarious livelihoods are inextricably interrelated for *char* dwellers. With experience of repeated agricultural land loss, homes and communities, they live in places that are now, more than in the past, marked by uncertainty. Their perceptions of vulnerability are thus influenced by this experience. As new *chars* accrete, they put their hopes on moving and building new houses and communities. Their adaptive capacity becomes stronger, seen in this chapter through investments in economic and social capital in relation to land, which is the key for them to live in such a fragile environment. However, *char* dwellers' vulnerability and resilience remain subject to the river as it inundates and erodes their villages.

Development programmes, be they for economic or social benefit, barely change the predicament of uncertainty; indeed they add to the complexity of living and making a living on *char* lands. All the programmes are built for the short term, which is not enough for building sustainable disaster resilience. The *char* dwellers criticise short-term development projects because support, whether material or ideological, does not last long. They have no faith in short-term projects, although they actively participate in activities as part of social fields – for example, attending meetings at local and national levels and arranging community meetings to share their views. To understand as well as to ameliorate the effects of floods and riverbank erosion, the state needs to consider disasters as a *national crisis*. Perhaps only then will *char* people's ambiguous position regarding uncertain landscapes be taken with the seriousness it deserves.

Notes

1 It is worth mentioning that a few well-off families temporarily live in *char* villages to utilise their land during the dry or agricultural season. They come back to *chars* when the flood water recedes. Moreover, compared to the mainland, *chars* are considered as relatively better places for rearing cattle because of available green grass.
2 CLP is a longitudinal livelihood development project jointly funded by the Department for International Development (DFID) and Australian Aid, sponsored by the Rural Development and Co-operatives Division of the Government of Bangladesh's Ministry of Local Government, Rural Development and Co-operatives, and implemented through Maxwell Stamp Plc. For details: http://clp-bangladesh.org/work/overview/ (accessed on 17 June 2015).

References

Ashley, S., Kar, K., Hossain, A. and Shibabrata, N. (2000) *The Chars Livelihood Assistance Scoping Study* (Crewkerne: In Development Ltd for the Department for International Development).

Baqee, A. (1998) *Peopling in the Land of Allah Jaane: Power, Peopling and Environment: The case of Char-lands of Bangladesh* (Dhaka: The University Press Ltd).

Basso, K.H. (1996) *Wisdom Sits in Places: Landscape and Language among the Western Apache* (Albuquerque: University of New Mexico Press).

Bourdieu, P. (1985) 'The social space and the genesis of groups', *Theory and Society*, 14:6, 723–44.

Bourdieu, P. (2004) 'The forms of capital', in S.J. Ball (ed.), *The RoutledgeFalmer Reader in Sociology of Education* (London: Routledge), 15–29.

Bourdieu, P. (2005) 'The political field, the social science field, and the journalistic field', in R. Benson and E. Neveu (eds), *Bourdieu and the Journalistic Field* (Cambridge: Polity), 29–47.

Brandt, C. (2011) *Educating Santals: The Seventh-day Adventist Church in Joypurhat (Bangladesh) and the issue of cultural alienation.* Working Papers on South Asian Studies 10. South Asia Section, Institute for Oriental Studies. Martin Luther University of Halle-Wittenberg.

Cliggett, L., Colson, E., Hay, R., Schudder, T. and Unruh, J. (2007) 'Chronic uncertainty and momentary opportunity: A half century of adaptation among Zambia's Gwembe Tonga', *Human Ecology*, 35, 19–31.

Debnath, M.K. (2010) *Living on the edge: The predicament of a rural Indigenous Santal community in Bangladesh*, unpublished PhD thesis (University of Toronto, Canada).

Fiske, S.J., Crate, S.A., Crumley, C.L., Galvin, K., Lazrus, H., Lucero, L., Oliver-Smith, A., Orlove, B., Strauss, S. and Wilk, R. (2014) 'Changing the atmosphere: Anthropology and climate change', Final report of the AAA Global Climate Change Task Force (Arlington, VA: American Anthropological Association).

Ford, A. and Norgaard, K.M. (2020) 'Whose everyday climate cultures? Environmental subjectivities and invisibility in climate change discourse', *Climatic Change*, 163, 43–62.

Gardner, K. and Lewis, D. (2015) *Anthropology and Development: Challenges for the Twenty-First Century* (London: Pluto Press).

Gluckman, M. (1963) *Order and Rebellion in Tribal Africa* (New York: Free Press of Glencoe).

Graeber, D. (2005) 'Value: anthropological theories of value', in G.J. Carrier (ed.), *A Handbook of Economic Anthropology* (Cheltenham: Edward Elgar), 439–54.

Holling, C.S. (1973) 'Resilience and stability of ecological systems', *Annual Review of Ecology and Systematics*, 4, 1–23.

Hossain, M.A. (2021) 'Political ecology of disaster vulnerability and people's limited agency on Char-Lands, *Rajshahi University Journal of Social Science and Business Studies*, 25, 35–48.

Kearney, A. (2017) *Violence in Place, Cultural and Environmental Wounding* (London: Routledge).

Lahiri-Dutt, K. and Samanta, G. (2013) *Dancing with the River: People and Life on the Chars of South Asia* (New Haven, CT: Yale University Press).

Nelson, D.R. (2011) 'Adaptation and resilience: Responding to a changing climate', *Wiley Interdisciplinary Reviews: Climate Change*, 2:1, 113–20.

Oliver de Sardan, J-P. (2005) *Anthropology and Development: Understanding Contemporary Social Change* (London: Zed Books).

Oliver-Smith, A. (2009) 'Anthropology and the political economy of disasters', in E.C. Jones and A.D. Murphy (eds), *The Political Economy of Hazards and Disasters* (Lanham, MD: AltaMira Press), 11–28.

Oliver-Smith, A. (2016) 'The concepts of adaptation, vulnerability, and resilience in the anthropology of climate change: Considering the case of displacement and migration', in S.A. Crate and M. Nuttall (eds), *Anthropology and Climate Change: From Actions to Transformations*, 2nd edn (New York: Routledge), 58–85.

Rashid, H. and Bimal, P. (2014) *Climate Change in Bangladesh: Confronting Impending Disasters* (Lanham, MD: Lexington Books).

Sakdapolrak, P. (2014) 'Livelihoods as social practices – Re-energising livelihoods research with Bourdieu's theory of practice', *Geographica Helvetica*, 69:1, 19–28.

Strauss, S. (2003) 'Weather wise: Speaking folklore to science in Leukerbad', in S. Strauss and B.S. Orlove (eds), *Weather, Climate, Culture* (London: Routledge), 39–60.

Turner, V. (1968) *Schism and Continuity in an African Society: A Study of Ndembu Village Life* (Manchester: Manchester University Press).

Turner, V. (1975) *Dramas, Fields, and Metaphors: Symbolic Action in Human Society* (Ithaca, NY: Cornell University Press).

Wacquant, L.J.D. (1989) 'Towards a reflexive sociology: A workshop with Pierre Bourdieu', *Sociological Theory*, 7:1, 26–63.

Wisner, B., Blaikie, P., Cannon, T. and Davis, I. (2004) *At Risk: Natural Hazards, People's Vulnerability, and Disasters*, 2nd edn (London: Routledge).

Zaman, M.Q. (1989) 'The social and political contexts of adjustments to riverbank erosion hazard and population resettlement in Bangladesh', *Human Organization*, 48:3, 196–205.

Zaman, M. and Alam, M. (2021) 'Rethinking Char development in Bangladesh', in M. Zaman and M. Alam (eds), *Living on the Edge: Char dwellers in Bangladesh* (Cham: Springer), 429–38.

Part III

Imagining an 'otherwise'

7

Ambiguity in Belgrade's bike activism: marginalised activists, powerful agents of change

Sabrina Steindl-Kopf

Introduction

Streets for Cyclists was the motto of a group of activists who organised monthly bike rides in Belgrade, hoping to motivate others to use bikes and highlight cyclists' presence in the city. The activists aimed to transform Belgrade into a bike-friendly city similar to other European capitals, such as Copenhagen or Amsterdam. The monthly bike rides were also understood as a way to convince local authorities of the benefits of cycling as a means of urban transportation and to push forward activists' claims for the introduction of cycling infrastructure. Originating in 1992 in San Francisco, joint bike rides have become a global phenomenon in hundreds of cities worldwide. The monthly bike rides, which are often titled 'critical mass events', are conceptualised as a peaceful protest by which cyclists reclaim the streets in a safe and celebratory manner. Although bike rides are not characterised as political events, several examples, such as in Belgrade, show they are linked to political activism. In the case of Belgrade, cycling was constructed as a serious issue of life in a city that after years of painful postwar transformation was still seeking to gain a status as a European metropolis. However, activists did not frame their engagement as a form of urban contestation. Rather, they perceived it as 'collective problem-solving in everyday life' (Jacobsson, 2015: 10), an immediate reaction to daily problems, which had been caused by corrupt authorities, urban planners and politicians, leading to what many saw as 'moral decay'. Hence, activists were convinced that their engagement would improve the overall quality of life in Belgrade.

In Belgrade, the local appropriation of this global phenomenon marked the emergence of a new movement that represented activism *of* the city and experimented with new forms of organising and articulating citizens' claims. Around 2012, various urban activist groups emerged and voiced their resistance to large-scale construction projects and the restructuring of the city. Besides the emergence of groups promoting cycling as a mode of sustainable mobility, other activists were protecting inner-city green areas from rezoning and subsequent demolition, promoting the further development of public transport, or resisting the expulsion of vulnerable social groups from the city centre. At the same time, the mobilisation of people around such issues was part of a broader shift to city-oriented activism in the post-Yugoslav region. From the establishment of small-sized activist groups in Belgrade to the formation of protest movements with hundreds to thousands of followers in the cities of Dubrovnik, Zagreb or Skopje, 'the urban' was at the core of activism. Previous movements had been concentrated in cities, including student, anti-regime and anti-war movements, and were immediate responses to violent conflicts in the 1990s during which Milošević and his supporters attempted to maintain an authoritative regime. In contrast, 'the urban' was now the starting point for a new generation of activists, identity formation and the articulation of goals, as Bilić and Stubbs (2015: 119) note.

This chapter explores how global phenomena, such as the monthly bike rides and imaginations of what makes a city liveable, are adopted and reinterpreted by locals who are engaged in bike activism. I argue that ambiguity is an integral force in the bike-activist movement, induced by their narration of a 'moral decay' among state and civil society actors. Ambiguity was entrenched in activists' narrative of an 'Other Serbia' (*Druga Srbija*) as a powerful marker of their own identity and their imagining of a better future. The idea of an 'Other Serbia' invokes particular tropes of crisis, morality and Balkanism, giving rise to contested notions of normality (Gilbert et al., 2008; Greenberg, 2011), public 'decency' (Tazreiter, 2010) and accountability among authorities. Activists' desire to build an 'Other Serbia' entailed the creation of boundaries through which activists hoped to legitimise their engagement with cycling. Activists differentiated themselves from the state and other civil society actors which, in their eyes, had failed to initiate the transformation of Belgrade into a modern capital. Such a conception of themselves and others further entailed demarcations between modernity and backwardness, corruption and decency.

The ethnographic material on which this chapter draws was collected during fieldwork in Belgrade between 2012 and 2013. My interest was to examine the everyday organisation, activities and spatial practices of activist groups, their members' individual perspectives of the city, society and activism, and their relations to each other and public institutions. Since activities took place on various sites within and outside of Belgrade – including in parks, main squares, roads, cafés, cultural centres and so on – as well as in virtual spaces – such as email, Facebook or YouTube – I decided to not only 'follow the people' but also their ideas and activities (Marcus, 1998: 79; Lazar, 2017) in order to grasp how they perceived, interpreted and tried to act upon their social worlds. Aiming to promote cycling in the city, activists chose various strategies, from 'Do-It-Yourself' actions and events on the streets, such as festivals or the monthly bike rides, to petitioning or the elaboration of suggestions for bike infrastructure, and consequently ended up 'doing politics'.

I begin by analysing bike activism in Belgrade by positioning social movements as sites of ambiguity, arguing that although complexity and conflicts have been recognised as central characteristics of such phenomena, they are still widely neglected in anthropological research. I then discuss activists' narratives of an 'Other Serbia' which entailed a black-and-white thinking of their relation to the state and civil society actors. In the latter part of the chapter, I show that activists were able to manoeuvre ambiguous situations and thus minimise ambiguity through the conceptualisation of their engagement as the moral and affective opposite of politics. In turn, ambiguity is positioned throughout this chapter as a force that can stifle political goodwill and lead to disagreement about how the future of a city and its people ought to be constructed. Yet ambiguity is also shown to be part of activism; it promotes a challenge through which certainty can emerge out of uncertainty and identity can be built through an alter-politics.

An 'Other Serbia': activists' marginality in 'backward' Serbia

Ambiguity is commonly taken to be a situation or statement that is unclear because it can be comprehended in more than one way. Definitions of ambiguity are linked to and have been differentiated from 'experience' (Throop, 2005), 'everyday knowledge' (Herzfeld, 1993), 'collective sense-making' (Merkus et al., 2017), 'ambivalence' (Augé, 1998), ontological 'uncertainty' (Dein, 2016) and 'clarity', The analytical value, then, of ambiguity in ethnographic research is that it is a strategic resource carrying the potential for the reconciliation of seemingly contradictory interpretations. Linking the concept to the study of social movements helps to demonstrate how ambiguity constitutes an effective tool to negotiate situations of uncertainty and conflict inherent in Belgrade's contemporary bike activism. As Jeffrey Juris and Alex Khasnabish (2015: 581) suggest, social movements are 'complex fields defined by social and ideological heterogeneity, not only as vehicles for struggle but sites of struggle'. As such, social movements are characterised by conflicts over ideology, organisation, decision-making, strategy and tactics. These internal dynamics are thus also a valuable field of inquiry because they allow for insights into the ways activists construct and negotiate shared culture, identity or politics.

Explorations of the internal dynamics of social movements, however, are still rather marginal. In anthropology there has been an increasing interest in the study of social movements in the Balkans (e.g. Greenberg, 2014; Mikuš, 2013; Razsa, 2015), yet these studies either treat movements as homogeneous, unified and without frictions or mention ambiguity and conflicts only as an aside. Following the suggestion of Ortner (1995: 179), the task of disentangling 'the internal political complexities' of bike activists in Belgrade is significant for understanding their internal conflicts as well as the ambiguity in activists' narrations and their concrete practices, both of which I discuss further below. This is important because such a focus highlights activists' attempts to make meaning of their social worlds, despite perceived challenges and unclarified futures, and to open spaces for activist agency where identities and actions can solidify. As explored by Clifford and Heffernan (both this volume), state–society conflict provides a useful backdrop to explore the construction and elaboration of emergent protester identities, their subjective agency amid uncertain conditions, and claims for social and political renewal.

A core example of activist agency through which new meanings about the social world can be made includes emerging narratives on building an 'Other Serbia', positioned against proponents of strident nationalism and invoking a rural–urban divide that has long been present in the country's recent history. Although the idea of an Other Serbia allowed activists to make sense of the political realities at the time, it created various ambiguous situations – for example, when activists were looking for cooperation with authorities whom they criticised for being unaccountable, unresponsive and corrupt. The term 'Other Serbia' (*Druga Srbija*)[1] was introduced in the early 1990s by dissenting Serbian intellectuals to demonstrate a different, non-nationalist Serbia against the agitation of both nationalist politicians and the intelligentsia. The term was accompanied by the sense of a distinct identity among activists who felt that they represented a Serbia that was open-minded, tolerant and peaceful and opposed to a supposedly nationalist, narrow-minded and violent Serbian majority. Although the identification with an 'Other Serbia' was closely tied to the experience of Milošević's authoritarian regime, the notion prevailed in the years after 2000 and served as a central marker of identity among contemporary activists. Even though the relations between civil society and the state have improved since the emergence of the term in the 1990s through examples of cooperation between NGOs and state actors, my interlocutors still felt they were marginalised by authorities in their engagement with cycling in the city.

In October 2012 the decision of the Belgrade municipality of Stari Grad to prohibit a monthly bike ride, based on bad weather forecast, stirred a heated debate among activists. Given that the week in question turned out to be quite mild and warm for the end of October, the alleged weather forecast was interpreted as a false pretence of the authorities to keep cyclists off the streets. For activist Dean, the prohibition of the bike ride reflected the city authorities' standpoint towards cycling-related issues, which in his opinion was marked by ignorance and indifference. Furthermore, he viewed the short-term banning of the ride as a deliberate act by the authorities to control space and maintain cyclists as a marginal group in urban traffic. Dean's criticism was in line with activists' claim that Belgrade's authorities not only missed the chance to position Belgrade as a modern and inclusive city by promoting cycling as a sustainable mode of mobility but also demonstrated their backwardness by prohibiting cyclists' appropriation of space and their articulation of demands. For instance, by perceiving themselves as 'invisible people' (*nevidljivi ljudi*) whose access to urban space was deliberately restricted and whose demands were being disregarded by the authorities, activists equated their position in society with that of other vulnerable social groups, such as the homeless and the LGBTQ community. Activists argued that the authorities masked their intolerance towards cyclists as well as their disregard for the groups' appropriation of urban space by putting forward supposed security risks couched in bad weather forecasts. According to this group, references to public security were made arbitrarily by the authorities because groups that did pose a threat to public security (e.g. hooligans and right-wing nationalist groups) were not prohibited from participating in street marches.

Serbian hooliganism is not only limited to football fan groups but also assembles members of radical groups or individuals engaged in criminal activities. Nationalist, right-wing organisations and hooligans are also said to receive major financial and ideological support from political and clerical elites. Due to their close connections to the state, nationalist and right-wing organisations are not regarded as outside the power of the state but rather as an extension of it.

Activists' narration of marginality was an essential part of their narrative of an 'Other Serbia' and consequently reinforced the idea of a supposed dichotomy between civil society as a peaceful and tolerant associational sphere and the state as hostile and corrupt. This particular notion of civil society reproduced a Western model of liberal individualism which saw civil society as a private realm in opposition to the public realm of the state (Hann, 1996). Located outside the direct influence of the state, civil society was further equated with the voluntary or non-governmental sector. Discussing civil society in the context of transformation processes in Eastern Europe, Hann (1996: 7) notes that it serves as 'a slogan, reified as a collective, homogenised agent, combating a demonic state'. Similarly, my interlocutors claimed that civil society was not only opposed to, but rather marginalised by, the state. Activists' understandings of their opposition to the state coincides with a dominant strand in literature in which nationalist and right-wing religious associations came to be excluded from the realm of Serbian civil society (Kostovicova, 2006), while left-wing and human-rights organisations, which were seen to possess greater civility, were believed to form civil society proper.

The narration of a culturally divided Serbia: modern activists and the backward rest

Activists' narration of the 'Other Serbia' was grounded on a distinct comprehension of Serbia as divided by two antagonistic value systems. Activists claimed to represent the modern, tolerant and Europeanised layer of society, while emphasising that they constituted a minority that was opposed by a backward and nationalist majority. To position themselves as modern European actors, activists resorted to the trope of a Balkanist 'other' on to which they could project images of the state and nationalist actors as backward. Activists' identity discourse was couched in an essentialist understanding of 'self' and 'other' that harkened back to Balkanist images and 'nesting divisions' (Bakić-Hayden, 1995), such as progressive/reactionary, advanced/backward, rational/irrational, urban/rural. In particular, the 'urban' was central in activists' self–other configurations.

Identifying themselves as inhabitants of the city (*gradani*) activists drew on long-standing urban–rural dichotomies reproducing the idea of naturalistic differences between urban, educated, civilised citizens and their peasant, primitive and backward counterparts (Jansen, 2005; Živković, 2011; Bilić and Stubbs, 2015). Besides referring to city dwellers, the term *gradanin* also means 'citizen'. However, during my research activists continually stressed the former meaning by using their supposed urban belonging as a distinct marker of their own European and modern mindset, an identity that was differentiated from villagers (*seljaci*) as their cultural, social and moral opposite.[2] Elaborating on this distinction, activist Milan noted the political elite in Serbia consisted of 'village people'. For instance, President Tomislav Nikolić had announced publicly that 'he is proud to own a little farm where he produces *rakija*' (fruit spirits). Instead of associating the president's references to village life with a lifestyle marked by small-scale farming, Milan viewed it as a marker of a distinct identity characterised by an allegedly backward and uncivilised mindset that was consequently extended to state actors and the country's supposed elite. Activists' characterisation of 'village people' relates to a particular power discourse in the construction of the Balkans. Maria Todorova (1994: 469) stresses that from the beginning the perception of the Balkans was shaped by an internal bourgeois perspective. During citizens' protests against the Milošević regime and its warmongering in the winter of 1996/97 and again in 2000, protesters reproduced the confrontation of the primitive, uneducated villager (*seljak*) with the civilised, educated city-dweller (*građanin*) (Jansen, 2001, 2005). The urban–rural divide was in fact 'not a topographical, but rather a moral or civilizational issue' (Jansen, 2001: 48) that retained its significance in the postsocialist and postwar period and that was now being taken up by my interlocutors.

Looking at the social background of Belgrade's activists, it becomes clear that they did not represent 'ordinary urbanites', which they perceived themselves to be, but rather belonged to a specific part of the population. As such, they spoke out on marginality and modernisation from a privileged position. Activists were mainly young and educated people from the urban middle class. The majority held a higher educational degree or were currently studying at the University of Belgrade. Furthermore, most activists were fluent in English and had left Serbia at least once, travelling around or visiting family abroad. Although there were some who experienced unemployment, several activists had found employment in creative branches, such as journalism, web design, architecture, photography or the arts. Although claiming that they were 'ordinary urbanites', activists nevertheless believed that they were role models for fellow citizens because the engagement with improving life in Belgrade was discerned as altruistic and selfless. For some, their engagement was driven by a 'calling', a spiritual mission. Local activism was thus a vehicle through which activists realised personal and societal development. With their essentialist understanding of 'self' and 'other', immanent to the narration of another Serbia, activists aimed not only to differentiate themselves from the authorities and politicians in terms of morality and culture but essentially to demonstrate their authority regarding the future development of Belgrade.

While activists were the ones who were able to provide solutions, the city authorities were portrayed as ignorant as well as simply unable and unwilling to grasp the need for a sustainable and visionary urban development. The authorities and politicians were accused of lacking any interest in a 'true' development of Belgrade, which was why their plans for urban transformation were just 'make-up' and 'all kippers and curtains', merely meant to impress both their electorate and foreign politicians and investors. The differentiation between 'modern' activists and the supposedly 'backward rest' was also expressed in activists' relation to the Serbian majority, which was viewed as too narrow-minded and self-involved to have an interest in the future development of the city.

The disappointment, distrust and general uncertainty described by my interlocutors was triggered by feelings that the state was unaccountable and unresponsive to its citizens. In particular, the lack of accountability was linked to a moral decay that had spread among the political elite and state actors and consequently impeded the introduction of extensive changes to spur Serbia's development. In this regard, the narration of a moral decline constituted an important feature of local discourse because it characterised people's understanding of politics. Politics was equated with self-interest, corruption and nepotism, values which were not only associated with politicians and state actors but rather extended to parts of the NGO sector, described as being marked by corruption and inefficiency. In the eyes of my interlocutors, many NGOs were just 'fake organisations' that were dominated by political parties and external investors or served as institutions for money laundering, as activist Boban emphasised. Activists asserted that, while many NGOs regularly received external funding and had thus grown considerably, they were completely inactive and unresponsive to the needs of their beneficiaries. Instead, NGOs' activities and projects appeared to my interlocutors as functioning as ends in themselves to sustain the livelihood of professional staff. Further, NGO leaders were seen as utilising their societal engagement as a stepping stone to make their way into politics, demonstrating the inherent close connection between Serbia's political and public arenas.

Activists therefore hoped that pursuing an Other Serbia would separate their engagement from allegations of immorality and hence legitimise their cause. Yet the boundaries between bike activists, authorities and other civil society actors were not as clear-cut as my interlocutors believed. Rather, contradictions were to follow because activists' practices differed greatly from the image which they had created of themselves and their engagement. Not everyone who was engaged in the bike-activist scene was guided by pure altruism and the will to serve the common good. Instead, some activists admitted that they hoped to transform the symbolic capital of their voluntary work into an economic one. While some viewed the voluntary investment of free time and energy as a way to gain work experience and thus improve their employability, others used activism as a form of self-employment.

Some believed that activism consequently had a positive impact on one's personal development – it was seen as a valuable personal experience and a form of self-fulfilment – while others volunteered simply because they wanted to have a good time and to meet like-minded people. What is interesting here is the variety of reasons for engaging in activism, which reflects the ambiguity in activists' attempts to enforce clear-cut boundaries between themselves and 'corrupt' actors. Although activists claimed to reject neoliberalism, they nevertheless took up neoliberal ideas of individualisation in their longing for individual self-realisation and their aspiration towards 'good times' through aligning themselves with capital accumulation. However, activists not only shared these commonalities with other civil society actors; they also sought to establish relations with foreign and local donor organisations and city authorities for funding and support. In the following section I discuss how activists manoeuvred ambiguous situations in their daily practice, arguing that they sought to minimise ambiguity through the conceptualisation of their engagement as 'anti-politics'.

Manoeuvring ambiguity: the 'concreteness' of anti-politics

Although Belgrade's bike activists opposed NGOs and the state, they nonetheless experienced difficulties in gaining public credibility and trust. 'You are automatically guilty' of corruption and clientelism when starting an initiative, activist Boban complained. Similarly, fellow activists confirmed that it was hard to persuade the public and required great efforts to show their independence and neutrality from other actors. Furthermore, activists continually emphasised that they did not want to get engaged in politics. Since politics was inflected by immorality, the boundaries of what constituted politics were drawn according to the values that activists ascribed to a particular sphere. Thus, the realm of dirty politics encompassed not only political parties, the government or authorities but was further extended to the NGO sector, which activists accused of having been corrupted by the prevailing state of immorality. In order to build legitimacy and distance themselves from the allegation of immorality, activists conceptualised their engagement for cycling as 'anti-politics', in which morality was 'the primary order' (Ticktin, 2011: 20) and positive emotions replaced the experience of disappointment associated with politics. In his analysis of the economic collapse in Iceland, Heffernan (this volume) elaborates the analytical value of affective atmospheres to understand processes of meaning-making in times of crisis and pursuing moral reform. Seeking new moral frameworks, bike activists in Belgrade hence defined anti-politics as the positive counterpart of politics which came to represent qualities that the realm of mainstream politics supposedly lacked. In so doing, activists aimed to minimise ambiguity in their daily practices by inducing transparency and clarity into ambiguous situations, thus reasserting their emphasis on civil decency and putting forward their own trustworthiness and efficiency.

Defining politics and the drawing of boundaries between politics and anti-politics has generated various lines of discussion in anthropology. From the 1960s onward, political anthropology has been expanded from structural functionalism to the study of 'political processes' (Swartz, Turner and Tuden, 2002: 102) and 'the politics of life itself' (Rose, 2006). This focus on the non-political consequently led to a neglect in defining the political as a category for ethnographic and analytical considerations, as noted by Candea (2011). Departing from Rancière's (2011) definition of politics, Candea treats the political and the non-political as 'performative projects' (2011: 321) that are 'mutually constitutive' (Spencer, 2011: 327) in the production of the other. Consequently, Candea concludes that 'the political is itself a result and condition of non-political action' (2011: 321) and vice versa. Likewise, politics and anti-politics represented mutually constitutive categories. Grounded in narrations of morality and emotions the two notions were conceptualised in opposition to one another. Anti-politics presupposed the existence, and effected the realisation of politics and vice versa. Abner Cohen has investigated the dialectical relationship between power and symbolism in *Two-Dimensional Man* (1974), emphasising that symbols are manipulated in the struggle for power (see also Clifford, this volume). Activists' striving for a moral engagement for the common good illustrates both the interrelationship between politics and anti-politics and the instrumentalisation of 'culture' to claim their authority in the future development of Belgrade.

Even though activists denounced politics as the realm of the immoral and disappointment, they were nonetheless actively involved in politics in their attempt to turn cycling into a political issue and push for the enactment of fairer laws and bureaucratic procedures. My point is that activists were 'bringing politics in' with their construction of cyclists as a particular group in need of state care, while at the same time they were 'taking politics out' by positing their activism as a depoliticised form of engagement (Ferguson, 1994). Likewise, examining Serbian student activism in the 2000s, Greenberg (2014) showed that students separated their engagement from politics. Arguing that their activism was anti-political because it was grounded in claims for innocence (as youth) and authenticity (as organisers of previous protests against Milošević), students struggled to legitimise their involvement in university laws and administrative processes. Similar to the activists I studied, Greenberg's students found themselves in a situation in which they had to find justification for their engagement in politics. Student activists legitimised their call for proceduralism by asserting that laws and administrative procedures were 'a form of compulsion that would force democratic behavior by creating consistency between intention and deeds' (2014: 173). Proceduralism was thus viewed as a way to *purify* politics.

I suggest that activists' politicisation of cycling was justified in a different manner. Activists' engagement was inspired by the imagination of an 'Other Serbia' in which certainty and predictability ruled out the murkiness of the immoral. For activists their longing for these qualities could be realised only within politics. They were therefore pushing for the enactment of laws and regulations befitting the image of this Other Serbia in the belief that such a move would result in another version of politics becoming the primary order. Activists sought to purify politics through doing politics in a contested space. Despite their hope for a purified politics, activists emphasised that anti-politics, as a moral and affective opposite, was only to be realised in the way activism was enacted.

In mid-December 2013 the Road Traffic Safety Agency organised a workshop dealing specifically with the safety of cyclists for the first time. More importantly, bike activists had also been invited to participate in the event and were asked to present their suggestions. Even though activists were hesitant toward the outcomes of the workshop, they nevertheless hoped that their arguments would convince authorities and lead to the implementation of new measures. In particular, the activists put their hopes in the organiser of the workshop. 'He is OK, he is on our side,' Dean remarked, implying the organiser not only shared the same visions of cycling but was a trustworthy person and thus a potential ally for activists. Although traffic safety represented only a small part of the agency's responsibilities, Dean hoped that the organiser would have enough time to deal with modern visions of cycling. Further, he believed that the organiser's intentions were good, noting that the latter had announced the formation of a working group with state actors and bike organisations as participants for the amendment of the Law on Traffic Safety.

The organisation of the workshop by the agency contrasted with activists' self-characterisations as marginal and the supposed backwardness of state actors. In fact, activists were quite successful in making themselves seen and their demands heard by the authorities. They were able to initiate meetings with the authorities and ensure their own involvement in decision-making processes. Activists interpreted the previously mentioned prohibited bike ride as a deliberate strategy of the city authorities to keep cyclists marginal. Yet at the same time, activists were involved in several cycling-related issues. Their participation in the workshop, the subsequent creation of a 'committee for bike-related issues' in which representatives of public institutions, researchers and activists exchanged suggestions for the amendment of the Law on Traffic Safety,[3] as well as the adoption of activists' ideas within the introduction of a public bike system in Belgrade point to the fact that activists had been able to establish relations with the authorities and articulate their demands vis-à-vis the state. What limited activists' agency, however, was the fact that the bike-activist scene was fragmented – various activist groups competed against each other for funding and influence which consequently made it difficult to act as a joint movement. Additionally, their participation in the workshop shows how activists attempted to manage ambiguous situations through the particular conceptualisation of their engagement. Unlike student activists or traditional NGOs whose work was 'done behind curtains', they were said to reside in official offices and rush from one meeting with politicians and authorities to another; my interlocutors believed that activism had to be a 'concrete' (*konkretan*) form of engagement for the common good. This 'activism of the concrete' was marked by a number of qualities that activists assigned to their strategies and practices. They had to be perceivable, visible and tangible in order to be identified as concrete and thus anti-politics.

First and foremost, activists staged their activities carefully and with caution; they were either organised directly in public or, in the case of there being no immediate audience, evidence was provided to prove the visibility of activists' actions. Since not every action could be joined by activist followers, my interlocutors resorted to the open platform of Facebook to distribute pictures and videos as evidence of their work. During their participation in the workshop and in the subsequent committee for bike-related issues activists thus shared information about the current situation regarding traffic security and their interactions with the authorities with their followers on Facebook, giving them the possibility to comment on the events. Activism of the concrete, activists believed, prevented them from corrupting their ideals. Instead, other civil society actors could not be trusted and had exposed themselves to rightful critique, since their work did not reach out to the public and hence lacked the necessary corrective. While NGOs were not answerable to anyone except nebulous donors, activists had to justify their activities to their supporters – both in real life and the world of social media.

Activists' engagement was based on the fact that there were 'concrete problems', such as the lack of bike infrastructure that called for 'concrete solutions'. According to activists, the logic of politicians, authorities and NGOs was that of always 'seeking big things'; they pursued large-scale projects, such as big construction projects or the amendment of legislation, which were described as expensive, abstract and time-consuming. Activists, on the other hand, were interested in solutions that didn't require a lot of financial resources or time. For instance, a small group of activists organised the symbolic marking of a bike track on one street that was heavily used by cyclists on their way to the city centre, after having grown frustrated by the idleness of the authorities (Figure 7.1). This do-it-yourself action was seen as a proof that improvements for cyclists could be achieved easily and fast. However, in situations where activists worked on the implementation of

Figure 7.1 Marking of a bike track at Poenkareova Street, Belgrade

bigger, more time-consuming projects, such as the amendment of the Law on Traffic Safety or the drafting of a model for a public bike system in Belgrade, they were eager to emphasise that they would withdraw their participation as soon as their cooperation with the authorities lacked progress.

Activists' practices further differed from conventional forms of engagement because they took place outside the formalised realm of NGOs; they were organised by 'associations of citizens', informal groups of people as well as individuals. Activists presented themselves as 'ordinary urbanites' (*obični gradani*) yet 'experts on the city' who, unlike the professional staff of NGOs, were driven by altruism and the selfless wish to engage for the common good. Activists' 'expertise on the city' originated from their personal experience as cyclists and their technical knowledge from studying laws, bureaucratic procedures and plans of urban development. Furthermore, the fact that their engagement came with personal sacrifices – it was based on hard work and the investment of time, energy and emotions – enabled activists to emphasise their trustworthiness. Activists participating in the workshop on traffic security thus legitimised their cooperation with the authorities by their own expert authority – a quality that overruled the competences of authorities, academic researchers and other civil society actors.

Conclusion

Studying the recent emergence of bike activism in Belgrade, the chapter has shown that ambiguity was an intrinsic part of activists' imaginations and essential to the dynamics of the movement. Ambiguity was entrenched in activists' narration of an 'Other Serbia' as a powerful marker of their own identity. While activists tried to make sense of Serbia's postsocialist and postwar transformation with their narration of an 'Other Serbia', it consequently produced ambiguous situations in their day-to-day practices.

The distinct configuration of the activists' self as representing another Serbia required the enforcing of demarcations to the state and other civil society actors and consequently led to a reduction of the complexities of their social world. Activists employed binary modes of classification and evaluation, believing that society and politics were divided into antagonistic entities, such as politics versus anti-politics, modernity versus backwardness, and marginality versus agency. In so doing, activists realised their claims for difference, while at the same time moral simplifications were the necessary consequence of their desire to develop Belgrade and build a modern, decent society in which trust in state actors and institutions can develop (Tazreiter, 2010). Although activists understood their classifications of their social world as definite and clear-cut, they turned out to be fuzzy when looking at their daily practices.

Activists minimised ambiguity by inducing transparency and clarity in their actions. They legitimised their cooperation with the authorities by positioning themselves as 'experts on the city', possessing an expertise that stemmed from their personal cycling experience and their technical knowledge of laws, bureaucratic procedures and plans of urban development. Activists produced transparency in their practices by ensuring the visibility of their actions – they were either organised in public or evidence of their work was communicated through social media. Furthermore, they emphasised their accountability to the needs of cyclists by fixing 'concrete problems' in the city with their do-it-yourself actions. With their 'activism of the concrete' activists put forward their trustworthiness vis-à-vis followers and the wider public and consequently assured themselves of the legitimacy and rightfulness of their cause. In so doing, activists gained the capacity of acting – the ability to take action and initiate concrete activities that were believed to improve the lives of cyclists in Belgrade.

Activists manoeuvred ambiguous situations in their interactions with the authorities through the particular conceptualisation of their activism as the moral and affective opposite of politics. Activists' attempts to purify politics led to greater integration between authorities and activists, perhaps charting the way for a more decent society in Serbia that coalesces the neoliberal and anti-political agendas that are variously held by authorities and activists.

However, at the same time, activists' understanding of their activism downplayed their commonalities with the authorities and other civil society actors, hindering them from establishing broader networks of cooperation. Activists' exclusionary understanding of civil society and the state made it difficult for them to realise the existence of common interests and the possibility of collaboration in the long term. Furthermore, perceiving their vision of Belgrade and Serbia as the only legitimate one made activists blind to those changes that had already been achieved as well as the realistic potentials of their engagement.

Analysing the contradictions in activists' engagement with cycling, I do not aim to conclude by dwelling on the shortcomings of Belgrade's contemporary bike activism. Rather, I want to point to the positive moments and potentialities that arise from ambiguity. The current generation of activists has been able to promote an alternative vision of Belgrade and Serbia in a relatively short period of time, even though they were themselves far more critical of their engagement and did not recognise their achievements as such. Even more, I want to emphasise the analytical and practical value of ambiguity in social movements because they testify to the complexities of the social worlds in which we all live and in which some people find incentives to become active and work together for a common purpose.

Notes

1 In Serbian the term *Druga Serbia* also means 'Second Serbia'. Although activists employed both meanings, 'Other Serbia' was far more prevalent and meaningful.
2 Studying the urban–rural divide in post-Yugoslav discourse Bilić and Stubbs (2015: 120) point out that one had to distinguish between 'real' and 'symbolic' reproduction.
3 Ideas for the amendment of the law comprised the opening of one-way streets for cyclists and the expansion of traffic-calmed areas.

References

Augé, M. (1998) *A Sense for the Other: The Timeliness and Relevance of Anthropology* (Stanford, CA: Stanford University Press).

Bakić-Hayden, M. (1995) 'Nesting Orientalisms: The Case of Former Yugoslavia', *Slavic Review*, 54:4, 917–31.

Bilić, B. and Stubbs, P. (2015) 'Unsettling "The Urban" in Post-Yugoslav Activisms: "Right to the City" and Pride Parades in Serbia and Croatia', in Kerstin Jacobsson (ed.), *Urban Grassroots Movements in Central and Eastern Europe* (Farnham: Ashgate), 119–38.

Candea, M. (2011) ' "Our Division of the Universe": Making Space for the Nonpolitical in the Anthropology of Politics', *Current Anthropology*, 52:3, 309–34.

Cohen, A. (1974) *Two-Dimensional Man: An Essay on the Anthropology of Power and Symbolism in Complex Society* (Berkeley: University of California Press).

Dein, S. (2016) 'The Anthropology of Uncertainty: Magic, Witchcraft and Risk and Forensic Implications', *Journal of Forensic Anthropology*, 1:1, 1–7.

Ferguson, J. (1994) 'The Anti-Politics Machine: "Development" and Bureaucratic Power in Lesotho', *The Ecologist*, 24:5, 176–81.

Gilbert, A., Greenberg, J., Helms, E. and Jansen, S. (2008) 'Reconsidering Postsocialism from the Margins of Europe: Hope, Time and Normalcy in Post-Yugoslav Societies', *Anthropology News*, 49:8, 10–11.

Greenberg, J. (2014) *After the Revolution: Youth, Democracy, and the Politics of Disappointment in Serbia* (Stanford, CA: Stanford University Press).

Greenberg, J. (2011) 'On the Road to Normal: Negotiating Agency and State Sovereignty in Postsocialist Serbia', *American Anthropologist*, 113:1, 88–100.

Hann, C. (1996) 'Introduction: Political Society and Civil Anthropology', in Chris Hann and Elizabeth Dunn (eds), *Civil Society: Challenging Western Models* (London: Routledge), 1–26.

Herzfeld, M. (1993) *The Social Production of Indifference: Exploring the Symbolic Roots of Western Bureaucracy* (Chicago, IL: University of Chicago Press).

Jacobsson, K. (2015) 'Introduction: The Development of Urban Movements in Central and Eastern Europe', in Kerstin Jacobsson (ed.), *Urban Grassroots in Central and Eastern Europe* (Farnham: Ashgate), 1–32.

Jansen, S. (2001) 'The Streets of Beograd: Urban Space and Protest Identities in Serbia', *Political Geography*, 20:1, 35–55.

Jansen, S. (2005) 'Who's Afraid of White Socks? Towards a Critical Understanding of Post-Yugoslav Urban Self-Perceptions', *Ethnologia Balkanica*, 9, 151–67.

Juris, J.S. and Khasnabish, A. (2015) 'Immanent Accounts: Ethnography, Engagement and Social Movement Practices', in Donatella Della Porta and Mario Diani (eds), *The Oxford Handbook of Social Movements* (Oxford: Oxford University Press), 578–91.

Kostovicova, D. (2006) 'Civil Society and Post-communist Democratization: Facing a Double Challenge in Post-Milošević Serbia', *Journal of Civil Society*, 2:1, 21–37.

Lazar, S. (2017) *The Social Life of Politics: Ethics, Kinship and Union Activism in Argentina* (Stanford, CA: Stanford University Press).

Marcus, G. (1998) 'Ethnography in/of the World System: The Emergence of Multi-Sited Ethnography', in George Marcus (ed.), *Ethnography Through Thick and Thin* (Princeton, NJ: Princeton University Press), 33–56.

Merkus, S. et al. (2017) 'A Storm is Coming? Collective Sensemaking and Ambiguity in an Inter-organizational Team Managing Railway System Disruptions', *Journal of Change Management*, 17:3, 228–48

Mikuš, M. (2013) 'What Reform? Civil Societies, State Transformation and Social Antagonism in "European Serbia"' (PhD dissertation, London School of Economics).

Ortner, S.B. (1995) 'Resistance and the Problem of Ethnographic Refusal', *Comparative Studies in Society and History*, 37:1, 173–93.

Rancière, J. (2011) 'The Thinking of Dissensus: Politics and Aesthetics', in Paul Bowman and Richard Stamp (eds), *Reading Rancière* (New York: Continuum), 1–17.

Razsa, M. (2015) *Bastards of Utopia: Living Radical Politics after Socialism* (Bloomington: Indiana University Press).

Rose, N. (2006) *The Politics of Life Itself: Biomedicine, Power, and Subjectivity in the Twenty-First Century* (Princeton, NJ: Princeton University Press).

Spencer, J. (2011) 'Comment to the Article of Matei Candea', *Current Anthropology*, 52:3, 327.

Swartz, M.J., Turner, V.W. and Tuden, A. (2002) 'Political Anthropology', in Joan Vincent (ed.), *The Anthropology of Politics* (Oxford: Blackwell), 102–109.

Tazreiter, C. (2010) 'Towards Decent Society: The Demands of Justice and the Demands of Civility', *Thesis eleven*, 101:1, 97–105.

Ticktin, M. (2011) *Casualties of Care: Immigration and the Politics of Humanitarianism in France* (Berkeley: University of California Press).

Throop, J. (2005) 'Hypocognition, a "Sense of the Uncanny," and the Anthropology of Ambiguity: Reflections on Robert I. Levy's Contribution to Theories of Experience in Anthropology, *Ethnos*, 33:4, 499–511.

Todorova, M. (1994) 'The Balkans: From Discovery to Invention', *Slavic Review*, 53:2, 453–82.

Živković, M. (2011) *Serbian Dreambook: National Imaginary in the Time of Milošević* (Bloomington: Indiana University Press).

8

Adding (ambiguous) value: interfacing between alternative economics and entrepreneurial innovation in Ecuador

Alexander Emile D'Aloia

Introduction

The bridge impressed everyone. Made from coloured card and glue, the group who constructed it not only finished within fifteen minutes and under budget but also found time to attach a sign, presenting the name of their association. This was clearly the '*valor agregado*' (added value) that our trainer had been looking for. Eduardo was the head of AssoTrain, a non-profit association dedicated to training organisations in Ecuador who were engaged in the Popular Solidarity Economy (PSE) in tax obligations and administration. Others present were all representatives from small PSE enterprises. Eduardo held the bridge aloft for the room to admire. The murmurs of appreciation demonstrated that we all agreed – the bridge was clearly an example of *valor agregado*. What exactly this added value was, however, went unspoken.

The editors of this volume have highlighted the importance of thinking through how ambiguity manifests locally and how anthropologists can study and explore it. To this end, in this chapter, I explore the ambiguity of *valor agregado* in economic and policy terms, as used by my interlocutors, primarily bureaucrats and others working to promote alternative economies. I focus on this ambiguity not as grounded theory, but as an analytical tool for anthropologists to think with. In particular, I focus on how, in a policy context, it helps anthropologists to examine how disparate forms of policy and economy can be integrated.

As a theoretical concept, the PSE is an alternative form of economy based on 'relations of solidarity, cooperation and reciprocity' and 'privileging labour and human beings … over appropriation, profit and the accumulation of capital' (Asamblea Nacional, 2018). Coraggio (2011: 34–5), a theorist often referenced by my interlocutors, places the PSE on a long list of alternative economic concepts, including the social and communitarian economies, noting that these terms are largely fluid and cannot 'crystallise' into firm definitions (see Nelms, 2015). What sets the PSE apart from other alternative economies is that it was written into the Ecuadorian constitution in 2008 by leftist president Rafael Correa. It was subsequently cemented as a policy framework in 2011 with the Organic Law of the Popular Solidarity Economy, which provided the legislative structure for the government to both promote and regulate the new economy. Since then, it has waxed and waned in favour with successive governments but continues to provide a structure around which a small contingent of bureaucrats, NGO staff, and small enterprises cohere, self-identifying as a group dedicated to promoting alternative economies.

In the tradition of the Manchester School, extended case studies were used to understand the interplay between structuring processes and the actions and decisions taken by individuals (Gluckman, 1961). I take as a case study the ambiguous space between policymaking and its realisation as such. In 2017 and 2018, I conducted fieldwork in Ecuador and followed how the theoretical construct of the PSE became realised in policy.[1] While spending most of my time with the staff of the Institute of Popular Solidarity Economy (IEPS), a government organisation created in 2011 to grow and strengthen the PSE, my field site was effectively the wider networks through which PSE policy was enacted, including among academics, NGO staff, and economic actors. AssoTrain, Eduardo's association, was from this wider cohort.

In Ecuador, with the advent of the PSE, 'association' has taken on the specific legal meaning of a small enterprise that is formally registered as part of the PSE. In comparison to a small business, an association must distribute profits evenly between all members and leadership positions must be rotated between members via voting. AssoTrain was a not-for-profit association created by a group of accountants to provide training to other PSE associations. As Eduardo described it, 'it's part of giving back as professionals'. For AssoTrain members, workshops were part of a social obligation, rather than a source of income. It was how they marked themselves as participating in something other than the capitalist economy.

The last key actor in the workshop was not present that day – the staff of the IEPS. The six-day workshop had been organised at the behest of the institute, with the IEPS inviting attendees. My fieldwork occurred during what was a year of near paralysis for the institute. The workshop was one of the largest projects organised by the local team and also one of the most popular events among programme beneficiaries that I saw. Although the training was not run by IEPS staff, it was one of the strongest embodiments of the PSE during my fieldwork. The workshop was also representative of the types of support offered by the IEPS. Since the oil price crash in 2014, their budget had been slashed, creating the previously mentioned paralysis. Staff turnover was immense, with only half of the local team keeping their positions during my fieldwork. In response, institute staff were constantly on the lookout for opportunities to run workshops and training sessions, especially if they involved free labour from other organisations.

The workshop was also representative of the topics covered at PSE training sessions. Some were exclusively about practical business skills – a workshop on cooking, for example. The majority I observed, however, blended practical economic concerns with wider social and political ideas. At most training sessions, it was ambiguous whether the advice was for the purpose of improving the profits of associations or to induct their members into the political philosophy of the PSE. As such, the promotion of the PSE in Ecuador offers an excellent extended case study as to the ambiguity of how the PSE was conceptualised, practised and ultimately understood, bringing together the everyday happenings, frictions and convergences between policymaking as a set of abstract, systemic forces and the real-world realisation of policy among government functionaries and PSE actors (Gluckman, 1961). Here, ambiguity is taken as a multiplicity of overlapping meanings within the concept of *'valor agregado'*. Importantly, this polysemy was not just about different people offering different meanings to words. Instead, people used the concept differently in different contexts, often strategically to place themselves on certain sides of political divides (Tesch and Kempton, 2004). As highlighted by Steindl-Kopf (this volume), ambiguity can integrate diverse perspectives and reconcile potentially contradictory interpretations, especially in the arena of policy and politics, even when political actors themselves attempt to reject said ambiguity.

Eduardo's bridge activity represented this well. The activity involved participants being split into groups of five or six. We had a budget of $7,000 to complete a bridge for the government, with measurements drawn on a whiteboard. We were given access to paper, glue and scissors, which all had prices. We had fifteen minutes to finish. It was a fast and fun activity, with smiles and laughs all around. It was when Eduardo assessed the bridges that the explicit lessons were imparted. After checking whether each bridge held up, Eduardo then quizzed each group about their process, asking if they had plans, what they would do with profits, and where the added value was. The tight budget and time limit meant that almost all the bridges were identical. When he asked the first group where their added value was, for example, they had no reply. 'You didn't do anything more than the requirements,' he said, with a touch of sadness. 'This happens a lot in the PSE, when often a touch is all you need.' There were murmurs of agreement around the room. 'That's how it is' (*Así es*), a fellow participant said.

In this context of almost uniform bridges, the addition of the sign clearly stood out. This was apparently *valor agregado*, though it was never clarified whether the sign's value came from the bridge's aesthetics, the sense of group cohesion (they gave themselves a name on the sign), or simply the presence of the sign. No one ever felt the need to question or elaborate on what that value was. Rather than treating this lack of specification as either an oversight or a strategic move for social cohesion, I examine the ambiguity of added value and how it itself added value for those involved in the PSE as a policy platform. I do so to make a methodological intervention into techniques for ethnographic analysis of policy and economics, proposing an alternative analytical framework to that of 'strategic ambiguity' which is often the approach of anthropologists of policy (Tate, 2015).

I begin with a brief discussion of how ambiguity has been treated in anthropological literature on policy, noting that previous approaches tend toward cynicism, as the motivation of policymakers is necessarily thought to be anything other than the explicit goals of policy (e.g. Ferguson, 1994; Mosse, 2005; Tate, 2015). A push for a more explicit discussion is then offered on how ethnographers examining ambiguity can pursue novel analytical techniques. I then return to a discussion of the ambiguity of *valor agregado* and how it added value to the PSE by bringing together both entrepreneurial and social solidarity concepts under the same label. I use this example to offer an alternative analytical technique for anthropologists of policy to study ambiguity. Not only did *valor agregado* help the IEPS bring together a host of different stakeholders, it allowed the PSE as both a policy framework and an alternative economy to interface with the wider economic context, especially at a time of fiscal austerity and instability.

In examining the ambiguity of policy, I want to highlight the importance of making methodologies more explicit. Ballestero and Winthereik (2021: 1) observe that most discussions on ethnography as a form of knowledge production stop at 'the point at which we are called to specify how we perform analysis'. With few exceptions, the actual techniques anthropologists use to analyse their data are rarely made sufficiently explicit or circulated widely.[2] I follow the example of Ballestero, Wintereik and their colleagues in offering not perfectly delimited instructions but an example of a technique to help anthropologists to reconsider what we think we already know. By focusing on the concept of ambiguity, I wish to make my own analysis explicit while also demonstrating the alternative insights it is possible to glean by using the concept of ambiguity differently to produce methodological specificity.

Thinking with ambiguity in policy analysis

When assessing the ambiguity of policy, Tate (2015) and Mosse (2005) build on the work of Ferguson (1994) and consider policy as primarily a post hoc rationalisation of existing action. For them, policymaking involves producing narratives to 'unite disparate bureaucratic projects' (Tate, 2015: 4). While they are unique in dealing directly with ambiguity, they speak to a long-standing anthropological tradition in which policy is examined not as a rational strategy for governing, but as a series of discourses and practices used by governments and other authorities to pursue a course of action. Generally, there is an emphasis on how policy shapes people's actions and relationships.[3] For anthropologists, therefore, 'the key question is not "What is policy?" but rather, "What do people do in the name of policy?" ' (Wedel et al., 2005: 35).

As a discipline, anthropology lacks a simple, neat definition of what policy 'is' beyond what actions are undertaken in the name of government. This complicates anthropologists' work. Describing how policy 'unfurls as a series of project stutters, misdirects, and meanderings' (Lea, 2020: 15) is a useful reminder of how it is not the neat, systematic, cyclical process that policymakers portray. Tate's (2015: 4) suggestion that policy is a uniting force, a set of narratives for 'disparate bureaucratic projects', means that 'strategic ambiguity' is essential in policy work. From this perspective, policymakers intentionally create ambiguous policy, or at least maintain ambiguities within policy, to 'create coherence among disparate programs that are already underway' (Tate, 2015: 5). This helps create the appearance of success, with 'successful' policy attracting more resources and institutional allies. Such additional support helps generate further 'success', creating a cycle of growth for policy initiatives as long as they can unite ever more projects (Ferguson, 1994; Mosse, 2005).

In contrast, as highlighted by Marshall (this volume), the power policymakers wield can at other times be felt through attempts to suppress ambiguity. Denying the varied and unpredictable effects of policy through compartmentalisation can itself be an act of bureaucratic power and control. If encouraging and tamping down on ambiguity can be leveraged by policymakers, there is an analytical question of how anthropologists address these different strategies. If we follow authors like Mosse (2005), Tate (2015) and Ferguson (1994), for example, and assume that the key purpose of policy is to make the disparate appear coherent, then it is essentially impossible to ever consider policymakers as actually being motivated by the stated aims of policy. At the same time, consistently highlighting the contradictions of policy is not necessarily enlightening. Many of those working in policy often already know that its outcomes can contradict the stated intentions of policy actors (van Ufford, 1993).

Central to my argument about the ambiguity of policy is a potential contradiction that sits at the heart of the PSE and other alternative economies more broadly. PSE proponents intend for it to be an alternative to capitalism, although the extent to which it is a wholesale replacement of capitalism or simply complementary to it is generally left unspoken. However, as highlighted by Steindl-Kopf (this volume), even though ambiguity can lead to conflict, it is an essential part of an alter-politics premised on moving away from capitalist accumulation. Because the PSE is miniscule relative to the wider economy, its proponents, like alternative economy proponents globally, find themselves in need of integrating with the dominant capitalist economy. In doing so, alternative economies take on many of the characteristics of the mainstream economy that proponents are opposed to (Maurer, 2005, 2013).

Precarious integration of the PSE in Ecuador took shape through the linking of the ideals of entrepreneurialism and social solidarity. Luis Razeto (1997, n.d.), a heterodox Chilean economist and early adopter of the term Popular Solidarity Economy, provides an excellent example. Aside from traditional factors of production – financing, technology, labour, material resources, and management – Razeto (1997, n.d.) identified 'factor C'. He came up with the term because, in Spanish, many of the words that set apart the PSE and other forms of the solidarity economy begin with 'c': *compañerismo* (fellowship), *cooperación* (cooperation), *comunidad* (community), *compartir* (share), *comunión* (communion), *colectividad* (collectivity) and *carisma* (charisma). That factor C could be a source not only of social good but of economic success is a vein of PSE theorising that has continued into the present (e.g. Sabín Galán et al., 2012; Cotera Fretel, 2010).

Central to the discourse of PSE theorising, including Eduardo's lessons, was the idea that the social values of the PSE were both morally correct and sensible business strategies, such as solidarity and reciprocity. Where the motivation to embody solidarity stopped and profit motivation started was never made clear. This intentional interpolation of social values with economic strategy had material effects on the realisation of PSE policy, with Razeto being explicitly referred to by my interlocutors who engaged in Eduardo's or other organisation's training sessions. For example, ConQuito, a provincial government organisation, also ran PSE workshops. Working in the metropolitan district of Quito, the organisation was well regarded and well known in the region, making it an important local player. ConQuito trainers explicitly used a variety of business model templates from the tech industry, further demonstrating the precarious integration of capitalist and alternative economic principles. Their training expressly used strategies from modern entrepreneurs to support what they saw as social values of solidarity.

Teresa, a government employee who was a big fan of Razeto, had worked previously in the entrepreneur sector, supporting business startups. During my time in Ecuador, she was the head of the PSE team at ConQuito. For Teresa, one of the hardest aspects of her job was convincing association members that 'innovation isn't just for technology'. She went on to explain that the organisation believed in three kinds of innovation: social, productive and commercial. Teresa was an explicit fan of Razeto's factor C, telling me that it was both what separated 'solidarity enterprises' from 'capitalist enterprises' and what let the solidarity enterprises compete in the market when they often lacked the technology and resources of capitalist businesses.

Despite the interpolation of entrepreneurialism and social solidarity, PSE proponents still distinguished between them. Their commonly expressed worry that they were accidentally creating 'little capitalists' rather than solidarity actors evinced this. Although proponents pushed for a reunification of 'the social' with 'the economic', this goal and their associated fears that 'the economic' would overwhelm 'the social' only made sense in the context of a distinction between the two. 'Valor agregado' was one of the key tools by which my interlocutors conceptualised this reunification.

The overlap between 'valor agregado' from PSE proponents and 'value added' from entrepreneurial businesses was no coincidence. Despite Teresa's argument that innovation wasn't just for technology, many government functionaries working with the PSE found inspiration in the tech industry. In training sessions for associations, government organisations used business tools, such as 'Business Model Canvas', that originated in the tech industry. This cross-pollination of ideas affected how the PSE operated as a social construct that united policy, social values such as 'solidarity', and specific economic forms. Here, it is possible to see the utility of ambiguity, through contradiction and cross-pollination, in the creation of new economic forms. In his examination of cryptocurrencies, Swartz (2018) highlights how the ambiguous purpose of Bitcoin in many ways led to its success. Importantly, he notes that the community around Bitcoin (and other cryptocurrencies) is comprised of two 'techno-economic imaginaries', one based around its speculative value and another founded upon its (speculated) ability to act as a mutualistic yet independent form of communication. For a period of time, it was unknown whether Bitcoin and other cryptocurrencies were a tool for rampant speculation or a new form of 'mutualistic self-help' (Swartz, 2018: 632). Swartz argues that, at the height of its popularity, Bitcoin's success was largely due to these two imaginaries being undifferentiated.

Elsewhere in the tech industry, it is often the 'ambiguous novelty' of new tech firms that gives them their market value (Hogarth, 2017: 261). Uber's early success largely hinged on its ambiguous status as a taxi company and software platform. Similarly, the DNA analysis firm 23andme was attractive to investors because it exploited the ambiguity in the minds of consumers, investors, policymakers and regulators about whether it provided software or healthcare. It was the collapse of this ambiguity that transformed the firm's business model into more traditional forms of regulatory compliance and government lobbying (Hogarth, 2017). At the same time, value creation itself can form a justification for 'radical forms of disinhibition' (Muniesa, 2017: 445–6; see also Geiger, 2020). Many, perhaps most, entrepreneurial strategies 'add value' through blurring the lines between different categories. At the same time, the value creation itself can be a powerful force for further overcoming previous inhibitions. The process is self-reinforcing.

The ambiguous value of social solidarity

In the case of the PSE in Ecuador, organisation staff members who were tasked with strengthening and growing the alternative economy felt value creation, variously understood, was in large part their value added. *Valor agregado* did not simply paper over the gaps between contradictory concepts or ideals. The key qualities of PSE associations – the equal distribution of profits and democratically elected, rotating leadership – meant that PSE policy was not simply micro-entrepreneurialism in another guise. As in other contexts where tight social bonds interact with small business structures, the solidarity of association members motivated them to often work extremely excessive hours to generate value and success in the marketplace (Shever, 2008; Yanagisako, 2002). At the same time, success in the marketplace reinforced solidarity. Many PSE association members I spoke to noted that it was always easier to show solidarity when things were going well. The social added value to the entrepreneurial at the same time as the entrepreneurial added value to the social. It was the ambiguity of where one started and the other ended that allowed for this mutually reinforcing situation.

The way my interlocutors sometimes treated the entrepreneurial and social solidarity aspects of the PSE as distinct and at other times as almost synonymous complicated my analysis. I could not create a hard distinction between them, but nor could I usefully treat them as a single amorphous mass. Instead, similar to Walford's (2021) use of 'analogy' as an analytical technique, I set my task as using one set of logics to unpack the other and vice versa, in a non-reductive way.[4] Rather than using analysis to pare back the ethnographic data until only a core remained, I used one set of logics or 'imaginaries', after Swartz (2018), to explain the other. Importantly, as highlighted by Walford, this technique involves conserving, extending and even transforming those concepts we wish to examine. Ideas of economic value helped in understanding the social solidarity foundations of associations. This, in turn, offered insights into how those social solidarity practices also help achieve success in the market. At the same time, they are 'conserved' in that they are not allowed to collapse into each other. Teasing apart the different strands that make up ambiguous policy can certainly be useful; however, allowing those different strands to wrap together into whole threads also offers its own insights. This, in turn, enabled me to explore how these insights are formed in the PSE.

Indeed, the words 'valor agregado' appeared to follow me around Ecuador, being used by government staff, NGOs, academics and associations alike. The sheer number of uses of *valor agregado* recorded in my notes revealed how central it was to IEPS staff, though its definition was never fully elaborated. Here, I explore the specific uses of the term in greater depth, demonstrating how it obscured, but did not eliminate, a division between 'the social' (*lo social*) and 'the economic' (*lo económico*), as perceived by my interlocutors. During fieldwork, I asked people how they would define 'valor agregado', especially outside the context of training sessions, where this term was rarely interrogated. Most gave examples that fit with classical economic theory – it was the enhancement made to a product before selling it to a customer. A common example was taking bread, cheese and ham to construct a sandwich for sale.

In daily conversation, however, the term was used in many ways. In comparison to the economic theory of added value, *valor agregado* in quotidian settings was closer to the marketing concept of 'value-added proposition' – a statement of why a customer should choose your product or service over that of a competitor. Occasionally, the *valor agregado* was used in a context to refer to the social values of the PSE itself, such as when an attempt to create specific PSE branding (similar to Fair Trade labelling), was described as 'adding value' to PSE products. In that case, it was not clear if the speaker was referring to the potentially improved asking price for the labelled products, or whether they were saying that the solidarity of the producers added value in the eyes of potential consumers. I heard *valor agregado* used in both ways.

Explicitly asking interlocutors a relatively standard question about their definition of 'valor agregado' proved useful. It highlighted one of the ways that this policy and its application was rendered ambiguous. People were not simply using a word with multiple definitions. Instead, it stemmed from everyone using a word differently but, when asked, typically defining it in similar ways. This reflected the illusion of coherence around policy that can be described as either 'strategic ambiguity' (Tate, 2015) or 'productive ambiguity' (Mosse, 2005). Many could potentially say the same words and appear to be saying the same thing. This was not simply some linguistic ploy made possible by multiple definitions or homonyms; ambiguity stemmed from the way that the term had a high level of coherence when people thought about it explicitly. That was what let people leave their specific usages of *valor agregado* largely unquestioned.

The work done in the name of PSE policy reflected this ambiguity. While some workshops organised by the IEPS were entirely focused on workplace skills (such as cooking) to improve production, the focus of many others tacked back and forth between topics focused on smart business sense and social values, such as solidarity. The workshop with AssoTrain was no exception. Eduardo's advice moved between business and morals. The activity on bridge building was not only about business (he also spoke about the importance of planning and budgeting), it was also about lessons on *asociatividad* (associativity), on how *to be* an association. During the training session that this chapter opened with, my group was the last to present, and we were 'the bad' group. We were the last to finish, and the moment Eduardo picked up our bridge, a leg fell off. 'The government won't accept this,' said Eduardo. 'They won't pay.' This sparked a bit of back-and-forth discussion with our group, with some insisting that the government had to pay. Eduardo met them halfway, saying that we would have to repair the bridge at our own expense and make a loss. What would we do? 'All pay equally!' came the emphatic response in unison. 'That's good,' he replied. 'That is the idea of the PSE. But what if one of the ladies (*señoras*) can't pay the full amount?' he asked, gesturing to one of our group members. 'Then I would lend it to her,' came the instant response from another group member. Eduardo nodded and looked genuinely impressed.

The answer embodied what was seen as the collective spirit of the PSE. A common refrain during my fieldwork was that 'You share the profits, but you also share the debts' (*deudas*). This was often implicitly contrasted with a regular business in which debts were held by the owner, but all profits went to them as well. Eduardo's activity could so easily tack back and forth between the economic and social aspects of running an association because they were considered to be closely tied in the PSE and, at times, treated as one. The ambiguity of what was valued within the PSE – commercial success, social solidarity or otherwise – allowed a diverse range of actors to participate in a workshop on ostensibly divergent topics. Administrative duties and tax obligations sat alongside moral guidance on how to show solidarity, all interspersed with entrepreneurial tips. The common sense that these different topics added value to the PSE made the workshop feel like a coherent activity for all to engage in.

Harmonising ambiguity

At this level, it is possible to see how such an analysis of ambiguity is largely similar to that of other anthropologists of policy: ambiguity helps policy actors paper over gaps in the motivations and actions of different stakeholder groups. The polysemy of an ambiguous term is strategically used by different groups to position themselves and opponents on different sides of political divides (Tesch and Kempton, 2004). This analytical approach, however, produces a cynical account, in which the motivations of policymakers cannot be considered the same as the stated goals of policy. It treats ambiguity as a pragmatic strategy for mobilising people, with a sense that actors have their own motivations and that any lack of detail in policy work is to avoid highlighting discrepancies between those motivations, whether intentional or not.

With reference to *valor agregado* and the PSE in Ecuador, I propose an alternative approach to studying policy ambiguity. While the acknowledgement of incompleteness and ambiguity is essential to the formation of policy, as argued by Marshall (this volume), its full impact when applied can never be known by its originators. Therefore, rather than treating it as valuable solely for its ability to bring different stakeholders together, studying ambiguity can be useful for examining how actors integrate different systems and for unpacking the interconnectedness of said systems. To this end, Burawoy (1998: 5), the student of Mancunian anthropologist Jaap van Velsen, makes useful recommendations on the use of the extended case method. He proposes several 'extensions' for case studies. Of relevance here is the need to '[trace] the source of small difference to external forces' (Burawoy, 1998: 19). If increasing and collapsing ambiguity are tools for policymakers, it is important to assess under what circumstances they choose one over the other. In the case of the PSE, much of the need for ambiguity came from its position. Similar to the cases studied by Mosse (2005) and Tate (2015), it was their relative inability to affect external forces that rendered strategic ambiguity necessary. With limited funding, the ability to latch on to other, more popular discourses was essential.

In this style of analysis, I step away from looking at the overlap between social solidarity and entrepreneurialism as 'strategic'. For example, a traditional critique would be to show how the ambiguous concept of *valor agregado* functioned as cover to unite government actors and proto-entrepreneurs under the banner of social solidarity, often with the additional critique that it was somehow all a trojan horse for neoliberal capitalism.[5] In economic anthropology, as in Science and Technology Studies, a classic analysis would be to show how 'practices of measuring, counting, and numbering actually have a hand in sculpting and shaping the worlds that they measure, count and number' (Walford, 2021: 209). While this approach can certainly generate insightful analysis, it also pushes the ethnographer to 'conveniently ignore' what researchers, economists and other policymakers understand they are doing (Walford, 2021: 210). Perceptions of their own actions are devalued and rendered as self-deception, at best, and deception of others, at worst.

As an alternative to emphasising contradictions, I follow my interlocutors and look at how entrepreneurial and social solidarity work together. Similar to Walford's use of 'analogy', I concentrate on how my interlocutors described these different aspects of the PSE, often expressed through *valor agregado*, as not only supporting one another but each in terms of the other. To return to Eduardo's bridge activity, any added economic value was valuable for the additional resources it provided to help the bridge builders cohere as a unit. In turn, any growth in solidarity was valuable for the additional economic resources it could generate to help the association grow. Any tensions between economic success and social solidarity were rendered harmonious by the ambiguity of added value. In a formulation I saw repeated throughout my fieldwork, one conception of *valor agregado* was expressed in terms of the other and vice versa.

In another, more concrete example, several young adults in a small town started a PSE enterprise making ice-cream. The key organiser said their goal was to 'add value to the local [fruit] production' and create work so that he and his friends did not have to move to the city. Making ice-cream added value to the fruit and created employment. At the same time, it was the solidarity of all working together that was often described as the key to success for the PSE. Where capitalist businesses had the money to buy more advanced machinery, PSE enterprises had to make up for their lack of financial capital through the labour of members. In the case of the ice-cream store, it was a recent start-up that was only surviving through the additional labour and funding of several young émigrés from the town who wanted their friends to be able to stay, and to perhaps return themselves one day and work in the town. The *valor agregado* of a product created the funds to help avoid emigration and reinforce the solidarity of a township; however, the solidarity of PSE enterprises and communities as a whole was the value they could add to the production process to be successful in the economy. Rather than simply being a strategy for creating unified action, the ambiguity of *valor agregado* was central to the translation of different conceptions of value between different conceptions of the PSE so the alternative economy could function.

Conclusion

The ambiguity of the conceptualisation and application of PSE in Ecuador, as both a form of entrepreneurialism and an alternative economy, was central to why it was valued by the Institute of Popular Solidarity Economy

(IEPS), the wider government, and a host of NGOs. In a precarious context in which support for an alternative to capitalism appeared to be under threat, the ability to interface with that self-same capitalist economy made the PSE an appealing policy platform for different groups. Ambiguity, when considered as something overlapping and yet remaining unspecified, allows many different purposes to be ascribed to policy without any apparent sense of contradiction. For the central government, supporting the PSE was a strategy to encourage micro-enterprise while maintaining left-wing credentials. For PSE actors, the ambiguity of the alternative economy was essential for their incomes. Preferential government contracts were predicated on associations being entrepreneurial while also embodying solidarity and reciprocity. Finally, for the IEPS, the ambiguity of the PSE allowed them to interface with more organisations, inside and outside of government, as well as direct more support to associations, nominally in the form of programmes to enter the private market.

At the same time, to simply dismiss this ambiguity as 'strategic' (Tate, 2015) misses the opportunity to examine the contours of that ambiguity in depth; to this end, as explored by Puszka (this volume), professional strategising casts a light on the ways policies are understood by those implementing them, as well as the kinds of behaviours and actions that lead on from the invocation of certain policies. Certainly, political actors can intentionally use ambiguity to paper over different motivations and ideologies between themselves and allies, real or hoped for. However, to describe the ambiguity of the PSE as 'strategic' would ascribe far too much agency to the IEPS and PSE actors in a context of extreme precarity, in which staff came and went far too rapidly to realise any 'strategy'. Instead, I have proposed examining ambiguity itself, both in this instance and as an analytical technique for other anthropologists of policy.

Rather than teasing apart the different set of logics that made up the PSE and highlighting how they were held in a creative tension, the approach I proposed involves following my interlocutors and examining those logics through the lens of a harmonious ambiguity premised on understanding the cross-overs between the economic and the social. Without attempting to collapse everything into 'entrepreneurialism' or 'economic alternative', we can examine what ambiguity makes possible. In the case of the PSE, this was more than the strategic alliances of government. The ambiguous position of the PSE and *valor agregado* led PSE associations to a particular strategy for success in the market. At the same time, this same ambiguity was responsible for the slow restructuring of that alternative economy, as its purpose shifted from a wholescale alternative to capitalism to a way for those of a leftist political persuasion to engage in entrepreneurial activities, either directly or vicariously through the associations they supported. It is not simply that the value added by PSE supporters was ambiguous, but that ambiguity was one of the key values they were able to add to the economic policy environment.

Accepting this ambiguity does not simply mean everything has to be a melange, however. My interlocutors often acknowledged that there were both economic and social considerations to the PSE as one of the explicit purposes of the alternative economy. Instead, working with ambiguity requires sitting uncomfortably with multiple potential understandings and asking what this multiplicity does for those we work with. Following in the footsteps of the Manchester School, detailing locally salient understandings of ambiguous concepts can be extended toward systemic issues, such as the ever-increasing spread of entrepreneurial logics and ideals. Importantly, while cynical, almost functionalist, interpretations have their place, so too do more credulous explanations. Experimenting with different forms of analysis and examining the differences in our findings can reveal novel insights into local and global systems. After all, if our interlocutors experience their own actions as ambiguous, collapsing that ambiguity would undermine the ethnographic principle of exploring the experiences of those we talk to.

Notes

1 This research is supported by an Australian Government Research Training Program (RTP) Scholarship.
2 They note two famous exceptions: the 'implosion' method conceived by Haraway and subsequently developed by Dumit (2014) and Fortun's (2009) memo system.
3 For example, see Ansell (2014), Greenhalgh (2008), Nelms (2015), Shore and Wright (2011), Trouillot (2001) and Wedel et al. (2005).
4 Walford herself borrows the concept of 'analogy' as an analytical technique from Strathern (2006).
5 See, for example, Amsler and Shore (2017), Faas (2018), Falconer (2018), Schild (2000) and Soederberg (2016).

References

Amsler, M. and Shore, C. (2017) 'Responsibilisation and leadership in the neoliberal university: A New Zealand perspective', *Discourse: Studies in the Cultural Politics of Education*, 38:1, 123–37.
Ansell, A. (2014) *Zero Hunger: Political Culture and Antipoverty Policy in Northeast Brazil* (Chapel Hill: University of North Carolina Press).
Asamblea Nacional, Republica del Ecuador (2018) Ley Organica de Economía Popular y Solidaria, in T.4887-SNJ-11–664, ed. SEPS (Superintendencia de Economía Popular y Solidaria), Quito.

Ballestero, A. and Winthereik, B.R. (2021) *Experimenting with Ethnography: A Companion to Analysis* (Durham, NC: Duke University Press).

Burawoy, M. (1998) 'The Extended Case Method', *Sociological Theory*, 16:1, 4–33.

Coraggio, J.L. (2011) *Economia social y solidaria: el trabajo antes que el capital* (Quito: Abya-Yala).

Cotera Fretel, A. (2010) 'Respuesta a la Crisis desde la Economía Solidaria', *Materiales de Reflexión*, 72.

Dumit, J. (2014) 'Writing the Implosion: Teaching the World One Thing at a Time', *Cultural Anthropology*, 29:2, 344–62.

Faas, A.J. (2018) 'Petit capitalisms in disaster, or the limits of neoliberal imagination: Displacement, recovery, and opportunism in highland Ecuador', *Economic Anthropology*, 5:1, 32–44.

Falconer, C.A. (2018) '(En)Gendering Equality? Conditional Cash Transfers as National Development in Post-Neoliberal Ecuador', *Journal of Latin American and Caribbean Anthropology*, 23:2, 320–37.

Ferguson, J. (1994) *The Anti-Politics Machine: 'Development', Depoliticization, and Bureaucratic Power in Lesotho* (Minneapolis: University of Minnesota Press).

Fortun, K. (2015) 'Figuring Out Theory: Ethnographic Sketches', in D. Boyer, J.D. Faubion and G.E. Marcus (eds), *Theory Can Be More than It Used to Be: Learning Anthropology's Method in a Time of Transition* (Ithaca, NY: Cornell University Press).

Geiger, S. (2020) 'Silicon Valley, disruption, and the end of uncertainty', *Journal of Cultural Economy*, 13:2, 169–84.

Gluckman, M. (1961) 'Ethnographic Data in British Social Anthropology', *Sociological Review*, 9:1, 5–17.

Greenhalgh, S. (2008) *Just One Child: Science and Policy in Deng's China* (Oakland: University of California Press).

Hogarth, S. (2017) 'Valley of the unicorns: Consumer genomics, venture capital and digital disruption', *New Genetics and Society*, 36:3, 250–72.

Lea, T. (2020) *Wild Policy: Indigeneity and the Unruly Logics of Intervention* (Stanford, CA: Stanford University Press).

Maurer, B. (2005) *Mutual Life, Limited: Islamic Banking, Alternative Currencies, Lateral Reason* (Princeton, NJ: Princeton University Press).

Maurer, B. (2013) 'The Disunity of Finance: Alternative Practices To Western Finance', in Karin Knorr Cetina and Alex Preda (eds), *The Oxford Handbook of the Sociology of Finance* (Oxford: Oxford University Press), 413–30.

Mosse, D. (2005) *Cultivating Development: An Ethnography of Aid Policy and Practice* (London: Pluto Press).

Muniesa, F. (2017) 'On the Political Vernaculars of Value Creation', *Science as Culture*, 26:4, 445–54.

Nelms, T.C. (2015) '"The problem of delimitation": Parataxis, bureaucracy, and Ecuador's popular and solidarity economy', *Journal of the Royal Anthropological Institute*, 21, 106–26.

Razeto, M.L. (1997) 'Charla de Luis Razeto: Factor "C"', Economía Solidaria, www.economiasolidaria.org/sites/default/files/el_factor_c.pdf (accessed 27 August 2022).

Razeto, M.L. (n.d) 'El "Factor C": La Fuerza de la Solidaridad en la Economia (Entrevista)', www.luisrazeto.net/content/el-factor-c-la-fuerza-de-la-solidaridad-en-la-economia-entrevista (accessed 8 August 2022).

Sabín Galán, F., Fernández Casadevante, J.L. and Bandrés de Lucas, I. (2012) 'Factor C: Factores de resistencia de las microempresas cooperativas frente a la crisis y recomendaciones para un fortalecimiento cooperativo del sector de lo social', XIV Jornadas de investigadores en economía social y cooperativa, Madrid.

Schild, V. (2000) 'Neo-liberalism's New Gendered Market Citizens: The 'Civilizing' Dimension of Social Programmes in Chile', *Citizenship Studies*, 4:3, 275–305.

Shever, E. (2008) 'Neoliberal associations: Property, company, and family in the Argentine oil fields', *American Ethnologist*, 35:4, 701–16.

Shore, C. and Wright, S. (2011) 'Conceptualising Policy: Technologies of Governance and the Politics of Visibility', in C. Shore, S. Wright and D. Peró (eds), *Policy Worlds: Anthropology and the Analysis of Contemporary Power* (Oxford: Berghahn), 10–38.

Soederberg, S. (2016) 'Introduction – Risk Management in Global Capitalism', in Susanne Soederberg (ed.) *Risking Capitalism* (Bingley: Emerald Group Publishing), 1–22.

Strathern, M. (2006) 'Useful Knowledge', *Proceedings of the British Academy*, 139, 73–109.

Swartz, L. (2018) 'What was Bitcoin, what will it be? The techno-economic imaginaries of a new money technology', *Cultural Studies*, 32:4, 623–50.

Tate, W. (2015) *Drugs, Thugs, and Diplomats* (Redwood City, CA: Stanford University Press).

Tesch, D. and Kempton, W. (2004) 'Who is an Environmentalist? The Polysemy of Environmentalist Terms and Correlated Environmental Actions', *Journal of Ecological Anthropology*, 8:1, 67–83.

Trouillot, M.R. (2001) 'Anthropology of the State in the Age of Globalization: Close Encounters of the Deceptive Kind', *Current Anthropology*, 42:1, 125–38.

van Ufford, P.Q. (1993) 'Knowledge and ignorance in the practices of development policy', in Mark Hobart (ed.), *An Anthropological Critique of Development: The Growth of Ignorance* (New York: Routledge), 135–60.

Walford, A. (2021) 'Analogy', in A. Ballestero and B.R. Winthereik (eds), *Experimenting with Ethnography: A Companion to Analysis* (Durham, NC: Duke University Press), 209–18.

Wedel, J.R., Shore, C., Feldman, G. and Lathrop, S. (2005) 'Toward an Anthropology of Public Policy', *The ANNALS of the American Academy of Political and Social Science*, 600:1, 30–51.

Yanagisako, S.J. (2002) *Producing Culture and Capital: Family Firms in Italy* (Princeton, NJ: Princeton University Press).

9

The sovereign's road: checkpoints and the ambiguity of exception during Aotearoa's lockdown

Joe Clifford

Introduction

States of emergency are characterised in ways that emphasise the uncertainty of an unfolding situation. They function as a threat to a sense of normality and demand interventions by authorities (Calhoun, 2013: 55). Such interventions are linked to an imaginary held by the body politic that is tied to the perception of emergencies as abnormal, brief and unpredictable (Calhoun, 2004: 375). For Carl Schmitt intervention is directly linked to sovereignty, as the sovereign is 'he who decides upon the exception', and it is the decision by the sovereign on the necessity of intervention that defines the exception (1985 [1922]: 5).[1] This places the sovereign in the dual role of simultaneously belonging to and being outside the law: they exist in the realm of juridical procedure and the manufacturing of norms and yet suspend and act independently of legal and political norms (Schmitt, 1985b: 7–13). The theoretical lineage following Schmitt, however, has oriented us too strongly towards analyses of exception and emergency that prioritise the coercive and controlling aspects of the state. Studying states of emergency as they unfold orients us to a range of ambiguous actions and occurrences, explored here through Aotearoa New Zealand's pandemic experience. Indeed, ambiguous actions and occurrences often arise as non-state actors set about establishing new methods for responding to and repurposing state-imposed emergency measures and generating new imaginaries. In Aotearoa New Zealand, ambiguity arose as competing conceptions of legitimacy, sovereignty and territoriality co-existed and produced an Indigenous-led crisis-response in a settler colony.

During the first lockdown in March of 2020, Māori groups (iwi) began to help enforce the state's ban on non-essential travel to remote communities in the North Island (Te Ika-a-Māui). Iwi are the largest social and political group in Māori sociality, comprised of different hapū (a kinship group comprised of a group of families with a common ancestor), which are in turn comprised of whānau (extended families), the smallest unit of Māori political structure. This decision was justified in reference to the structural and historical violence and health inequity that Māori have been disproportionately exposed to. In political anthropology, political units or political communities have been taken to mean 'the most inclusive aggregate of persons who identify with each other as a group, and who are prepared to regulate their differences by means of decisions accepted as binding because they are made in accordance with shared political norms and structures' (Easton, 1959: 229). In this sense, we can think of iwi as political units. Sovereignty is usually attached to the political unit in the form of a nation-state and anchored in specific paradigms of power, such as biopolitics where the populations' physiological wellbeing and statistical construction become part of the process of governing (Foucault, 2008). Here, the idea of the political unit is extended and explored with reference to Indigenous groups and their activism within settler colonies. What is also considered is the ability of Māori to engage in a biopolitics of their own.

The consequence of iwi groups engaging in their own biopolitics was the establishment of checkpoints on key roads into remote communities. Checkpoints were framed as a duty of care towards those most at risk from exposure to the virus (Ngata, 2020). Unlike the emergencies which Schmitt theorised, often involving war or uprisings, COVID-19 emerged in Aotearoa New Zealand from a nonhuman source. In these examples, sovereignty, emergency and territory were all co-constitutive of one another but with a greater level of ambiguity and plasticity than is typical in Schmitt's theorising where one actor is shown to be sovereign through their enacting of an emergency. In this chapter I understand ambiguity to be a situation which is defined by a lack of clarity but also boasts an opportunity to remould and remake the situation in a novel way. For this reason, contradiction and plasticity are key terms in understanding how the checkpoints generated an ambiguous political situation in Aotearoa New Zealand.

The pandemic interrupted anthropology's usual ethnographic research methods due to the severity of the virus and the introduction of health restrictions on non-essential travel. During the first half of 2020, I was involved in the state-led COVID-19 response in quarantine hotels (Clifford, 2020), and being physically present at the location of these checkpoints would have been illegal and undermined the response that those manning the checkpoints desired. While states of ambiguity and potential contradictions have always been inherent in fieldwork through the meeting of different persons and lifeways, the pandemic has heightened this sense of ambiguity in how ethnography is conducted in response to local contexts. As a consequence, instead of building insights from typical ethnographic research practices, I draw on a range of public sources to examine how iwi fashioned their own understanding of exception as well as examining those who criticised them. This approach prioritises public explanations of the need for checkpoints by members of these iwi groups and has given sharper focus to public debates about these checkpoints and the ambiguity of the coherence of the state during emergencies.

The state's pandemic response

On 28 February 2020, Aotearoa New Zealand reported its first case of COVID-19. By 23 March, Prime Minister Jacinda Ardern and Director General of Health Ashley Bloomfield had introduced restrictions on gatherings, instructed returning travellers to quarantine for two weeks, and created a tier system of 'alert levels' outlining different gradations of freedoms available to the public. On 25 March, a state of emergency was declared, placing the entire country into level four, the most restrictive level. The publicly stated goal was the eradication of the virus. This was considered valuable enough to require a public health response encompassing one of the strictest lockdowns in the world. Alerts were sent to all smartphones in the country, instructing the public to 'act as if you have COVID-19', that close contact was only permitted among households, and that only essential workplaces could remain open. A state of emergency was in place from 25 March to 13 May, declared by the Minister of Civil Defence, Peeni Henare, and Ardern. This response showed how the notion of 'the public' is flattened in times of crisis, with citizens asked to work toward a common outcome.

Around the world, epidemiologists and public commentators used Aotearoa New Zealand's response to the COVID-19 pandemic as a point of reference in contradistinction to other country contexts, such as in the Untied States (see Marshall, this volume) and Sweden (Jefferied et al. 2020). The presentation of Aotearoa New Zealand's early handling of the pandemic was typified by early, proactive lockdowns and the closure and strict policing of borders. The personable communication style of Ardern and Bloomfield was also notable. In this approach there was an understanding of the state as building legitimacy by marshalling its bureaucracies and resources towards a goal of eradicating the virus with the public good in mind. This understanding of the public good is similar to Bear and Mathur's (2015: 18–19), where bureaucracies are conceived as functioning through a contract between officials and the citizenry. In this instance, intervention by the state was framed as a contract where the state would act to protect the population from a novel disease in return for strict limits on movement and gatherings, and other measures to mitigate the spread of the virus.

For New Zealanders, then, there is now a well-known timeline for the national COVID-19 response in 2020, centred around two lockdowns which acted as collective temporal markers for events in that year. The first of these lockdowns was the national one described above and accompanied by a state of emergency; the other was specific to those living in Tāmaki Makaurau (Auckland) from 11 to 30 August, when the city moved from Alert Level One to Three, with the rest of the country experiencing a shift in alert levels but not a lockdown. National collective time was here marked by bureaucratic determinations of alert and severity, which was marshalled to affect all or part of the country. While this timeline characterises the initial pandemic response experienced by many New Zealanders, among many Māori there is a deeper historical memory of pandemics that underlay a different temporality and intersect with settler colonialism and 'viral vulnerability' (Norman et al., 2021), which iwi ultimately came to draw upon through community responses to the pandemic.

While the extent of the lockdown and the role of Ardern's leadership and communication strategies have been widely discussed, much less time has been given to how the lockdown was enforced and how political actors outside of parliament have approached this. Among these include placing teddy bears in windows to make the lockdown less worrisome for children, protests against the lockdowns, and a whole new suite of work and learning practices (Trnka, 2020). As Matthewman and Huppatz (2020: 677) have shown, the response to the pandemic saw an explosion of community-minded actions in the tradition of mutual aid. They note that disasters are always socially shared and produce phenomena with collective adversity creating social solidarity within groups, as shown in Heffernan's ethnography (this volume) of protest culture and collective imaginaries of building a new moral framework following a banking collapse in Iceland. The question for anthropologists is how we determine the boundaries of who forms which groups; in other words, how has belonging been redefined in this emerging solidarity, and what kind of logic are these actions based upon? Different responses to those enacted by the state can shed light on this. Indeed, community responses, such as those mounted by Indigenous populations, are capable of highlighting the ambiguity at the heart of a dominant theory of sovereignty and the practices and discourses of the state in Aotearoa New Zealand.

The Treaty of Waitangi as a source of legitimacy

Unlike other British settler colonies with which Aotearoa New Zealand is typically compared (i.e. Australia, Canada and the United States) there is no singular written constitutional text. Instead, the state claims its foundational moment to be the 1840 signing of Te Tiriti o Waitangi (The Treaty of Waitangi) as the establishment of the New Zealand polity. In official discourses and histories, the state makes sense of itself through a declared partnership between Māori and New Zealand European settler-colonial descendants (Pākehā), both of which emerge as founding groups, regardless of the diversity of practices and interests among them.

There exist long-standing debates in the historiography of the Treaty regarding the intentions of the signatories representing the Crown. The Treaty text itself was initially written in te reo Māori and signed by 540 rangatira (leaders) at Waitangi. A subsequent English-language version toured Aotearoa New Zealand with significant language differences (Ministry of Culture and Heritage, 2012). Scholars have argued that the translation should be read as a text independent of the original (Mutu, 2010). The ongoing relevance of the Treaty is key to the state's framing of itself as possessing moral legitimacy, and an ongoing point of controversy for both Indigenous groups who seek greater autonomy and for the more conservative elements of the country's political landscape who would use the Treaty as a way to dissolve political notions of difference entirely.

Despite the claim that the Treaty is the foundational document for New Zealand as a nation-state, the original manuscript spent many years rotting in a basement in Wellington. What is more, the Treaty was effectively absent from law until the 1975 Treaty of Waitangi Act, which does not take the literal text of the Treaty but tries to isolate its key principles. This history came to the fore in the early stages of the pandemic as iwi groups, unhappy with the absence of Māori in decision-making processes, established their own checkpoints on key roads to remote communities. The linking of autonomy and self-determination to the Treaty is important in framing the language as iwi presented themselves as fulfilling the role of partners in a relationship (Ngata, 2020). For example, Julia Whaipooti, a Māori activist, said 'community-led checkpoints, working with police, is a practical expression of the Tiriti relationship and I think that's something to be upheld' (Hurihanganui, 2020). The Human Rights Commission (2020), an independent Crown entity, published a report on the lockdowns that broadly agreed with this assessment. What this history points to is the disparity between the nominal and formal construction of a singular national identity and a history of exclusion and colonialism.

The checkpoints and their justifications

Prior to the arrival of COVID-19, Aotearoa New Zealand was already a country with marked disparities in health outcomes between Pākehā, Māori and other groups. Notable are the premature mortality rates for Māori and Pacifica, being twice that of non-Māori or non-Pacifica populations (Walter, 2018: 254). Virulent pandemics emerging among immunologically at-risk populations are not new; they constitute a key part of the experiences of colonisation in the South Pacific (Barber and Naepi, 2020; Snowden, 2019: 85). An extreme example of this is the 1875 measles outbreak in neighbouring Fiji, which had a mortality rate of between 20 and 25 per cent (Morens, 2015: 123). For Pacifica people these issues are not simply historical. Pacific Islanders have continued to face adverse health outcomes after migrating to Aotearoa New Zealand, including higher rates of noncommunicable diseases and being less likely to have collected prescriptions due to the cost (Ministry of Health, 2019). Māori likewise saw long-term population decline with the introduction of smallpox and other diseases during European settlement, as well as a fatality rate more than seven times that of Pākehā during the Spanish Flu (Reid et al., 2019; Rice, 2019). Available epidemiological evidence suggests that, if early variants of COVID-19 had spread widely, these groups would have been disproportionately affected, with the expected infection fatality ratio (IFR) up to 50 per cent higher for Māori (Steyn et al., 2020). These discrepancies in health outcomes and a radically different historical experience with epidemics are part of what has complicated the notion of a shared national identity in the pandemic response.

The construction of a population via health modelling and statistical data is key to the biopolitical project of treating, governing and controlling populations (Foucault, 2009: 474). Equally key is the move from the statistical presentation of populations to the types of narratives that they are used to engender (Gupta, 2012: 111). In Aotearoa New Zealand conservative groups and political parties have considered the poor health outcomes of Māori to be due to poor personal decisions or genetics rather than structural factors. However, it was the framing and biopolitical construction of a population as vulnerable that was the basis for legitimacy claims made by iwi in their own emergency response. It was the perceived sense of the state improperly enforcing its own declared emergency that led to the establishment of checkpoints across Te Ika-a-Māui (The North Island). Checkpoints across the island included those established by members of the Ngāpuhi, Te Whānau-ā-Apanui, and Ngāti Porou iwi, respectively, as well as eight iwi in Taranaki. These groups cover diverse areas of the island but all are in remote communities.

While hapū representatives originally signed the Treaty of Waitangi, iwi steadily became the group that the state preferred to deal with due to their ability to represent larger groups of people. This is part of an ongoing contentious process of the Crown making Māori social structures legible to the Crown's project of rule (Scholtz, 2010; Scott, 1998). Rendering iwi legible is a double-edged sword in that it provides a group for the state to engage with but also makes them well-suited to raising political issues related to the historical experiences of Māori, and to critique the government's emergency on its own terms. In mid-century political anthropology, Abner Cohen (1969: 5) of the Manchester School made the case that, in Indigenous social structures, politics 'refers to the processes involved in the distribution and exercise of, and struggle for, power within a social unit'. Working among urban African Hausa, Cohen sought to challenge Eurocentric conceptions of politics and kinship by breaking down the scholarly silos imposed around these domains. For Cohen and the Manchester School crises presented opportunities to understand productive socio-political tensions, including ideas of order and disorder, maintaining that such crises provided insights into socio-political functioning. More recently, Thelen and Alber (2018) have shown how notions of belonging and descent continue to structure political organisation in many localities. The checkpoints understood in the wider historical trajectory of Aotearoa New Zealand show exactly this.

Iwi checkpoints were manned alongside police checkpoints on various occasions. The Police Commissioner estimated up to fifty checkpoints were in operation across the country (Burrows, 2020). Typically, these checkpoints involved stopping traffic, inquiring where drivers lived, questioning their connections with the local community, and using police to turn around non-essential travellers. Tina Ngata, an Indigenous rights activist, highlights the Māori duty to protect their own in relation to the checkpoints. Detailing the devastating effects of colonisation and disease on Māori, Ngata (2020) writes that due to many Indigenous groups globally experiencing disease as a genocidal weapon and the state's long history of failing to protect her ancestors – 'you can understand why we could not wait for anyone to come and save us'. We can read this and much of Ngata's article as a rejection of the desire to, in Agamben's (1998) terms, be reduced to bare life. Instead, the pandemic led to Indigenous actors drawing on duties to care for and protect one's community. We see here not only a type of bio-citizenship that links health and social identity (Rose and Novas, 2005: 442–5), but the mobilisation of these based on Māori values. When paired with Cohen's thesis on the function of discrete political units, Indigenous checkpoints highlight the ways that cultural ideals and symbols may be leveraged in times of crisis (in contrast to official state policy models) to promote ideas of equity and cultural responsibility in working towards building a shared sense of security.

The Te Tai Tokerau Community Borders group used this line of argument in their reasoning for establishing checkpoints. In an online flyer (Ngapuhi, 2020) the members of the Ngāpuhi iwi, like Ngata, cite the continuity between colonisation and the likely impacts of allowing the virus to spread through the community. Tellingly, they note 'a lot of the contributors such as socioeconomic opportunities, housing standards and community isolation haven't really changed in the last hundred years', a reference to the vastly different health protections and IRF infection fatality rate experienced by Māori during the Spanish Flu. Comparable to the established links between sovereignty, territory and emergency, there is a strong continuity in the biopolitical literature that frames the oppressive and power-laden dimensions at play in state-enacted public health measures. For example, Foucault's (2008: 24–5) reading of plague response measures is a classic example of how control over a population's biological life and wellbeing becomes part of the political project of ordering society.

Biopolitical paradigms of control, especially how Māori and their health are constructed, are certainly problematic (see Reid et al., 2019). However, the biopolitical framing of populations was also a key to the justification for iwi groups making claims for their own enactment of checkpoints. Not satisfied with state-proposed measures for protection, iwi groups claimed higher risks based on the health data (outlined above) and sought to enact their own virus mitigation. The presentation of Māori as a population that is less healthy and more susceptible to negative experiences of viral illnesses was key to the legitimation of restricting movement into lands where iwi claimed authority. This is a clear example of adherence to a political unit (iwi) being mobilised against the actions of the state to resolve the complexity of vulnerability imposed by a biopolitical model of health and wellbeing on minority groups.

The structural violence, then, that contributes to Aotearoa New Zealand having consistently unequal outcomes in health was seen as the motivating factor for these iwi groups to enact their own exception and enforce the state's own restrictions on mobility among the wider population. Thus, narratives that had previously been used to render Māori as peripheral or unable to enact their own agency were repurposed and used as an imperative for Māori to enforce something of their own emergency.

Sovereignty, exception and territory

The actions of iwi groups point to a larger question in how we come to understand the making and remaking of sovereignty in Aotearoa New Zealand, both through the discursive construction of populations and the on-ground actions that reproduce the state. Sovereignty, exception and territory are crucial terms for the framing of the modern nation-state. How they constitute one another through various practices and discourses has long drawn the attention of anthropologists interested in the state apparatus. So too, the way in which narratives of sovereignty differ from the on-ground realities has gained traction by practitioners (Das and Poole, 2004; Ferguson and Gupta, 2002). Much existing literature on emergencies tends towards the idea that declaring a state of emergency is something that is imposed on a population, and which they must endure and are often overwhelmed by (Trnka, 2020: 13). However, the electoral success of the New Zealand Labour Party in 2020 and the continued high support for lockdown measures amongst the public (Manhire, 2021) speaks to the popularity of the pandemic response, and further showcases, after Rosner (this volume), how crises can spark creative or lateral responses. For many, including the government, inaction would have been considered an impossibility. This is in contrast to the more famous theorising of exception by Schmitt and Agamben. Agamben's (2005: 2) claim that a permanent state of emergency has become paradigmatic of modern government is a key point of departure or contrast for the study of emergencies or states of exception. This characterisation of emergencies has long coloured theoretical interpretations of exception as moments of an intense strengthening of state power. Yet, as Heffernan and Puszka (both this volume) show, emergencies can spark new socio-political relations between citizens and government in times of collective crisis.

For both Schmitt and Agamben emergencies were primarily theorised as involving political actors, be it internal uprisings or the threat of invasion or terror. Schmitt's theorising did not give much consideration to a pandemic or natural emergencies. While Agamben's theorising of emergency is more applicable to the pandemic, where he directly extended his analysis of exception to the current pandemic, the analysis has been largely uninspiring. In February 2020, he insisted that the Italian government's response to the pandemic was 'frantic, irrational, and [includes] absolutely unwarranted emergency measures'. For Agamben, responses that politicise biological life constitute an unjustifiable decision. Despite this, it was the potential of the state not to extend an equal level of care or proper enforcement of its own emergency that resulted in iwi adopting the measures they did. The differential outcomes in health between Māori and Pākehā were part of the repurposing of the logic of exception. This repurposing of the health response is not surprising given so many emergency responses are tied to the re-establishment of a pre-existing normal rather than being premised on structural alterations that would reduce the exposure of certain groups to undue risk (Calhoun, 2013: 47).

This repurposing also requires the tethering of a third term: territory. Sovereignty and territory are of course foundational to both the Westphalian and Weberian conceptualisations of the state (Weber, 1946). In both of these the state apparatus and its authorities figure control to be spatialised across a territory which corresponds with a sense of national belonging and is tied to a vertical chain of command (Ferguson and Gupta, 2002), with control over movement and entry into particular territories being one of the primary expressions of sovereignty. Unsurprisingly, then, the suspension of the norm in a state of emergency often involves the closure of borders, and restrictions of movement spatially and temporally through use of curfews. Pandolfi's (2003) conception of mobile sovereignties shows how movement is inherent to the construction of sovereignty. In her account, the ability of NGO and aid workers to freely cross borders between the former Yugoslavian nation-states demonstrated an inherent distinction between the international workers and the communities they were helping. This being the case, the enactment of checkpoints was not an act of absolute sovereignty. Instead, they were justified as a partnership between iwi and the Crown (Ngata, 2020). These checkpoints were also an extension of the state's policy and its decision to enact an exception in conjunction with the wishes of those manning the checkpoints. Neither actor in this situation exercises absolute sovereignty (iwi or Crown), although, with the later closure of checkpoints, the Crown seized a political opportunity to reassert its authority. Within the functioning of the state apparatus, the act of restricting the movement of people from one place to another, then, is at least partially an act of sovereignty involving both control and the territorialisation of land.

For Māori, however, restriction over access to different areas was interpreted differently and was not new to Māori culture or law (Tikanga). The temporary restriction of access to land is a well-established practice in Māori culture, called *rāhui* (McCormack, 2011; Wheen and Ruru, 2011). Throughout the pandemic there were various attempts to brand lockdowns as a form of *rāhui*. Further, Fitzmaurice and Bargh (2021, 56) found in their interviews with those manning the checkpoints that iwi groups were willing to work closely with police but ultimately saw their authority as deriving from Tikanga. While iwi checkpoints discouraged those who moved between territories rather than coercing them, they did so effectively. They sought to block off access to areas with which they had *mana whenua* (connection and right to manage an area of land) in order to protect a community they claimed to represent. This sort of claim cannot be disentangled from Indigenous sovereignty, regardless of how this concept is constructed. Not only was there a 'discursive pre-catastrophization' (Ophir, 2013) that rallied members of an iwi into response, thus defining an emergency, but the checkpoints were also justified with recourse to an alternative, local and cultural sense of identity away from the state's blanket claim across its understanding of an unbroken territory. This points to a wider ambiguity regarding notions of inclusion, exclusion, and of course, sovereignty in Aotearoa New Zealand.

The ambiguity of belonging and sovereignty

If ambiguity, as suggested earlier, is understood as a situation involving plasticity and lack of clarity, then iwi-led checkpoints point to an ambiguity in the framing and enactment of sovereignty and exception in Aotearoa New Zealand. The early pandemic response in Aotearoa New Zealand has often been marked out for the personable communication style of Prime Minister Ardern and reference to 'the team of five million' to describe the nation. The purpose no doubt was to frame the response to COVID-19 as a collective endeavour that the entire nation would participate in. By doing this, Ardern engendered a singular national public represented by a caring and effective state. However, the injunction to be kind and to interpolate oneself as part of a team of five million was not received in the same way across different populations. Likewise, the reaction from public conservative figures to the checkpoints, as unlawful and inconsistent with the state's power, is useful in telling us how strongly the concepts of sovereignty, exception and territory remain co-constitutive. Despite the comparatively measured response by iwi members on the ground, the response to the checkpoints by conservative commentators and politicians was overwhelmingly negative. Simon Bridges, then leader of the National Party, called the checkpoints illegal, stating: 'There's no scenario – this is law school 101 – in which a Kiwi is acting anything but unlawfully by stopping another Kiwi on a road in New Zealand' (Bridges quoted in Burrows, 2020).[2] Conservative groups such as Hobson's Pledge, led by former Governor of the Reserve Bank and sometime leader of both the National and ACT Parties, Don Brash, called the checkpoints 'vigilante roadblocks' (Hobson's Pledge, 2020).

The iwi checkpoints involved a plasticity over who was able to decide and enforce the exception. While traditional conceptualisations of the state hold that its territory is unbroken and populated by its citizens, these checkpoints showed the disjuncture between these narratives and the on-the-ground reality. A similar point is made by Steindl-Kopf (this volume) in Serbia, where activists' narratives are used to not only separate the actions of one group from another (e.g. elites and the public) under the banner of territorial identity, but demonstrate how disunity can be used as an impetus for change. Crisis, then, allows for the exposure of the plasticity of the sovereign nation-state and opens new opportunities for alternative conceptions of sovereignty to assert themselves. Cohen (1969: 5) noted that political groups are required to mobilise their resource towards solutions to organisational problems especially during crises. Further, Cohen (1969: 5) writes that 'formal political groups organize these functions legally and bureaucratically. Informal political groups organize these functions through the idiom of custom'; here these are elaborated as a responsibility and duty to care within Māori culture. The COVID-19 crisis did not create this ambiguity nor did the checkpoints, which may in time turn out to be a minor part of iwi–state relations. However, they remind us of the underlying ambiguities and inequalities that permeate both the emergency imaginary and the 'normal'.

Returning to Agamben's conception of the emergency, it is the shift from the rights of the citizen to the rights of man due to the politicisation of bare life (*zoe*) and the blurring of the distinction with social life (*bios*) which has come to be possible due to the state's representatives placing biological life at the centre of its concerns (1998: 11–12). This is what makes the pandemic response measures so problematic in his theorising. The biopolitical models that require states to effectively govern a population have engendered a situation that requires a permanent suspension of rights, and the pandemic supposedly provides a useful justification for the current suspension of norms (Agamben, 2020). The idea that the public health emergency was either exaggerated or unnecessary seems deeply unsatisfactory. Contra Agamben, whose theory assumes a strong conceptualisation of the state and sovereignty (Gupta, 2012: 17), and alongside Adi Ophir (2013: 71), we can see that the monopoly on exception no longer resides exclusively with the sovereign, modern nation-state, as new entities (especially NGOs and IGOs) and subnational actors such as iwi are increasingly able to frame crises as emergencies. Cohen's (1979) work remains valuable here as it points us towards an anthropological understanding of how the symbolic designation of something such as a crisis remains a thoroughly political and ambiguous process that pluralistic societies must negotiate.

Indeed, Cohen (1974) stressed both power and symbolism in political life, both of which are shown in the checkpoints. The presence of the roadblocks as symbols of bottom-up mobilisation and limited self-determination shows how symbolism and power act upon one another. In their conservative reading of the situation there is no ambiguity or contradiction to be found in the iwi-led response or in Māori–Crown relations. Don Brash, for example, quoted the use of te reo Māori by Governor Hobson when he concluded the signing of the Treaty – 'He iwi tahi tatou' (we are one people); those who present this line of reasoning claim the Treaty dissolved different notions of political belonging in the creation of a new identity: that of the 'New Zealander'. In a sense these groups understood the emergency in a completely 'Schmittian' sense. To repurpose or control an exception imposed upon you would suggest a form of sovereignty that was intolerable to the conservative position of one state, one nation and one political identity. Cohen (1974: 87) has made the point that in complex pluralistic societies there is often a contest between groups for political power but that these groups also crosscut and support one another. This leads to the question of how a functioning system can emerge that balances these interests and their intersections. As noted above, historically, this circle was supposedly squared by reference to the Treaty, as if a quick phrase from Hobson could dissolve centuries of political culture that predates colonisation.

The inability to accept an understanding of sovereignty as something that is negotiated, periodically reassessed, and is at times ambiguous points to another unfortunate parallel with Schmitt. This time with his *The Crisis of Parliamentary Democracy* (Schmitt, 1985), in which he argues that democracy is only sustainable among homogeneous populations. I am not suggesting the figures I have mentioned endorse Schmitt's wider political project but rather that their politics does not tolerate the existence of a core ambiguity in contemporary politics in Aotearoa New Zealand – that of competing identities and partial sovereignties. In the conservative reading of exception there is no room for alternative identities which can be used to compete with the national identity, even if there is good evidence to show markedly different experiences among groups within the nation. The enactment of checkpoints shows the ambiguity and tension in the relationship between sovereignty, territory and exception in Aotearoa New Zealand. Ambiguity here can be thought of as the dialectical movement between two forms of sovereignty engaging in an unequal negotiation that confuses existing and taken-for-granted categories.[3] This unequal negotiation involving the overlapping of identities and competing conceptual claims that occur between two cultural-political systems existing within a single nation-state shows how the contours of the relationship between state and iwi were able to be shifted using the creative reinvention and deployment of biopolitical narratives.

Conclusion

For those wishing to seek an anthropological understanding of exception, the pandemic situation in Aotearoa New Zealand points to the ambiguous and negotiated realities that occur in the production and reproduction of sovereignty and the enactment of states of exception. The history of Māori experiences with diseases that they were immunologically naïve to as a population should not be dismissed. Agamben's (1998) arguments regarding the state of exception becoming the dominant form of government for modern states have certainly been an influential and useful analytic for understanding how sovereignty is enacted via the suspension of political and constitutional norms and engendering classes or groups of people who are both inside and outside the law. Reading the establishment of these checkpoints suggests that to understand emergencies and the relationship between populations and the state requires us to complicate existing narratives of exception and emergencies. Amongst other actions from the New Zealand public the roadblocks showed the limitations to Schmitt and Agamben's theorising regarding exception. Too much emphasis has been placed on the top-down imposition of these measures, and not enough attention has been directed to understanding how these measures may be co-opted, reworked or supported by populations. However, this does not mean that sovereignty and exception should be detached from one another; instead there is ample room for theorising how less absolute conceptions of sovereignty are imagined and enacted during emergencies.

As a contribution to this, I have proposed a way of understanding the checkpoints led by iwi groups during the nationwide lockdown as a limited and temporary assertion of sovereignty over a group's own biopolitical construction. By drawing on critical political theory and political anthropology I have shown how sovereignty is not simply a will imposed from above or something that can be codified into law. Instead, it requires making and remaking on the ground and different groups find ways of co-opting processes designed to interpolate them into a broader expression of sovereignty shot through with ambiguity.

Notes

1 The use of Schmitt's theoretical work is in no way an endorsement of his political positions. Rather, like Chantelle Mouffe (1999), I consider Schmitt to be an adversary who demands a response, and an important figure in the theoretical lineage discussed in this chapter.

2 It is worth noting that during this period both leader and deputy leader of the opposition, Simon Bridges and Paula Bennet respectively, were of Māori descent, and while the state's discourses imagine and construct coherent groups this is of course not absolute.

3 For reading of the checkpoints as an enactment of rangatiratanga and having a distinct cultural and political logic, see Fitzmaurice and Bargh (2021).

References

Agamben, G. (1998) *Homo Sacer: Sovereign Power and Bare Life*, trans. D. Heller-Roazen (Stanford, CA: Stanford University Press).

Agamben, G. (2005) *State of Exception*, trans. K. Attell (Chicago, IL: University of Chicago Press).

Agamben, G. (2020) The state of exception provoked by an unmotivated emergency, http://positionspolitics.org/giorgio-agamben-the-state-of-exception-provoked-by-an-unmotivated-emergency/ (accessed 5 October 2021).

Barber, S. and Naepi, S. (2020) 'Sociology in a crisis: Covid-19 and the colonial politics of knowledge production in Aotearoa New Zealand', *Journal of Sociology*, 56:4, 693–703.

Bear, L. and Mathur, N. (2015) 'Introduction: Remaking the public good', *Cambridge Journal of Anthropology*, 33:1, 18–34.

Burrows, M. (2020) 'That's a disgrace': MPs, Police Commissioner in fiery clash over COVID-19 community roadblocks. 30 April. https://www.newshub.co.nz/home/new-zealand/2020/04/that-s-a-disgrace-mps-police-commissioner-in-fiery-clash-over-covid-19-community-roadblocks.html (accessed 1 March 2022).

Calhoun, C. (2004) 'A world of emergencies: Fear, intervention, and the limits of cosmopolitan order', *Canadian Review of Sociology/Revue Canadienne de Sociologie*, 41:4, 373–95.

Calhoun, C. (2013) 'The Idea of Emergency: Humanitarian Action and Global (Dis)order', in Didier Fassin and Mariella Pandolfi (eds), *Contemporary States of Emergency: The Politics of Military and Humanitarian Interventions* (New York: Zone Books), 29–58.

Clifford, J. (2020) Strange Work in Familiar places: Inside Aotearoa/New Zealand's Border Hotels. 17 August 2020. https://thefamiliarstrange.com/2020/08/17/inside-border-hotels/ (accessed 1 March 2021).

Cohen, A. (1969) *Custom and Politics in Urban Africa: A Study of Hausa Migrants in Yoruba Towns* (Berkeley, CA: University of California Press).

Cohen, A. (1974) *Two-Dimensional Man: An Essay on the Anthropology of Power and Symbolism in Complex Society* (Berkeley, CA: University of California Press).

Cohen, A. (1979) 'Political Symbolism', *Annual Review of Anthropology*, 8, 87–113.

Das, V. and Pool, D. (2004) 'State and its Margins: Comparative Ethnography', in Veena Das and Deborah Poole (eds), *Anthropology in the Margins of the State* (Oxford: Oxford University Press), 3–34.

Easton, D. (1959) 'Political Anthropology', *Biennial Review of Anthropology*, 1, 210–62.

Ferguson, J. and Gupta, A. (2002) 'Spatializing states: Toward an ethnography of neoliberal governmentality', *American Ethnologist*, 29:4, 981–1002.

Fitzmaurice, M. and Bargh, M. (2021) *Stepping Up: COVID-19 Checkpoints and Rangatiratanga* (Wellington: Huia Publishers).

Foucault, M. (2008) *The Birth of Biopolitics: Lectures at the Collège de France, 1978–1979*, ed. M. Davidson and M. Senellart, trans. G. Burchell (New York: Palgrave Macmillan).

Foucault, M. (2009) *Security, Territory, Population: Lectures at the Collège de France, 1977–78*, ed. Michel Senellart, François Ewald and Alessandro Fontana, trans. Graham Burchell (New York: Palgrave Macmillan).

Gupta, A. (2012) *Red Tape: Bureaucracy, Structural Violence, and Poverty in India* (Durham, NC: Duke University Press).

Hobsons Pledge (2020) 4900 Oppose Vigilante Iwi Checkpoints, https://www.hobsonspledge.nz/update_128_roadblock_petitionA (accessed 1 March 2022).

Human Rights Commission (2020) Human Rights and Te Tiriti o Waitangi: COVID-19 and Alert Level 4 in Aotearoa New Zealand.

Hurihanganui, Te Aniwa (2020) MPs' questioning of legal iwi checkpoints 'really is racism.' *Radio New Zealand*. 1 May, https://www.rnz.co.nz/news/te-manu-korihi/415617/mps-questioning-of-legal-iwi-checkpoints-really-is-racism (accessed 1 March 2022).

Jefferies, S., French, N., Gilkison, C. et al. (2020) 'COVID-19 in New Zealand and the Impact of the National response: A Descriptive Epidemiological Study', *The Lancet Public Health*, 5:11, e612–e623.

Manhire, T. (2021). Almost 90% of New Zealanders back Ardern government on Covid-19 – poll. The Spinoff. 8 April, https://thespinoff.co.nz/politics/08-04-2020/almost-90-of-new-zealanders-back-ardern-government-on-covid-19-poll (accessed 1 March 2021).

Matthewman, S. and Huppatz, K. (2020) 'A sociology of Covid-19', *Journal of Sociology*, 56:4, 675–83.

McCormack, F. (2011) 'Rāhui: A Blunting of Teeth', *Journal of the Polynesian Society*, 120, 43–55.

Ministry for Culture and Heritage (updated 20 December 2012). 'Differences between the texts', https://nzhistory.govt.nz/politics/treaty/read-the-Treaty/differences-between-the-texts (accessed 1 March 2022).

Ministry of Health (2019). Annual Data Explorer 2017/18: New Zealand Health Survey[Data File], https://minhealthnz.shinyapps.io/nz-health-survey-2017–18-annual-data-explore (accessed 1 March 2022).

Morens, D. (2015) 'Measles in Fiji, 1875: Thoughts on the history of emerging infectious diseases', *Pacific Health Dialog*, 5:1, 119–29.

Mouffe, C. (1999) 'Introduction: Schmitt's Challenge', in Chantelle Mouffe (ed.), The Challenge of Carl Schmitt (London: Verso).

Mutu, M. (2010) 'Constitutional intentions: The treaty texts', in Malcolm Mulholland and Veronica Makere Hupane Tawhai (eds), *Weeping Waters: The Treaty of Waitangi and Constitutional Change* (Wellington: Huia Publishers).

Ngata, T. (2020) COVID-19 and the Māori duty to protect, https://overland.org.au/2020/05/covid-19-and-the-maori-duty-to-protect/ (accessed 1 March 2022).

Ngāpuhi (2020) Te Tai Tokerau Community Borders, https://ngapuhi.iwi.nz/wp-content/uploads/2020/03/ZA20-COVID-flyer.pdf (accessed 1 March 2022).

Norman, D., Miller, J., Timothy, M., Friday, G. et al. (2021) 'From Sorcery to Laboratory: Pandemics and Yanyuwa Experiences of Viral Vulnerability', Oceania, 91:1, 64–85.

Ophir, A. (2013) 'The Politics of Catastrophization: Emergency and Exception', in Didier Fassin and Mariella Pandolfi (eds), *Contemporary States of Emergency: The Politics of Military and Humanitarian Interventions* (New York: Zone Books), 59–88.

Pandolfi, M. (2003) 'Contract of mutual (in)difference: Governance and the humanitarian apparatus in contemporary Albania and Kosovo', *Global Legal Studies*, 10:1, 369–81.

Reid, P., Cormack, D. and Paine, S.J. (2019) 'Colonial histories, racism and health – The experience of Māori and Indigenous peoples', *Public Health*, 172, 119–24.

Rice, G.W. (2019) 'Remembering 1918: Why did Māori suffer more than seven times the death rate of non-Māori New Zealanders in the 1918 Influenza Pandemic?' *New Zealand Journal of History*, 53:1, 90–108.

Rose, N. and Novas, C. (2005) 'Biological citizenship', in Aihwa Ong and Steven J. Collier (eds), *Global Assemblages: Technology, Politics, and Ethics as Anthropological Problems* (London: Blackwell), 439–63.

Schmitt, C. (1985a) *The Crisis of Parliamentary Democracy,* trans. E. Kennedy (Cambridge, MA: MIT Press).

Schmitt, C. (1985b) *Political Theology: Four Chapters on the Concept of Sovereignty,* trans. G. Schwab (Cambridge, MA: MIT Press).

Scholtz, C. (2010) 'Land claim negotiations and indigenous claimant legibility in Canada and New Zealand', *Political Science,* 62:1, 37–61.

Scott, J.C. (1998) *Seeing Like a State: How Certain Schemes to Improve the Human Condition Have Failed* (New Haven, CT: Yale University Press).

Snowden, F.M. (2019) *Epidemics and Society: From the Black Death to the Present* (New Haven, CT: Yale University Press).

Steyn, N., Binny, R.N., Hannah, K. et al. (2020) 'Estimated inequities in COVID-19 infection fatality rates by ethnicity for Aotearoa New Zealand', *New Zealand Medical Journal,* 133:1521, 28–39.

Thelen, T. and Alber, E. (2018) 'Reconnecting state and kinship: Temporalities, scales, classifications', in Tatjana Thelen and Erdmute Alber (eds), *Reconnecting State and Kinship* (Philadelphia: University of Pennsylvania Press), 1–35.

Trnka, S. (2020) 'From lockdown to rāhui and teddy bears in windows: Initial responses to Covid-19 in Aotearoa New Zealand', *Anthropology Today,* 36:5 (2020), 11–13.

Walter, P. (2018) 'Tackling inequalities to improve wellbeing in New Zealand', *The Lancet,* 392:10144, 254.

Weber, M. (1946) 'Politics as Vocation', in H.H. Gerth and C. Wright Mills (eds and trans.), *Max Weber: Essays in Sociology* (New York: Oxford University Press), 77–128.

Wheen, N. and Ruru, J. (2011) 'Providing for rāhui in the law of Aotearoa New Zealand', *Journal of the Polynesian Society,* 120:2, 169–82.

10

Grease Yakā in Sri Lankan political culture: humour, anxiety and existential ambiguities in the public sphere

Anton Piyarathne

Introduction

A society's public and political arenas, while often taken to be universal in character, are in effect shaped by very local factors. In turn, the public sphere becomes a site of political contention in everyday life where citizens freely discuss the nature and functioning of key power structures, including the credibility of government (Habermas, 1989). Responding to political crises linked to a perceived lack of government credibility since independence in 1948, the multi-ethnoreligious people of Sri Lanka have negotiated political distrust in the context of the public sphere. The underdevelopment of Sri Lankan democracy is an outcome of not having socially acceptable elite circulation, as elites adapt techniques to remain in power amid political scandal, often through invoking mythology to remain in control of state–society tensions (Kapferer, 1977; Obeyesekere, 1981). This enables elites to establish multiple interpretations of well-publicised scandals and, more generally, capitalise on political uncertainties. In response, satire, humour and cartoons have come to be used by the public to carve out a liveable space amidst state-led media suppression to criticise elite political culture in general and the ruling government in particular. In this context, whereby political scandal becomes a kind of panic mired in both mysticism and satire, public commentary is used to launch a critique that would not otherwise be tolerated. What is perceived negatively – political impropriety – is countered in positive terms, not with unrest but via thinly veiled humour that allows people to reshape and challenge the elite's narratives.

This chapter is based on two years of fieldwork and analysis of cartoons which appeared in leading national newspapers in 2010 and 2011 about public reports of night-time prowlers clad only in underwear, called 'Grease Yakā', who were said to be terrorising local communities in attempts to distract from allegations of political corruption. My grasping of the concept of ambiguity via the ethnographic information gathered during fieldwork (conducted in four locations) facilitated the analysis of the cartoons. Indeed, a sense of social unease and political ambiguity are shown to be stoked by elites during moments of tension and public panic. Yet ambiguity is also embraced in cartoons and the public sphere to critique elites' behaviour. To this end, the chapter demonstrates how the public sphere is not a space where the people are passive but rather active, as a place wherein subjectivity, connectivity and, crucially, independence from top-down structures can flourish. Against this backdrop of state–society tensions, the chapter discusses the public's response to political ambiguity stemming from the Grease Yakā scandal. This chapter takes an existential anthropological approach to understanding how political ambiguity is negotiated and how the public sought to promote agency in a reduced public sphere.

Ambiguity is defined in the chapter as a situation where different interpretations were provided in order to confuse people's clarity concerning a given phenomenon, creating a large number of anxieties and fear that political elites can sustain. Alternatively, it can also be read as a strategy of the political elite to confuse people about the actions of the government and ruling political elites while taking cover from the constitution and apparatuses of the state. Ambiguity is thus a powerful force in politics as dissidents may be subjected to surveillance by law enforcement authorities, potentially facing legal action under special laws such as the notorious Prevention of Terrorism Act (PTA) or any other legislation representing the interests of the ruling elites. This is not static in nature but open to social processes of negotiation, especially in the public sphere. Existential anthropology studies the experience and essence of being, and will thus enable me to discuss how people negotiate difficulties, especially in which there are no rational or traditional answers. I assert, following Jackson and Piette (2015), that while an individual's behaviour, reasoning and emotions are often located historically, socially and environmentally, every individual's survival is described by schemes, purposes, aspirations and results that outdo and, in some ways, alter these earlier situations. In the public sphere, counter discourses are mounted against political elites. This is linked to what Nancy Fraser (1990) identifies as a subaltern counterpublic, with Rajbharat Patta (2018) further expanding this argument to show how it is that people challenge and seek to influence the public sphere with reference to political satire and cartoons.

All major political parties in Sri Lanka, it should be noted, have been implicated in political disquiet – including postcolonial liberators and successive governments – with fear, threats, terror and intimidation associated with the increasing normalisation of militarisation by government.

Through a focus on the Grease Yakā phenomenon, the chapter shows how events can be mobilised and separately narrated by the state and citizens, leading to a range of tactics being used to variously maintain a sense of ambiguity or else launch critiques that would not normally be palatable. To begin my analysis of the Grease Yakā controversy, this phenomenon and its public response must be clarified in the context of Sri Lanka's history of colonialism and supplanted Western democracy combined with local traditions, beliefs and political hegemony.

Colonial democracy, majoritarian politics and political culture

Sri Lanka has a long colonial history, and a brief overview of how democracy was established in the country as a local–global hybrid, and the creation of a political culture around this, establishes the background for understanding the Grease Yakā scandal. So too, this history establishes political elites' strategies for stoking and using ambiguity to defeat opponents and gain and maintain power via maintaining optimal levels of uncertainty, rather than working to strengthen democracy. Sri Lankans have undergone various sociocultural, political and economic changes over 450 years through Portuguese, Dutch and, finally, British colonial administration. Though the Westminster parliamentary system was gradually introduced, in which majoritarian voting is important as a ruling mechanism, the colonists were incapable of establishing the principles required for a healthy administrative system of governance (Uyangoda, 2021).

Within a decade of independence in 1984, ethnocentric politicking began in earnest. The Buddhist-Sinhalas began dominating state institutions backed by powerful sections of society, such as Buddhist monks, security forces, civil servants and entrepreneurs. Post-independence, two elite groups emerged: those who had connections or hailed from the families close to colonialists and a new learned class who had undergone free education. Thus, post-independence Sri Lanka was ruled by a few elite families who considered politics as a 'way of life', but yet whose actions were critiqued by groups of educated youth protesting against them, ranging from violent uprisings to everyday protests called 'harthal'. In 1971 and again in 1988–89, two youth insurrections were led by (mainly) Sinhalas in the south, namely the Janatha Vimukthi Peramuna (the JVP or People's Liberation Front), and between the 1980s and 2009, the northern Tamil youth led by the Liberation Tigers of Tamil Eelam (LTTE). Ultimately, protests were suppressed, and corrupt politics continued, characterised by patron–client relationships concerning the distribution of state resources, the division of people along ethnoreligious lines, and the creation of segregationist sentiment for means of control, supported by academics, priests, artists and government officials. Political elites, then, appeared to construct ambiguous political conditions to, firstly, gain and maintain majority votes, to then run the government and divert the attention of the people, and finally, to ensure that the ruling class would always be in power.

In the process of maintaining control, elites used occult sciences and mythologies (Jayasinghe, 2015, 2021; Ratnaweera, 2021). The most recent and popular example was prevalent during the term of President Mahinda Rajapaksa at the time of the greased devil phenomenon. Rajapaksa called a snap election two years before the end of his term on the advice of his astrologer, Mr Sumanadasa Abeygunawardena (Jeyaraj, 2015). It is the general practice of Sri Lankans to refer to astrologers when embarking on significant events in their lives. President Mahinda Rajapaksa is known to be a firm believer in astrological interpretations and depended on these when required to decide upon dates for elections (Buerk, 2008). Several efforts were undertaken to publicly highlight Mahinda Rajapaksa as the 'reincarnation' of the great King Dutugemunu who was considered an extraordinary Sinhalese hero and leader who was brave and righteous and succeeded in defeating the Indian king, Elara, whilst liberating and uniting the country (Gunasekara, 2014). The history of colonial democracy in Sri Lanka highlighted the elites' strategies of fostering political ambiguity to perplex political optics and mobilise the majority towards the elites' own advantage. In this instance, political ambiguity was constructed by combining myths and the occult in a manner the public could not disentangle.

After Marshall (this volume), this is another example of the political co-option of ambiguity. In the tradition of the Manchester School, Gluckman (1963), following Durkheim and Radcliffe-Brown, suggests that society is a self-maintaining moral order, using this system of moral order to overcome membership conflicts. Kapferer (1983) explains that this moral order is connected to deep structures inherent in cosmology and social recognition given to it via discussions linked to the areas of healing rituals and exorcists' practices. This is suggested in a comparative analysis of nationalism in Sri Lanka and Australia, pinpointing the link between the 'logic of being in the world' (ontology) and collective violence (Kapferer, 1988) and sorcery practices (Kapferer, 1997). In this sense, local experience and wisdom (or knowledge) are entwined to establish a way of being in the world, yet one that is heavily inflected by the political culture of the elites and prior colonialists. Citizens also contribute to political ambiguity through speculation and rumour (Tambiah, 1996), leading to Sri Lanka being known as one of the most violent states (Kapferer, 2001).

Grease Yakā: the body and mythology in the creation of ambiguity

In 2010 people became aware of the 'Grease Yakā', who had appeared in the Kahawatte and Ratnapura area. The discussion below highlights the construction, spread and magnitude of public confusion, and the history of the ambiguity created by elites. Several elderly Sinhala women were murdered, after which the menace spread across the country, making the figure an omnipresent force. Various localities interpreted the Grease Yakā according to their ethnoreligious and political backgrounds. In this context, how do people from multi-religious and multiethnic backgrounds interpret, respond to and negotiate the fear inculcated by this phenomenon to construct a liveable social space? A large-scale social phenomenon of fear of this nature surfaced for the first time during the term of the third Sri Lankan executive president, Ranasinghe Premadasa (1989–93). Young women feared for their lives as there were rumours stating that virgins (S. *kanyāviyō*) were being abducted to bathe Premadasa in milk to protect his presidency, in accordance with the instructions given by Malayali black magic specialists. Such a phenomenon thereby created mass panic through the association with women's bodies, which are considered across ethnoreligious divides to be a source of protection, sustenance and nourishment of cultures, traditions and identities. Sri Lankans possess a long-standing fear over demons, identified as 'Yakku' (S.[1]) or 'Pēi' or 'Pisāsu' (T.[2]) or evil spirits which have become part and parcel of existing mythologies, irrespective of a person's ethnoreligious background.

Twenty years later, the Grease Yakā made a comeback, interpreted by the people as suspiciously connected with the political regime. When the authorities failed to secure the lives of the people, the people took things into their own hands when rumours spread that Grease Yakās were running into military camps or police stations. This pinpoints the scale of the confusion created by the fear and unease. This led to multiple deaths in Haputale, and Wellamboda in Kandy. Another death was reported when police fired at Muslim protesters in Pottuvil, during my fieldwork. These greased devils came at night to apparently grope women's breasts or, as the saying goes, to collect blood from the breasts of women. The narratives connected to greased devils varied slightly by location and, since they mostly came to houses where women lived alone, it resulted in creating considerable disturbances to daily life. Contrastingly to what was experienced in 1991, fear engulfed the country, coalescing with post-independence ethnopolitical tensions.

The issue of the greased devil was the main topic among the Pānama and Pottuvil villagers I met at the Ampitiye Dewalaya (shrine) dedicated for Goddess Pattini in 2011. A 45-year-old man who had been selected to work at the Sarvodaya Bank, and who was well-respected in the village, relayed to me and my research assistant the local version of Grease Yakā:[3]

> There are rumours about this incident. They say there is a sword made of gold hidden in Neela Maha Saaya in the Kotiyagala area, which is wanted by a senior politician. They have found an ola leaf (S. *puskola poth*) which gives instructions on how to obtain this massive wealth buried by ancient kings, possibly by King Dutugemunu. All these efforts were presided by making offerings to a dwarf (S. Bahirawaya) who supposedly guards it, and thereby obtain the hidden wealth. You might have seen some time back there was a greased devil in the Kahawatte area that killed old women. Why is it that these greased devils haven't been arrested? This is the mystery.

The term 'grease' means oil or liquid used for vehicles to provide necessary lubrication and enable effective functioning of various parts which are denoted as being slippery. Yakā is a term for a demon or devil. By looking at the shape of the Grease Yakā, it appeared that it was neither a demon nor an avatar appearing or possessing a human body; however, people responded to these figures assuming they were devils.[4] Nevertheless, this concept operates within the context of fear placed upon 'devils' and 'spirits' (especially evil ones). Senior police officials, such as Prashantha Jayakody, then police spokesperson, identified Grease Yakās as people with 'mental disorders' and, in certain instances, some such persons arrested on suspicion were found to be wearing more than twenty pairs of women's undergarments (Aneez and Sirilal, 2011). Such individuals were pathologised and their behaviour was seen in local terms as 'abnormal' or 'disordered'. The post-1970s escalation of this situation, due to the changes in the postcolonial period, should be analysed in relation to Gluckman's 'total context of the plural society' (Lindgren, 2008: 286). The second lot of devils mentioned above were the widespread 'unusual' within the existing normal 'abnormality'. The emergence of the later form of grease devils caused widespread panic, resulting in fatalities and clashes between protesters and authorities. It led to suspicions towards strangers, avoidance of unfamiliar areas, and limited night-time activities outside the home. This pinpoints the power of constructed ambiguities by political elites in creating confusion among the ordinary citizens towards the state, government, law and order, own existence, etc.

In this context, how are anthropologists to make sense of ambiguity as it is unfolding in the field, and when they come to collect sense-making elements via ethnography? One night in August 2011, I was walking through the paddy fields to arrive in the Pattini Kovil and participate in the Ankeliya ritual with my research assistant, when suddenly a few men with clubs appeared. There was a full moon and clear night sky, meaning we were visible to our acquaintances. They approached us slowly and I was very nervous and afraid for the safety of our lives given the numerous killings that were reported across the country in connection with this phenomenon. Fortunately, when they drew close they recognised us; Aravinda called to them 'Hi, elder brother,' confirming our loyalty and non-threatening behaviour. They too cracked some casual jokes. 'These people are known as grease devils, aren't they?' The long discussion we had with them revealed that they had been ambushing the Grease Yakā and warned us to be cautious when walking along the village off-roads at night. This created significant concern in my mind, as I attempted to be very careful when collecting ethnographic data. I collected several narratives on the Grease Yakā, witnessing people's suspicion towards us and their reluctance to meet or be contacted, urging us to refrain from visiting their homes temporarily.

Against this backdrop, sarcastic references to the Grease Yakā from both sides were common to confirm the non-threatening nature of our research and to be transparent regarding our identity. People alleged that the government used state military or intelligence services to create panic among the public. Certain close associates referred to us as 'Ah, see the Grease Yakās are coming ... be careful, they may come in the night to harass us ... Hey, you guys, come during the daytime to see the arrangements here so that you can come back in the night, won't you?' This was owing to the need to create healthy interactions with interlocutors. People tend to believe 'once this grease is off, it could be anyone, ah?' The above remarks were concealed warnings of danger, threats posed to our lives as well as theirs. This displayed the social complexity of the Grease Yakā as well as the open possibility in this context of anyone and everyone 'appearing' as Grease Yakā, threatening everyday lives. Moreover, this pinpoints the complexity and risk to anthropologists in such a setting, since they engaged with people during the heightened times, evoking suspicion. Consequently, I postponed data collection during the peak of the phenomenon.

Everyday strategies of negotiating political ambiguity

'Grease Yakā is truly a Sri Lankan concept ... he represents our identity ... but not secondary to Batman[5] or Superman,'[6] people stated mockingly during fieldwork. There they referred to chauvinistic and patriotic sentiments through which the then government had come into power. As the panic increased, people began to suspect everyone: fathers, teachers, postmen, breadmen commencing from demons to living clergy, which made public life very difficult, though new tactics for launching political critique came to surface in the form of satirical cartoons.

The cartoons published on the Grease Yakā attacks appeared in widely circulated national newspapers. Among them are *Divaina* and *Lankadeepa* published in Sinhala, *Virakesari*, a popular Tamil newspaper, and the *Daily Mirror*, an English-language newspaper. The cartoons embraced the widespread fear held by the general public, and were used to mock the situation and politicians. The Samayan cartoon which appeared in *Divaina* on 15 August 2011 was comprised of two pictures, a man in full black holding hands with a woman wearing a skirt and a blouse. The moon and the clear dark sky are the background. It suggests an occasion where romantic lovers meet secretly at night. The man says, 'Honey, I am very scared – how long can we meet like this in the night?' The girl asks the man, 'Why is that, my loving grease demon?' 'Who knows whether they will increase the price of grease in a bid to eradicate us?' the man replies. Sarcasm was used here to suggest that the Grease Yakā situation was an opportunity for certain individuals to enjoy their lives at night, as others hid, or that it was a gifted opportunity.

A cartoon which appeared in the *Divaina* on 26 August 2011 suggests the opportunism behind the phenomenon. This referred to a critical view of the malpractices which generally occur in prisons (and other similar incidences) with special reference to extramarital affairs which are considered a social stigma in the country. A cartoon appeared in the *Virakesari* Tamil newspaper on 11 August 2011, titled '*appidippodu*', which depicted a husband coming home very late after the office and his wife attacking him due to mistakenly identifying him as the grease devil. This was a significant example which emphasised the serious mistakes which occurred across the country due to hasty decisions being taken by people panicking.

While grease is often thought to be opaque, sticky and aligned with dirt and muck, the commentary in the cartoons shows how it is embraced to provide clarity on the situation through the lubricating quality of humour in the public domain. Indeed, the above-mentioned cartoon highlights how everyday strategies of people are adapted, to deal with the ambiguity constructed by politicians. The analysis of the cartoons and my ethnographic data suggests that the Grease Yakā attack was very powerful in rural settings as opposed to urban areas. Gluckman highlighted the value of studying phenomena not as isolated events but as interconnected. In general, the fear of devils, evil spirits and ghosts was connected with darkness whilst most of the villages and estates did not have the facility of electricity supply and it was not economically viable to power the streetlights or light the gardens and houses of the families. More prominently, it did not happen in Crow Island, my urban middle-class research site, where the majority were well-educated and employed in high positions in government and private sector organisations, and were recognised as a 'highly rationalised' and 'organised' community, having access to all the powerful organisations and individuals in society, demonstrating that the socioeconomic backgrounds of individuals and families played a role in the uptake of this panic.

The cartoon named '*kumbidurerunga*' which appeared on 11 August 2012 in *Virakesari* highlights this concern. The cartoon portrays two characters – an old man and a woman. One says, 'a mysterious man (T. Marma manithan) 'because of the grease man issue a tense situation had arisen in the estates' and the other person responds to this with 'stating something and doing another thing which is contradictory'. This suggests that the creators of the issue have something up their sleeve. This is a very popular idiom among Tamils and the Sinhalas. This cartoon openly raises concerns expressed by the public on the reasons why the Grease Yakā is appearing in the estate, the resulting actions that the politicians intend to take and how this recourse may have an impact (mostly negative) on the estate's Tamil community in general. This appears as a casual conversation between two persons (male and female). It is likely that this could be connected to transfers of estate management, salary issues, and concerns over work norms which are likely to create mainly negative influences on the everyday lives of the workers and their families. In the meantime, people in the estate sector were suspicious of the increasing political rivalries prevalent among emerging and established politicians.

However, as shared by a villager, 'all our politicians' are a special group of animals and treat people as a 'meadow to munch away in a way benefiting the politicians'. This was a statement made when I was collecting ethnographic data on politically led election violence, regarding the incident in 2009 when the killing of ten supporters of the Sri Lanka Muslim Congress (SLMC) in Udathalawinna, Kandy took place (Höglund and Piyarathne, 2009).

'Grease Yakā must be some low-class shanty bugger ...' was a sentence uttered by one of the middle-class interlocutors in Colombo, emphasising the class dimension. However, when I visited Crow Island people sarcastically mentioned, 'look, even last night Grease Yakā has come'. My experiences in the field suggested that this sentiment was mostly reported in the areas where the communities were significantly deprived, economically and socially. Similarly, in the middle-class setting of Colombo, it happened mostly in the camp setting patronised by the Muslim refugees, who had been displaced due to the three-decades-long internal war. The second location comprised an urban 'dis-organised' community of low income. The middle-class people looked at these stories more sarcastically rather than trying to understand the situation empathetically. The existing political culture favoured one or other class at the expense of the masses. The middle class – the bilingual and Sri Lankan urban community – were able to negotiate the 'fear' and engage in a critical discussion on the power abuses of political elites.

Meanwhile, people on the ground who were in charge of the investigation suspected there were 'powerful people behind this mayhem'. This suspicion could have influenced the depiction of politicians in cartoons, as reflected in the narratives collected during the fieldwork. It has always been similar around the world that humour has a very intimate relationship with politics (Petrovic, 2018: 202). People in the localities in Pottuvil or elsewhere found that, when they chased the Grease Yakā, it ran into either a military camp or a police station, after which people could not find any trace. Despite the cartoonists refraining from highlighting the characters depicted in the cartoon as politicians, they drew the characters with burly figures and bald heads and wearing national dress. The 'kumbidurerunga' cartoon which appeared in *Virakesari* on 8 August 2011 includes two old men engaged in a conversation. One says, '*Grease man intrudes*' while the other responds, '*friends of irresponsible politicians*'. The grease man intrudes into private spaces and the phenomenon was considered similar to the politicians and, therefore, the grease man was labelled as the friend of the politicians, the designers of the ambiguity.

While the cartoon which appeared in *Virakesari* played a key role in leading to this assumption, all the cartoons which appeared in other papers also mainly concentrating on the critical role played by politicians. Additionally, during the Mahinda Rajapaksa government, several taxes were imposed on various goods. The taxation is considered as a way of funding required resources to run the governments led by a certain class of political elites. A big demon identified as 'TAX' was found to be chasing the ordinary person who was running behind the Grease Yakā. The political cartoon drawn by Awantha Artigala, which appeared in the *Daily Mirror* of 22 August 2011 (Figure 10.1), depicts three characters: a man with a club chasing a man with 'Grease' written on his body, and a massive buffalo-faced demon with horns titled 'Tax'.

The *kurahan satakaya* (S. maroon shawl) was draped around the neck of the demon with two horns. The maroon shawl represented millet farmers of the remote villages in Hambantota, symbolising the oppressed people, patriotism and nationalism. The two horns represent a buffalo, which is used to refer to idiotic persons among Sri Lankans. The buffalo-faced demon wearing a *kurahan satakaya* signified the Rajapaksa regime in the eyes of the viewers and was considered to be the real threat. The people were being hoodwinked by the Rajapaksa regime, by being persuaded to focus on a trivial subject such as the Grease Yakā and thereby having their attention diverted from the atrocities conducted by the regime. This seemed to be a very safe strategy to communicate a powerful message under a repressive government.

The politicians created a massive opportunity to plunder the nation's wealth (as testified by revelations from the release of the 2021 Pandora papers leaked by international journalists) by increasing Sri Lanka's ties with the Chinese government whereby Mahinda Rajapaksa opened the Sri

Figure 10.1 The Grease Yakā scandal diverting ordinary people's
attention from real issues

Lankan economy to Chinese investment, namely the Hambantota harbour
(creating an inland harbour), and the Port City Project (creating an island by
land-filling a section of the sea next to Galle Face Green). Ultimately, these
projects benefited China more than Sri Lanka, entangling Sri Lanka in a
debt burden that ultimately resulted in its bankruptcy in 2022. The cartoon
which appeared in *Virakesari* on 11 August 2011 depicted two men, one
resembling Mahinda Rajapaksa with a crimson shawl, '*Kurahan satakaya*'
(S.), draped across his neck and another labelled as China. In between these
two there was a stool with a large sum of money. In addition, there was a man
coloured in black and drawn to highlight the Grease Yakā. Consequently,
this cartoon depiction highlighted the possibility of politicians engaging in
financial abuse while the citizens were in mass paranoia regarding the greased
devil rumour. This premise should be understood and interpreted within
the suspicions and mistrust of interethnic relations, especially between the
Sinhalas and the Tamils in postwar ethnic relations. The Tamils feared that
Sri Lanka was getting closer to China with the intention of balancing the
Indian pressure on Sri Lanka with the intention of sidelining the concerns
of Tamils by offering significant benefits and encouraging prosperity in

the Sinhala areas. Meanwhile, there had been sufficient social whispering regarding the potential white-collar malpractices occurring within the economic relationships between Sri Lanka and China (cf. Pathak, 2016).

The cartoonists pursued indirectly and more powerfully highlighting the criminal nature of the then Mahinda Rajapaksa government, by giving a voice to the concerns of the people. The popular Sumathipala-Jothipalas' 'Samayan' (meaning nonsense in English) which appeared on 19 August 2011 in *Divaina* featured two men engaged in a discussion. One states, 'Ranil[7] has only wasps'; the other says, 'how can they have the grease devil?'

Thereby, the cartoonists highlight the power of the then Rajapaksa government, who were responsible for manipulating the opinion of the people, through either acceptable or unacceptable means, which was expressed in blurring the line between the serious and humorous as always, as observed by Petrovic (2018).

However, the political entrepreneurs were essentially careful to refrain from allowing people to realise their own power and to confuse them as to the appropriate action. The cartoons projected the masses or the citizens of the country as a group of silent sufferers or as a 'powerless', 'weak' and marginalised community, but with massive potential. This was significantly evident and was experienced during my fieldwork, where I found people let their imagination run riot and took the law into their own hands against the backdrop of the unavailability of formal institutions such as law enforcement authorities, politicians or regimes. This dimension was significantly highlighted in a cartoon published in the *Daily Mirror* on 24 August 2011. The cartoon depicts a man, terrified of his own exaggerated shadow on a wall, which suggested the widespread turmoil and panic that hindered people's ability to critically assess the situation and make rational decisions and thus avoid mass agony.

Horror and humour: addressing ambiguity in a distorted democracy

It was necessary for people to meet their everyday needs such as livelihood, food, shelter and safety as an existential need, even within an environment which was fearful and threatening. Therefore, people became significantly creative and invented mediums to meet their essential needs (Piyarathne, 2018). The everyday jokes and cartoons served this purpose with the intention of directing humour towards the rulers, which subsequently served as the 'weapons of the weak', as suggested by Scott (1985). Fraser's (1990) subaltern counterpublic spaces are informal spaces where ordinary people invent novel ideas, multiple ways of making jokes to ridicule bourgeois hegemonies and circulate counter-discourses, which eventually become mainstream via cartoons in a manner not irritating to the ruling elites. Most of the postcolonial regimes who ruled the country, especially after the introduction of the executive presidency in 1977, maintained a suppressive approach towards citizens. The motivation of politicians is always centred around their office and maximising their chances of re-election, with the power not extending beyond the political elite. Therefore, the incumbent ruling elites were seen to be stoking ambiguity (Alesina and Cukierman, 1990) throughout postcolonial political history rather than trying to completely eliminate it and improve the democratic space. Indeed, myth and traditional Sri Lankan tropes played an important part in the construction of cartoons, providing a useful medium to build up the weapons of the weak. This further elaborates Gluckman's idea about people's capacity to form and re-form a range of bonds with others that eventually facilitate challenging social problems and maintaining the stability of the system.

The explanation provided by Joseph Campbell (1991) regarding myths is that they serve four basic functions: mystical, cosmological, sociological and pedagogical. The sociological function consists of 'supporting and validating a certain social order' (Campbell, 1991: 12) that varies from place to place. In the Sri Lankan context, myths have contributed immensely to maintaining ethnoreligious group identities, creating and maintaining an ideology which favoured the ruling politicians belonging to a few families, and overall shaping the public sphere. Gunasekara (2014) argues that the

> post-war Rajapaksa meta-narrative was aimed at reinforcing the connection between the majority ethnoreligious community and the country's new rulers. It is premised on three main myths – the myth of eternal national insecurity, the myth of miraculous development and the myth of the infallible hero-king. The three myths reinforce each other; and in confluence they create and sustain the socio-psychological soil necessary for the new Rajapaksa dynasty to take root and flourish.

Therefore, by extending this analysis, it is possible to argue that the regime in power during this period benefited from the Grease Yakā phenomenon by successfully diverting the attention of the public through confusion to pursue their political agenda.

Cartoons, in this way, show the possibility of constructing social lives and a liveable social space through dark comedy, particularly within the context of tense relationships between oppressive regimes and their ethnically divided citizenry. For their survival, people were required to be aware of the ambiguous conditions created by ruling elites and were compelled to reduce the phenomenon to a manageable level, which had an impact on shaping the safety, prosperity and wellbeing of individuals, families and communities. The stories constructed around the myth of the greased devil pinpoint atrocities, and the people adopted the traditionally learnt art of 'living with' evil spirits as part and parcel of their everyday social life experience. Anthropologists evidenced emotions as a socially constructed and performed phenomenon and most of the feelings cannot be simply reduced to either culture or phylogeny (Jackson, 2010: 35). The masses who live within suppressive regimes with a high level of political ambiguity have become creative and invented mediums of constructing social lives and a social space to meet their essential needs. Consequently, this space was created through the use of sarcasm, everyday jokes, applying a language with double meanings, and so on, to create an environment conducive to the interaction of the possible within impossibility. Furthermore, it is not only the language itself but also the manner in which it is spoken, utilised and conveyed through bodily expressions.

Therefore, the cartoons and everyday humour of the people largely consisted of signifiers rather than considering the signified, which could easily make the perpetrators angry, and would have invited unnecessary trouble for the reporters and their family members including connected persons within the context of the highly militarised nature of state suppression. In such situations, if the contradictions were favouring the opposition rather than the ruling party, they might resort to occult sciences and myths such as Grease Yakā to resolve those contradictions.

Conclusion

The illogical 'fear' and 'anxiety' formed in the minds of the people amid the Grease Yakā phenomenon successfully diverted the attention of the people from politicians, showing how ambiguity can be an opportunistic force for political impropriety. At the same time, the provision of numerous humorous acts such as jokes, comedic mimicking, irony, satire, parody and lampooning, and the use of many cynical acts unique to individuals and communities, created a space in which the people could fulfil their needs even within a politically ambiguous context which threatened their lives. It appeared that the female body was used as an agency to create ambiguity and generate mass panic and anxiety among the people by the vicious, since the female body was symbolically used as an ethnoreligious, cultural, impurity, superiority, power and happiness marker as well. This was a way of confusing people via a common moral order which unites all the groups, despite the existing divisions of the people of the country via ethnic, religious, class and communal party-political lines. Communication combined with humour and sarcasm in a situational and contextual way was an appropriate formula and appeared to be a mechanism which created liveable social space, despite tense situations. This has been the embodied practice of Sri Lankans who have mostly lived hand in hand with crisis situations, or else ambiguity in shared situations, rather than in pleasant circumstances in the post-independence society. In that sense, ordinary people displayed the possibility of dealing with political elites' constructed ambiguity by projecting reality on to fantasy and fantasy on to reality, gaining control and defeating disempowerment, which would continue in the foreseeable future in Sri Lanka until such time as good governance reigns.

Notes

1 Refers to Sinhala terminology used by Sinhalas predominantly.
2 Refers to Tamil terminology used by Muslims and Tamils mostly.
3 See also Perera (2011).
4 In most of the cases these Grease Yakās (S. ග්‍රීස් යකා) are referred to as 'Grease Miniha' (S. greased man (singular)) and 'Grease Minissu' (S. greased men (plural)) in Sinhala. In Tamil they are referred to as 'Grease Pei' similar to the Sinhala's Grease Yakā. Moreover, in Tamil they are referred to as 'Grease Manithan' (T: கிரீஸ்மனிதன்) or 'Marma Manithan' (T: மர்ம மனிதன்).
5 Superhero appearing in American comic books and movies.
6 A superhero character in American comic books and movies.
7 Ranil Wickramasinghe, the current president, the opposition leader when Mahinda Rajapaksa was in power.

References

Alesina, A. and Cukierman, A. (1990) 'The politics of ambiguity', *Quarterly Journal of Economics*, 105:4, 829–50.
Aneez, S. and Sirilal, R. (2011) ' "Grease Devil" panic grips rural Sri Lanka', Reuters, 12 August, www.reuters.com/article/us-srilanka-devil/grease-devil-panic-grips-rural-sri-lanka-idUSTRE77B46V20110812 (accessed 8 January 2024).
Buerk, R. (2008) 'Astrology holds sway over Sri Lanka', BBC News, 22 December, http://news.bbc.co.uk/2/hi/south_asia/7783842.stm (accessed 8 January 2024).
Campbell, J. and Moyers, B.D. (1991) *The Power of Myth* (New York: Anchor Books.
Fraser, N. (1990) 'Rethinking the Public Sphere: A Contribution to the Critique of Actually Existing Democracy', *Social Text*, 25/26, 56–80.
Gluckman, M. (1963) *Order and Rebellion in Tribal Africa* (New York: Free Press of Glencoe).
Gunasekara, T. (2014) 'War, Peace and the Manufacturing of Rajapaksa Myths', *Groundviews*, 28 May, https://groundviews.org/2014/05/28/war-peace-and-the-manufacturing-of-rajapaksa-myths/ (accessed 8 January 2024).
Habermas, J. (1989) *The Structural Transformation of the Public Sphere: An Inquiry into a Category of Bourgeois Society* (London: Wiley).

Höglund, K and Piyarathne, A. (2009) 'Paying the price for patronage: Electoral violence in Sri Lanka', *Commonwealth & Comparative Politics*, 47:3, 287–307.

Jackson, M. (2010) 'From anxiety to method in anthropological fieldwork: an appraisal of George Devereux's enduring ideas,' in James Davies and Dimitrina Spencer (eds), *Emotions in the Field: The Psychology and Anthropology of Fieldwork Experience* (Stanford, CA: Stanford University Press), 35–54.

Jackson, M. and Piette, A. (2015) 'Introduction: Anthropology and the existential turn,' in Michael Jackson and Albert Piette (eds), *What is Existential Anthropology?* (New York: Berghahn Books), 1–29.

Jayasinghe, S. (2015) 'This Picture of Mahinda Says Thousand Words', *Colombo Telegraph*, 12 May, www.colombotelegraph.com/index.php/this-picture-of-mahinda-says-thousand-words/ (accessed 8 January 2024).

Jayasinghe, S. (2021) 'This government has dangerously lost the plot', *DailyFt*, 28 August, https://www.ft.lk/opinion/This-Government-has-dangerously-lost-the-plot/14–722321 (accessed 8 January 2024).

Jeyaraj, D.B.S. (2015) 'Astrologer Sumanadasa Abeygunawardena predicts victory for president Mahinda Rajapaksa at Jan 8th Election'. DBSJeyaraj.com, 4 January, http://dbsjeyaraj.com/dbsj/archives/36203 (accessed 9 January 2024).

Kapferer, B. (1977) 'First class to Maradana: Secular drama in Sinhalese healing rites', in S.F. Moore and B.G. Myerhoff (eds), *Secular Ritual* (Assen, Netherlands: Van Gorcum), 91–123.

Kapferer, B. (1983) *A Celebration of Demons. Exorcism and the Aesthetics of Healing in Sri Lanka* (Bloomington: Indiana University Press).

Kapferer, B. (1988) *Legends of People, Myths of State: Violence, Intolerance, and Political Culture in Sri Lanka and Australia* (Washington, DC: Smithsonian Institution Press).

Kapferer, B. (1997) *The Feast of the Sorcerer: Practices of Consciousness and Power* (Chicago, IL: University of Chicago Press).

Kapferer, B. (2001) 'Ethnic nationalism and the discourse of violence in Sri Lanka', *Communal/Plural*, 9:1, 33–67.

Lindgren, B. (2008) 'The politics of ethnicity as an extended case: Thoughts on a chiefly succession crisis,' in T.M.S. Evens and Don Handelman (eds), *The Manchester School: Practice and Ethnographic Praxis in Anthropology* (London: Berghahn Books), 272–91.

Obeyesekere, G. (1981) *Medusa's Hair: An Essay on Personal Symbols and Religious Experience* (Chicago, IL: University of Chicago Press).

Pathak, D. (2016) 'Chinese Whispering in Sri Lanka: On Gossip, Anxieties and Politics', *Groundviews*, 3 November, https://groundviews.org/2016/11/03/chinese-whispering-in-sri-lanka-on-gossip-anxieties-and-politics/ (accessed 9 January 2024).

Patta, R. (2018) 'Towards a subaltern public theology for India', PhD thesis, Manchester Faculty of Humanities.

Perera, K. (2011) 'De-greasing Social Speculation over "Grease Devils" in Sri Lanka', *Groundviews*, 21 August, https://groundviews.org/2011/08/21/de-greasing-social-speculation-over-"grease-devils"-in-sri-lanka/ (accessed 9 January 2024).

Petrovic, T. (2018) 'Political parody and the politics of ambivalence', *Annual Review of Anthropology*, 47, 201–16.

Piyarathne, A. (2018) *Constructing Commongrounds: Everyday Lifeworlds Beyond Politicized Ethnicities in Sri Lanka* (Nugegoda, Sri Lanka: Sarasavi Publishers).

Ratnaweera, N. (2021) 'Gota's Lockdown Decision Hinges on Gnanakka: Soothsayer Says Covid-19 Deaths are Sacrifices to Kāli', *Colombo Telegraph*, 20 August, https://www.colombotelegraph.com/index.php/gotas-lockdown-decision-hinges-on-gnanakka-soothsayer-says-covid-19-deaths-are-sacrifices-to-kali/   (accessed 9 January 2024).

Scott, J.C. (1985) *Weapons of the Weak: Everyday Forms of Peasant Resistance* (New Haven, CT: Yale University Press).

Tambiah, S.J. (1996) *Levelling Crowds: Ethnonationalist Conflicts and Collective Violence in South Asia* (Berkeley: University of California Press).

Uyangoda, J. (2021) 'Parliament & Parliamentary Democracy in Sri Lanka: A Brief Political History', *Colombo Telegraph*, 30 June, https://www.colombotelegraph.com/index.php/parliament-parliamentary-democracy-in-sri-lanka-a-brief-political-history/ (accessed 12 January 2024).

Part IV

Self-realisation and disjuncture

11

Liminal ambiguity: the tricky position of being Black in white skin

Suzi Hutchings

Introduction

The difficulty I had in starting this chapter reflects my ambiguous position of living within the slipperiness of the identity I discuss. This ambiguity is born of the dichotomy between being an Aboriginal[1] person living within Australian[2] Aboriginal cultural meanings, on the one hand, and living as an Aboriginal person where, on the other hand, Aboriginality has historically been determined by the state according to cultural difference, physical appearance and skin colour. Indigenous scholar Irene Watson (2015: 84) describes the impact of this history where:

> Imposed colonial views of Aboriginality have worked towards death, invisibility and our final absorption into a clothed whiteness of being. In its attempts to extinguish Nungas [Aboriginal people], the muldarbi [colonisers] created categories of colour. We were named and managed by the Aborigines Acts of each Australian state in categories of 'mixed race' and 'full blood'. The acts administered our separation from our old people[3] and families, and the language of our songs and law.[4]

I am *Arrernte*; my mother's family are from *Mparntwe* (Alice Springs) in Central Australia. My mother and her brothers grew up as members of a well-known, traditionally knowledgeable Aboriginal family, sharing rights and interests in the *Arrernte Native Title Claim* determined in the Australian Federal Court in 2000. At age 12 my mother came to Adelaide in South Australia for schooling. I was raised in Adelaide.

This chapter is contemplative and creative. It is not intended as a general critique of anthropology as a colonial tool. I acknowledge the extensive self-reflection of anthropologists and political scientists (e.g. Taussig and Coulthard) and critiques by others (e.g. Sartre, Said and Derrida) since the early twentieth century (Coates, 2008). Instead, I take a personal position as a First Nation anthropologist seeking to explore the ambiguity of living as a fair-skinned Aboriginal person in modern Australia. I argue that embodying

Aboriginality invokes both a politics of being and a project of belonging, which falls within the realm of an ethics of ambiguity that Simone de Beauvoir (1962: 18) describes as 'one which will refuse to deny a priori that separate existants can, at the same time, be bound to each other, that their individual freedoms can forge laws valid for all'. I contend that de Beauvoir's ideas on ambiguity provide a freedom of technique allowing for discussion of the ambiguous positionality of being a First Nations woman of *Arrernte* descent with fair skin. This is because de Beauvoir postulates that a state of ambiguity can exist beyond the social structures or the history which created it, while still being attached ethically to the circumstances that led to it. I join Marshall and Hizi (both this volume) in adopting de Beauvoir's exposition of the ethics of ambiguity in contexts of state-wielded power that allow for disclosure of distinct technologies in self-cultivation in contexts marked by paradox. De Beauvoir wrote her ideas on ambiguity and freedom coming out of a context of invasion, oppression and domination during World War II, as many practical examples throughout her treatise attest. It is this aspect of de Beauvoir's work I concentrate on in the ideas I present. I argue that de Beauvoir suggests a philosophical position that allows for the individual's disembodiment from their circumstances of social oppression. Understanding her in this way enables the recognition of certain truths about the liminal position of the colonised.

The truth is that, in order for my freedom not to risk coming to grief against the obstacle which its very engagement has raised, in order that it might still pursue its movement in the face of failure, it must, by giving itself a particular content, aim by means of it at an end which is nothing else but precisely the free movement of existence (de Beauvoir, 1962: 29). As Indigenous people, our freedom is at constant risk, and in danger of 'coming to grief', as we navigate daily obstacles, which our identity raises. The hazards of being stuck in a vortex of perceived binary identities of Aboriginal or not Aboriginal are extremely exhausting to navigate when identity in reality is complex, gendered, multilayered and ambiguously fluid.

On a Saturday evening in 2022 I was travelling on a packed Melbourne tram with commuters from different ethnic backgrounds. Some were office workers. Others were parents with children. Many were of African background. At the next stop, a man of middle-age and white European appearance boarded, proclaiming loudly that many fellow passengers should not be on the tram taking up space. 'Why don't they drive their cars?' he shouted. Moments later he sat down in the only available seat, next to me. In his Western European accent, he tried to engage me in his complaints. He asked me where I was from. I said I was from here – meaning Australia. He replied that I could not be from Australia as I was not black and the people who are *really* from Australia are 'black Aboriginal people'. He repeated, 'so, where are you from – where are your family from, England?' At the next stop he abruptly alighted.

This fellow traveller could not possibly know – unless I told him – my genealogy, which is inevitably intertwined with colonist ancestors, reflecting the complex history of colonial possession. My father's ancestors were from England. My maternal grandmother was *Arrernte*. My awkward, albeit brief, encounter with the man on the tram reveals multifaceted social issues that run deep through Australia's colonial history. Such interactions delineate a dilemma encountered by many light-skinned Aboriginal people, especially when aggravated by questions about identity, racial origins and/ or genealogy. Indigenous academic Chelsea Watego (2021: 155) challenges the imposition of ambiguous positionality head-on, making the point, 'as a fair skinned Blackfulla I have to say it has primarily been whitefullas or non-Indigenous colonisers who have suggested I was "too white to be Black"'. Her statement is couched in a broader critique of colonisers who claim to know best about who 'real' Aboriginal people are, and how to interact with 'them'. She comments: such colonisers 'fail to address a core feature of Indigeneity as expressed by Indigenous peoples', this being our relationships to other 'Indigenous peoples, culture and country' (Watego, 2021: 155). Aboriginal identity is truly ambiguous in its dialogue with agents and institutions of the colonial state. However, as Watego's arguments point to, for Aboriginal people our identity is *solid*, to use an Aboriginal English expression to mean fantastic or real, without denying that Aboriginal people negotiate identity constantly with each other when discussing kin relations, connections to Country and culture.

The ambiguity of Blackness or Whiteness as identities possesses multiple meanings within the context of social encounters experienced by Indigenous people in modern colonial settings. Yet what is clear from my example is when you are not dark-skinned, but you are Indigenous, and you are with people who do not know your biography, the realness of your Aboriginality is undetectable to others. For Aboriginal people, as Watego pinpoints, any ambiguity in our identity that is based on appearance and skin tone (or its invisibility) emerges profoundly in modern colonial encounters and relationships with settlers. Such invisibility or sketchiness nevertheless contains a strange individual power for a person who, through such encounters, is inadvertently and momentarily removed from the colonial structures that define and control the Aboriginal families they belong to. These small moments of ambiguity provide ways of seeing, knowing and distilling how power can operate in the minutiae of social interactions in the wake of colonialism (Sharpe, 2016).

I argue elsewhere, in line with other Indigenous theorists (e.g. Moreton-Robinson, 2015; Watson, 2015) and some settler scholars (e.g. Wolfe, 1994,

2001, 2006), that colonisation is ongoing. This is because its logic remains embedded throughout Australia, despite Indigenous peoples achieving recognition through reconciliation initiatives, native title and land rights legislation (Hutchings, 2019: 196; cf. Coulthard, 2014; Watego, 2021). Wolfe concluded that policies underpinning native title failed to provide the radical disruptor to the colonial project promised under the landmark 1992 High Court decision in *Mabo v Queensland* [no. 2] that overturned the myth of *terra nullius*, of land belonging to no one (Wolfe, 1994). Watson is more specific, targeting the discipline of anthropology as a handmaiden to the success of laws controlling Indigenous peoples imposed by the settler state. Watson views Australian anthropology as a discipline which has historically supported the colonial project, consistently speaking for Indigenous peoples, thereby rendering our stories of ourselves as unreliable, simplified, not scientific or objective. In Australia, this colonial logic remains enduringly wedded to what Wolfe has described as 'a colour-coded lap count along the course of elimination' of Aboriginal people by the settler state (Wolfe, 1994: 114). As this is a race to extinction that can never be won, colonial structures controlling Aboriginal communities remain entrenched. Wolfe (1994: 116) reveals the inherent flaws in this apparatus of elimination. As he describes, 'the system sought to impose a negative or reducing exogamy, a *nubium* without exchange whose target was not Black genes but Aboriginal community, not physical but social relations'.[5] It was, and remains a system that justifies the colonial project.

Australia's Coloured Minority: Its Place in the Community (1947) by Chief Protector of Aborigines, A.O. Neville, with an introduction by anthropologist A.P. Elkin, presented theories of racial purity backed by eugenic philosophy, providing pseudo-scientific credibility to notions that race is genetically constructed. Aboriginal people were branded a separate race subject to mathematical divisibility by interbreeding, where their *colour* and, by implication, *race* could be bred out after three generations of intermarriage. *Half-Blood*, *Half-Caste*, *Quadroon* and *Octaroon* became terminologies of policy, while also gaining credence in common Australian parlance. Insidiously, this underpinned legislation that removed Aboriginal people from their communities, identities, families, languages and cultures (Read, 2006). These classifications remain extremely offensive, not least because they deny a person their Aboriginal identity by focusing on the degree to which they are allegedly *not* Aboriginal. Such notions, which demarcate 'real' Aboriginality, persist in the Australian imagination and the colonial narrative, continuing to impact government policy on Indigenous welfare, even though assimilation policies officially ended in the 1970s. Indigenous scholars have incisively dissected how the ongoing colonial project structurally reinforces white privilege by controlling bodies, with Moreton-Robinson (2011: 647) revealing it as the 'possessive logic' of state control.

Aboriginal identity in the hands of Aboriginal people never fits such state-defined, ordered patterns of gradations of Aboriginality; rather it dislocates colonial categorisations. In *Shamanism, Colonialism, and the Wild Man* (1987) Michael Taussig critiques Victor Turner's postulation that a universal or quasi-universal feature of ritual is the seeking of unity, of wholeness. Taussig's examination of ritual is that of ritual played out in the context of conquest and colonialism, where disorder manifests in relations with the colonised. Taussig (1987: 442) goes on to critique anthropology in general as having 'bound the concept of ritual hand and foot to the imagery of order, to such an extent that order is identified with the sacred itself, thereby casting disorder into the pit of evil'. In seeking to order the disordered subjects, the coloniser designs a mimetic contract that recognises itself in the colonised. Taussig analyses this phenomenon through the example of the Cuna Indians who invite European and American anthropologists to study their whiteness, their culture and the surrounding ecosystem as a way of the Cuna gaining autonomy from the 'Black' Panamanian state (Taussig, 1993: 142).

In moving my focus more explicitly to the social interactions between Aboriginal people and settlers, and between Aboriginal people themselves where these relationships are underpinned by the structures these theorists define as colonial, I hypothesise Aboriginal positionality as a state of disruption. I further argue, these conditions of existence for Aboriginal people are all at once imbued with power; sacredness and danger; purity and impurity; and are ultimately ambiguous, being derived from the very colonialism which produced them to be viable. Within anthropology the concept of liminality emerged out of the concerns of early French anthropology that concentrated on social structure and classification. The notion of liminality is attributed to van Gennep and his work *Rites of Passage* (Kertzer in van Gennep, 2019). Given the focus of my chapter, it seems poignant that the ideas in *Rites of Passage* emerged from van Gennep's examination of documents about 'Australian societies', that is, Australian Aboriginal societies. However, the idea of liminality as further developed by Turner I argue is not particularly useful for an understanding of the positionality I am attempting to convey – one that slips from one state of being to another and back again – and occurs for Aboriginal people in relation to the imposed reality of ongoing colonialism.

Turner undertook his anthropological work with Zambia's Ndembu people, a country that was colonised by the British in the late 1800s (Turner and Abrahams, 2017 [1969], 1970). In expanding van Gennep's ideas, Turner concentrated on the liminal phase of ritual in which participants are ambiguously positioned as neither part of society nor reincorporated back into society in a new state of being, as a full adult member. For the initiates during the liminal phase, they remain in *communitas* with fellow initiates in a condition of limbo or ambiguity. Regardless, there is a defined path forward for initiates to full status back into the society from which they came, albeit in a transformed state – emerging as new adults. Importantly, Turner's work does not discuss liminality for the Ndembu existing in relation to the British colonial regime under which they were subjugated. For Aboriginal people, liminality is our constant state of being in our relations with the colonial state. *Communitas*, on the other hand, is achieved in the company of family and community beyond the immediate gaze of the state. Watego (2021: 176) offers insight when she says 'that sense of belonging that Indigenous communities offer is really something, no matter where that Indigenous community exists'.

Black Lives Matter – Indigenous Lives Matter

In his song *Black Lives Matter* (2017) Indigenous rapper Birdz demands listeners' attention.[6] I remain awed by Birdz' astute lyricism speaking truth to power. He decries the 'war' between Indigenous people and law enforcement that has been going on for too long, but despairs that he cannot keep holding out for change. He cynically reveals the falsehood embedded in the rhetoric of the coloniser, rapping: 'Now we say black lives matter / But shit, the fact of the matter is / We just black matter to them / This shit keeps happening …'

In June 2020, Black Lives Matter (BLM) protests happened across Australia, organised in solidarity with protests around the globe condemning the death of George Floyd at the hands of law enforcement officers in Florida, USA. While in Australia protests embraced sympathies for the plight of oppressed African Americans, in the main they focused on local Indigenous issues. At rallies led by Indigenous activists the catch cries 'Black Lives Matter' alongside 'Always Was Always Will Be Aboriginal Land' were shouted loudly, combining our grief and reinforcing our enduring pride as First Nations peoples (Hutchings, 2021). The appalling death of Floyd serves to reinforce further the reality of our ongoing colonial oppression. It is a spark reigniting our years-long battle calling for substantial reviews by governments into the disproportionate levels and continuing incidence of Indigenous deaths in custody, and the persistent over-representation of Indigenous peoples in the criminal justice system.

2021 marked the thirtieth anniversary since the report from the Royal Commission into Aboriginal Deaths in Custody (RCIADIC), established by the Hawke Labor government in 1987, to examine ninety-nine Indigenous deaths across Australia. A key finding was that one of the most significant factors bringing Aboriginal people into contact with the criminal justice system is their social disadvantage and unequal position in Australian society. Collectively we have suffered relentless surveillance and brutality at the hands of the colonial state under policies designed to integrate us into settler society during the assimilation policy era (1930s–1970s). The suicide death of Malcolm Charles Smith in prison in 1982 epitomises the horror of colonialism and the continuing suffering of incarcerated Indigenous people. The RCIADIC report on Smith's case gives a harrowing description of the manner of his suicide.

> At 1.25 p.m. on 29 December 1982 Malcolm Charles Smith, an Aboriginal prisoner in the Malabar Assessment Unit (MAU) of the Metropolitan Reception Prison (MRP) at Long Bay, Sydney, went into a toilet cubicle, locking the door behind him. About half a minute later a piercing scream came from inside. Prison officers rushed to the door and, when there was no response, knocked it off its hinges and found that the handle of an artist's paint brush had been driven through Malcolm Smith's left eye, so that only the metal sheath and hairs were protruding ... Despite all possible care, he died at 11.41 a.m. on 5 January 1983. (Wootten, 1989: 1)

The death of Smith was memorialised in the 1992 documentary *Who Killed Malcolm Smith?* which stars Indigenous filmmaker Richard Frankland[7] (Adler and Sherwood, 1992). In 1996 Frankland made an autobiographical short film entitled *No Way to Forget*.[8] I remember vividly when this evocatively moving film was released. It starts with Frankland's character Shane Francis gazing across a paddock at sunset before he returns to his car to drive along a dusty country road. The visual narrative then enters twilight and a dreamlike space – a liminal space between past and present that collides with spectres of a young Aboriginal boy who has died and old Aboriginal men 'painted up'.[9] These images haunt Francis as he drives through the night on his way to investigate yet another death in custody. The audience joins Francis as visualised memories of details of the Aboriginal deaths he investigates resurface. Here the film draws explicitly from the genre of magical realism. But the story also extracts from Aboriginal tradition where we are all taught to listen and gain knowledge from the spiritual realm, from our elders and ancestors. Intermingled with the envisioned memories of Francis, the audience is further confronted with scenes of unfathomable loss experienced by an Aboriginal mother as she screams out for reasons as to why her son, 'a great artist', died.

Writers like academic Christina Sharpe and novelist Toni Morrison, whose ancestors experienced the generational violence of colonialism through institutional slavery; or others who have explored the embeddedness of colonial structures and the Christianity that supports these, such as novelist Gabriel García Márquez, offer pathways to interrogate the enduring intergenerational impacts of colonialism on individual bodies. Sharpe (2016) interweaves personal narratives with academic examination to expose truths in the horror of living as a Black person in the contemporary United States. Morrison (2004) and Márquez (2014) rely on the literary technique of magical realism to elevate their readers into an imaginative space of the fantastic that synthesises the personal with a history of structural oppression. Regardless of any disparities in their approach, all lead their readers on a journey into the heart of darkness,[10] institutional slavery, and colonialism. A key difference I draw from their writings to that of de Beauvoir, introduced above, is that for Sharpe and Morrison being Black is never ambiguous. The violent impacts of colonialism continue to be embodied in each generation as a lived reality of Blackness, even though slavery as an institution ended in 1865.

And herein lies a contradiction, for although as I have argued above, my Indigenous positionality is ambiguous because I am an Aboriginal woman with fair skin, the generational impacts and ongoing experiences and shared knowledge of the violence of colonisation are carried through each generation regardless of what we, as Indigenous people, look like, just as they do for those who suffer the legacy of transatlantic slavery. Sharpe (2016: 14) has developed the theory of wakefulness, or being in the wake, as consciousness that 'departs from scholars and those works that look for political, juridical, or even philosophical answers' to the problem of Black exclusion from society. Rather, revelations are exposed in the imaginary realm of Black literature, performance and visual culture that 'observe and mediate this un/survival' (Sharpe, 2016: 14). Coming from an Indigenous positionality that resonates with the concept of wakefulness proposed by Sharpe, I contend that it is in the liminal space of spirituality, magic and death that those oppressed by the machinery of colonialism escape to survive.

Surviving colonialism, slavery and conquest requires a reimagining of conquered identities. In 'Of Love and Other Demons' (2014) García Márquez repurposes a legend told to him by his mother about a young woman bitten by a rabid dog from which it was feared she had become stricken with rabies. The young woman is confined to a convent to be exorcised. This story takes the reader into an imaginary past when colonial rule in Latin America was inextricably linked to the church. In a society dominated by strict Catholicism the young girl poses a threat to the church because her insanity is also linked to a belief she was raised by African slaves. In Toni Morrison's *Beloved* (2004) the mother murders her child to save her from a life of continual slavery and oppression, only for the ghostly presence of

Beloved to haunt her family for generations as an embedded and personified memory of that very act of violent survival.

For many Aboriginal people their positionality is profoundly established within the colonial state via the threat of violence and its reality; violence that mirrors the historical frontier wars and devastation of the early days of invasion and settlement (e.g. Foster et al., 2001; Connor, 2002; Reynolds, 2006; Bottoms, 2013). The enduring violence inflicted on Aboriginal people was recently magnified with news of the assault of Cassius Turvey in Western Australia. The brutal attack led to the 15-year-old dying of his appalling injuries in hospital days later. Turvey was phenotypically Aboriginal with brown skin. In the immediate aftermath police and politicians, in attempts to ameliorate suggestions that the attack was racially determined, argued that the public should not jump to conclusions as to any motivations. In further efforts to control the narrative to normalise such a violent death, police argued the attack may have been a case of mistaken identity, where Cassius was in the wrong place at the wrong time. Aboriginal family and community strongly contested this, saying Cassius was in the *right* place at the *right* time as he was merely walking home from school. Palawa[11] political reporter Dana Morse stated: 'there is no safe place for First Nations children in a country that is yet to overturn the racism and disadvantage faced by so many. This includes the right of an Aboriginal boy to walk home safely from school' (Morse, 2022: paras 22–3). At the time of writing, this case was before the courts, with four individuals charged with murder, pending a legal outcome.

Aboriginality and being Blak

Aboriginal deaths in custody are First Nations deaths in custody are Black deaths in custody. Yet, as I have argued above, the legacy of colonialism in Australia has ensured that not all Aboriginal people are identifiably black, according to their skin colour, resulting from the assimilation logic of the elimination of colour as described by Wolfe (1994). The complexities of living an ambiguous Indigeneity, conversely, are not resolved merely on an understanding of the history of Australian colonisation. People like me, and there are many of us, inhabit our Indigeneity as being Black in white skin, but we are not necessarily members of what is called the Stolen Generations under official assimilation policy that sought to take Aboriginal children from their families (Read, 2006).[12] It may be easy for an outsider to assume that my skin tone is because I grew up in the city and not the Australian Outback where many settlers still believe 'real' Aboriginal people originate; or that I am a member of the Stolen Generations; or that I have only recently learned I have Indigenous ancestry, thereby justifying my claim to Aboriginality in a time when settlers are increasingly 'discovering' that they have distant Indigenous lineage. None of these definitions is correct and I baffle all these stereotypes.

The result of the mismatch between outside perceptions and lived reality is that I exist within an ambiguous space that is ultimately imposed by settler society. A space that is constantly shifting, is unstable and at times psychologically dangerous. An identity that is buffeted by unpredictable shifts in government policies and interference by academics, including anthropologists,[13] who deign to determine what constitutes Aboriginality. It is also an identity that faces challenges from other oppressed peoples. While undertaking research in the USA on minority Hip-Hop, I was often questioned as to how I could claim to be Indigenous when I was not black- or brown-skinned. In the scenarios presented to me by African American and Latino colleagues and Hip-Hop practitioners, being oppressed is synonymous with having black or brown skin. As I have already pointed out, this position is also explored theoretically by Black academics and writers, who link this reality to an intractable legacy of colonisation through slavery. It is in this fraught ambiguous space that I, as do many others, embody and enact Aboriginal identity.

In 1991 Kuku[14] and Erub/Mer[15] artist Destiny Deacon was first to record the use of the term blak in the title of her photographic piece *Blak lik mi* in an exhibition of the same name that included works by other Aboriginal artists. Russell-Cook in a review of the art of Destiny Deacon notes that it is widely accepted in Australia that this was the first time an Aboriginal person used the spelling 'blak' (2021). In her multidisciplinary works across photography, film, performance, installation and sculpture, Deacon reflects a term now used by many Aboriginal people to reclaim historical, representational, symbolic, stereotypical and romanticised notions of Black or Blackness. The term purposely separates Aboriginality and Aboriginal identity from skin colour, which may be confusing to other black people from outside Australia. In urban Australia the term Blak is fundamentally possessed by Aboriginal people. In a website campaign titled *Shades of Deadly*, the Aboriginal-owned, Melbourne-based fashion label Clothing the Gaps uses photos and quotes from Aboriginal people of a variety of genders, ages and skin tones to explore uses of the term Blak, providing this definition on their website: 'A term used to distinguish Aboriginal and Torres Strait Islander identity from skin colour. The term Blak is used throughout the *Shades of Deadly* campaign as an expression of taking back power. Blak is an expression of self-determination.'[16]

Despite our attempts to determine the narrative, Aboriginal identity constantly faces new challenges from representatives of the Australian settler state. This became all too clear when I first heard discussions about *Dark Emu* (2018) by Bruce Pascoe. The book is hugely popular among settler readers and many Aboriginal people. Yet debate rages among academics and commentators about whether Pascoe is Aboriginal, as he claims to be. As I have collaboratively argued elsewhere (Hutchings and Holcombe, 2022), some high-profile Aboriginal people such as journalist Stan Grant (Hardacker, 2021) and academic Victoria Greives (2021) have publicly questioned Pascoe's claims to Aboriginal kinship, whereas settler academics such as Sutton and Walshe (2021) have intellectualised the 'problem', shifting the focus from an investigation of Pascoe's Aboriginal genealogy, to questioning his scholarship. Other academics have weighed in, arguing that it is not the business of settlers to query the genuineness of an Aboriginal person's stated identity by disparaging their academic acumen (e.g. Cowlishaw, 2021), with historian Stephen Mueke (2021) calling these debates 'Whitefella[17] magic'.

Such analyses leave little room for Indigenous theorists to be heard. Importantly, Watego (2021: 165) calls people who perform Aboriginality the 'ambiguously Indigenous' and the 'new native police', whose colonially ascribed scripts symbolise 'an Indigeneity of the past, a past Blackness that has been remediated so as not to pose a threat or risk'. Watego mocks people who co-opt and whitewash Indigenous self-organisation and self-expression in their misuse of Indigenous cultural terms and practices to justify their own alleged Indigeneity. They 'hold healing circles and they like to "yarn" with message sticks';[18] they adorn their work places with Indigenous art and artefacts, while ensuring there are fewer Indigenous people around 'to disrupt the standard order of things' (Watego, 2021: 170).

In the unfolding of the *Dark Emu* debate the magic of mimesis is at play. Taussig describes this magic functioning in other contexts, whereby a colonial dialogue emerges *about* extant societies. In his analysis of Turner's essay about an African healer, Taussig implies that anthropology repossesses the rite of ritual in the act of representing the ritual. Taussig makes the point that such representation of ritual as theoretical argument validates the structure and naturalises the connections that hold the argument about the ritual together, benefiting the argument beyond the story as embodied by the African people it is about (Taussig, 1992: 150–2). This is the magic of mimesis – and it is the magic of the colonial contract that keeps the colonisers in power. A contract that is supported by academics who, in the case of *Dark Emu*, and in the examples of Aboriginal enactment among academics and senior public officials that Watego describes, deliberate about what constitutes authentic Aboriginality.

For their part, the 'race-shifters', as some have argued Pascoe to be (e.g. Grieve-Williams, 2021; Newman, 2022; Knott, 2022) have embodied the very mimetic contract that colonialism has offered them in recognising in themselves the Indigenous other. They have achieved this by embodying Indigeneity into their very being, while at the same time rejecting Indigeneity or bla(c)kness as disorderly, disruptive, inauthentic, dangerous and impure. These people bring colonial order to the perceived messiness or impurity (Douglas, 2003) of Aboriginality. In doing this, they become more Indigenous than the Indigenous (Grieve-Williams, 2021). This is an extraordinarily clever manipulation of the mimetic contract that is intrinsic to the colonial project as played out by individual actors. Indeed, such people become the 'white Indian' among the Cuna of Darien that Taussig (1993) depicts colonial anthropologists desperately seeking, as discussed earlier.

Indigenous peoples in Australia do not subscribe willingly to this mimetic contract of complicity like the white Indians of Darien or the race-shifters I portray above, and our resistance is dogged. In his significant anti-colonial work *Black Skin, White Masks,* Frantz Fanon (2021) argues that people who are colonised carefully negotiate their existence and survival by operating in two worlds performing *whiteness* when required. In order to survive in a world dominated by whites, the colonised Black person becomes masterful in the language of the coloniser. Saving Aboriginal people, by making them whiter, has been an important colonial logic embedded in policies of removal of Aboriginal children, and this creates ongoing challenges. Central to many contemporary discussions about the composition of Aboriginality is whether Aboriginal experiences of racism can be compared to those of 'people of colour', including whether light-skinned Aboriginal people experience white privilege. Celeste Liddle (2014), an Indigenous activist, highlights an inherent fallacy in this argument:

> fair skin privilege from an Indigenous perspective is incredibly limited. [It] … completely ignores the many assimilation practices that fairer skinned Aboriginal people have been exposed to in this country, such as the 'Stolen Generations'. Children of fairer skin being ripped away from their darker parents in order to be trained up in domestic chores and farmhand duties so they could then be given to settler communities as free labour.

Indigenous critical theorist Glen Sean Coulthard in *Red Skin, White Masks* (2014) acknowledges he has been heavily influenced by the anti-colonial arguments of Fanon. Coulthard (2014: 6–7) contends that a 'settler-colonial relationship is one characterised by a particular form of domination' which cements structures of power. His reference to the works of Fanon and Jean-Paul Sartre are enlightening for my own arguments. Coulthard comments (2014: 131) that 'Fanon … turns our attention to the cultural practices of critical individual and collective *self-recognition* that colonized populations often engage in to empower themselves, instead of relying too heavily on the colonial state and society to do this for them' (emphasis in original). He further postulates that Fanon mostly associated 'self-affirmative cultural, artistic, and political activity with *negritude*', this being a form of activism that emphasised the need for colonised peoples 'to purge themselves of the internalized effects of systematic racism and colonial violence by rejecting assimilation' (Coulthard, 2014: 131) and, instead, affirming their worth through identity-related differences. Importantly, Coulthard notes that Fanon shared Sartre's views that cultural self-affirmation constituted a means but not an end of anti-colonial struggle.

According to Coulthard's analysis of Sartre and Fanon's works on antisemitism and colonialism, the most common response to being colonised is 'flight' in order for the Jew in Sartre's case (*Anti-Semite and Jew*, 1948), or for the Negro in Fanon's case, to escape their situation and negate their differences that mark them as 'morally deficient and inferior in the eyes of the colonizer' (2014: 140). Coulthard (2014: 135) also points out that Sartre argues that the Jew that chooses to flee their situation as a Jew is inauthentic, whereby Sartre is equating inauthenticity with assimilation. This would imply that the mimetic contract as argued by Taussig can only truly work if the colonised is genuinely complicit. What Sartre fails to adequately account for are the myriad ways oppressed peoples, even if they appear to be complicit, also enact forms of resistance in their apparent acceptance of imposed identities. Fanon (2021: 117) moreover criticises Sartre for talking on behalf of black people when he 'forgets that the black man suffers in his body quite differently from the white man'. Coulthard (2014: 143) points out that Fanon (2021: 114) argues against essentialism in stating: ' "The Black experience is ambiguous" … "for there is not *one* Negro – there are *many* black men".'[19]

Conclusion

Ambiguity, coming back to de Beauvoir's ideas, is a multilayered form of individual freedom – a liberation – that allows for individual and embodied resistances and affirmations of identity in highly fraught, complex and often violent situations of ongoing colonial domination. Ambiguity, as it is lived by, and among, colonised peoples, and among Indigenous peoples as I have discussed, disrupts and confounds the imposed mimetic contract of ongoing colonisation in its actualisation. Literary devices, such as magical realism or the interweaving of personal stories with theoretical analysis to elevate a reader into the realm of the fantastic, are important devices to an anthropology attempting to explore identities in the contexts of enduring colonialism. There is persistent danger, nonetheless, of anthropology in its practice being a historical handmaiden to the state, ensuring the success of the colonial project by co-opting how we identify away from us as Indigenous and Black peoples. It is against this that we are compelled to remain vigilant, and define our own terms of identification, and our own terms of being.

Notes

1 I use Indigenous, Aboriginal and First Nation(s) interchangeably. We use these terms to name ourselves in different contexts. For example, in everyday practice 'Aboriginal' is often used when speaking with non-Aboriginal people, or among each other. More commonly we use 'Mob'. 'Indigenous' is used inclusively of Aboriginal and Torres Strait Islander people Australia-wide. 'First Nations' or 'First Peoples' are increasingly acceptable to identify ourselves, linking us with Indigenous peoples globally.

2 I use Australia/Australian to provide context for international readers. However, using these names is fraught because doing so legitimises the colonialism that has oppressed us since 1788. Increasingly, Indigenous activists and academics favour 'so-called Australia'. We do not have a single Indigenous name for Australia. This is unlike Māori who refer to New Zealand as *Aotearoa*, or Indigenous peoples in North America who call this place Turtle Island.

3 Ancestors and/or elderly relatives in Aboriginal English.

4 I use this quote from Watson elsewhere (Hutchings, 2019). I also use it here because of how aptly Watson describes, from an Aboriginal perspective, the impact of the colonial project, where extinguishment of Aboriginality is linked to categories of race and colour.

5 Emphasis in original.

6 Nathan Bird is from Butchulla Country near Katherine in the Northern Territory.

7 Frankland worked as a field officer for the RCIADIC.

8 'No Way to Forget', directed by Richard Frankland (1996), Golden Seahorse Productions Pty Ltd, www.youtube.com/watch?v=Uxfb7C15ly8 (accessed 1 February 2022).

9 'Painted up' is an Aboriginal English expression meaning someone who has their body decorated for ceremony.

10 I have purposely invoked Joseph Conrad's 1902 anti-colonial novella, *Heart of Darkness* (2015).

11 Tasmanian Aboriginal people use this term to refer to themselves.

12 Australian legal and welfare systems have historically targeted Aboriginal women for the removal of their children under assimilation policies. These children are known as the Stolen Generations.

13 Elsewhere, I argue that some contemporary anthropologists see themselves as unofficial arbiters of Aboriginal identity (Hutchings, 2019: 204). Their judgement

of Aboriginal authenticity emanates from a history where distinguished anthropologists worked on Aboriginal affairs policy for Australian governments.

14 Kuku Yalanji people originate from the rainforest regions of Far North Queensland.

15 Torres Strait Islander peoples.

16 Clothing the Gaps 'Shades of deadly campaign' https://www.clothingthegaps. com.au/pages/shades-of-deadly-v-log-campaign?_pos=2&_sid=1cc0a980d&_ ss=r (accessed 2 October 2021).

17 Mueke has adopted an Aboriginal English term identifying non-Aboriginal people.

18 Healing circles, based on traditional cultural practices, have been adopted mainly by urban Aboriginal people as a means of community self-healing. To yarn is to discuss. Modern use of message sticks by Aboriginal people is derived from traditional practices of communication between Aboriginal groups.

19 Emphasis in Fanon and Coulthard.

References

Adler, N. and Sherwood, C. (1992) *Who Killed Malcolm Smith?* Titus Films. Australia.

Australia (1989). Royal Commission into Aboriginal Deaths in Custody and Wootten, J.H. *Report of the inquiry into the death of Malcolm Charles Smith*. Australian Government Publishing Service.

de Beauvoir, S. (1962) *The Ethics of Ambiguity*, trans. B. Frechtman (Secaucus, NJ: Citadel Press).

Bottoms, T. (2013) *Conspiracy of Silence. Queensland Frontier Killing Times* (Crows Nest: Allen & Unwin).

Coates, B. (2008) 'Anthropological criticism, from Colonialism, Post-Coloniality, Nation and Race', in Christa Knellwolf and Christopher Norris (eds), *The Cambridge History of Literary Criticism* (online: Cambridge University Press), 265–74, https://www.cambridge.org/core/books/abs/cambridge-history-of-literary-criticism/anthropological-criticism/E4B00067E10546A2C0549DE5B69946FE (accessed 2 July 2022).

Cohen, S. (2001) *States of Denial* (Cambridge: Polity Press).

Connor, J. (2002) *The Australian Frontier Wars, 1788–1838* (Sydney: UNSW Press).

Conrad, J. (2015) *Heart of Darkness* (Minneapolis, MN: First Avenue Editions).

Coulthard, G.S. (2014) *Red Skin, White Masks: Rejecting the Colonial Politics of Recognition* (Minneapolis: University of Minnesota Press).

Cowlishaw, G. (2021) 'Misreading Dark Emu', *Pearls and Irritations: John Menadue's Public Policy Journal*, https://johnmenadue.com/misreading-dark-emu/ (accessed 4 October 2021).

Douglas, M. (2003) *Purity and Danger: An Analysis of Concepts of Pollution and Taboo* (London: Routledge).

Fanon, F. (2021) *Black Skin, White Masks*, trans. R. Philcox (Penguin eBook).

Foster, R., Nettelbeck, A. and Hosking, R. (2001) *Fatal Collisions: The South Australian Frontier and the Violence of Memory* (Adelaide: Wakefield Press).

Frankland, R. (1996) *No Way to Forget* (Golden Seahorse Productions).

Grieve-Williams, V. (2021) ' "It's cultural fraud": The growing act of race-shifting', *The Australian*, 10 July, https://www.theaustralian.com.au/inquirer/its-cultural-fraud-the-act-ofraceshifting/news-story/0e2d97e1a745957a6b36029a9f04f0cbT (accessed 9 December 2021).

Hardacker, D. (2021) 'The kinship question: Bruce Pascoe and the long search for his mob', *Crikey*, 15 July, https://www.crikey.com.au/2021/07/15/the-kinship-question-bruce-pascoe-and-the-long-search-for-his-mob/ (accessed 11 September 2021).

Hutchings, S. (2019) 'Indigenous Anthropologists Caught in the Middle: The Fragmentation of Indigenous Knowledge in Native Title Anthropology, Law, and Policy in Urban and Rural Australia', in R. Aída Hernández Castillo, Suzi Hutchings and Brian Noble (eds), *Transcontinental Dialogues: Activist Alliances with Indigenous Peoples of Canada, Mexico, and Australia* (No. 7) (Tucson: University of Arizona Press), 193–219.

Hutchings, S. (2021) 'Aborigenes en Australia: Las Personas Mas Encarceladas De La Tierra', *Debates Indigenas*, Online Journal (Spanish language edition).

Hutchings, S. and Holcombe, S. (2022) 'Anthropology and Activism in the Global South: An exploration in activist scholarship with Indigenous peoples in the global south', *AlterNative,* 18:2, 225–34.

Knott, M. (2022) ' "Tick-a-boxes": Tackling the "growing problem" of who identifies as Aboriginal', *The Sydney Morning Herald*, 16 February, https://www.smh.com.au/national/tick-a-boxes-tackling-the-growing-problem-of-who-identifies-as-aboriginal-20220212-p59w0e.html (accessed 27 January 2023).

Liddle, C. (2014) 'Fair-skin Privilege? I'm sorry, but things are much more complicated than that', http://blackfeministranter.blogspot.com/2014/03/fair-skin-privilege-im-sorry-but-things.html (accessed 27 January 2023).

Márquez, G.G. (2014) *Of Love and Other Demons* (London: Penguin).

Muecke, S. (2021) 'Whitefella Magic: A Posthumanist Take on the Dark Emu Debate', *Overland*, https://overland.org.au/2021/08/whitefella-magic-a-posthumanist-take-on-thedark-emu-debate/ (accessed 16 August 2021).

Moreton-Robinson, A. (2011) 'Virtuous racial states: The possessive logic of patriarchal white sovereignty and the United Nations Declaration on the Rights of Indigenous Peoples', *Griffith Law Review*, 20:3, 641–58.

Moreton-Robinson, A. (2015) *The White Possessive: Property, Power, and Indigenous Sovereignty* (Minneapolis: University of Minnesota Press).

Morrison, T. (2004 [1987]) *Beloved* (New York: Vintage).

Morse, D. (2022) 'Peter Dutton says too many Aboriginal children aren't safe in their homes. The reality is so much worse', *ABC News On-Line*, 29 October, https://www.abc.net.au/news/2022-10-29/cassius-turvey-dutton-royal-commission-sexual-abuse-walk-home/101592104 (accessed 29 October 2022).

Neville, A.O. (1947) *Australia's Coloured Minority: Its Place in the Community* (Sydney: Currawong).

Newman, M. (2022) 'Rise of the race shifters, Governments are incentivising the growth of Aboriginal identity fraud', *Spectator/Australia* https://www.spectator.com.au/2022/08/rise-of-the-race-shifters/ (accessed 27 January 2023).

Pascoe, B. (2018) *Dark Emu: Aboriginal Australia and the Birth of Agriculture* (Broome: Magabala Books).

Read, P. (2006) *The Stolen Generations: The Removal of Aboriginal Children in New South Wales, 1883 to 1969* (Surry Hills: New South Wales Department of Aboriginal Affairs).

Reynolds, H. (2006) *The Other Side of the Frontier: Aboriginal Resistance to the European Invasion of Australia* (Sydney: UNSW Press).

Russell-Cook, M. (2021). 'DESTINY: the art of Destiny Deacon', NGV [National Gallery of Victoria], https://www.ngv.vic.gov.au/essay/destiny-the-art-of-destiny-deacon/ (accessed 10 January 2024).

Sartre, J-P., et al. (1948) *Anti-Semite and Jew* (New York: Schocken Books).

Sharpe, C. (2016) *In the Wake: On Blackness and Being* (Durham, NC: Duke University Press).

Sutton, P. and Walshe, K. (2021) *Farmers or Hunter-gatherers?: The Dark Emu Debate* (Melbourne: Melbourne University Press).

Taussig, M. (1987) *Shamanism, Colonialism, and the Wild Man: A Study in Terror and Healing* (Chicago, IL: University of Chicago Press).

Taussig, M. (1992) *The Nervous System* (London: Routledge).

Taussig, M. (1993) *Mimesis and Alterity: A Particular History of the* Senses (London: Routledge).

Turner, V. (1970) *The Forest of Symbols: Aspects of Ndembu Ritual* (Ithaca, NY: Cornell University Press).

Turner, V. and Abrahams, R.D. (2017 [1969]) *The Ritual Process: Structure and Anti-Structure* (London: Routledge).

van Gennep, A. (2019) *The Rites of Passage*, trans M.B. Vizedom and G.L. Caffee (Chicago, IL: University of Chicago Press).

Watego, C. (2021) *Another Day in the Colony* (St Lucia: University of Queensland Press).

Watson, I. (2015) *Aboriginal Peoples, Colonialism and International Law: Raw Law* (London: Routledge).

Wolfe, P. (1994) 'Nation and miscegenation: Discursive continuity in the post-Mabo era', *Social Analysis*, 36, 93–152.

Wolfe, P. (2001) 'Land, labor, and difference: Elementary structures of race', *American Historical Review*, 106:3, 866–905.

Wolfe, P. (2006) 'Settler Colonialism and the Elimination of the Native', *Journal of Genocide Research*, 8:4, 387–409.

12

The ambiguous path of self-cultivation in contemporary China

Gil Hizi

Introduction

Market-driven technologies for self-cultivation have expanded and become accessible to people in most walks of life in China, shaping life objectives and social responsibilities. Discursive practices such as self-help literature, psychotherapeutic workshops, public-speaking training, and commercial teaching of classical Chinese texts guide individuals in cultivating communicational and moral capacities. Nevertheless, self-cultivation is partly shaped by people's inconsistent standpoints and the multiplicity of ethical requirements, i.e. prescribed behaviours and roles in the realisation of models of personhood and sociality. In China today, the authority of state institutions coexists with demanding social obligations and the burden of individual responsibility for securing a livelihood. Moreover, individuals draw on various capitalist, socialist and more localised repertoires when configuring their ethical pathways. Thus, the capitalist tenets of self-cultivation tend to emerge within complex prescriptions, in addition to impasses in individuals' pursuit of financial security and social mobility. Young adults in China who engage with relevant practices and expertise seek to combat this puzzling reality and enhance their mastery over their life circumstances. However, these attempts often reify their challenge of achieving ethical coherence across social life by underlining conflicting subject positions as well as inconsistent ways of negotiating between them.

In this chapter, I focus on one interlocutor, Guo Feng, a 33-year-old divorcee whom I met in a workshop for communication skills run by a psychology centre. I depict her multiple ethical standpoints as she tries to embrace market ideologies while adjusting to other gendered and familial expectations. In her different engagements, she repeatedly attempts to configure how to enhance her self-esteem and moral competency, while negotiating with the oppressive aspects of both the labour system and heteronormative roles. Elsewhere (Hizi, 2021) I demonstrate how programmes for personal development in

China produce unique registers that individuals cannot easily transpose to behaviours and relationships outside workshops. Here, I look at more subtle variations of ethical prescriptions and subject positions in relation to self-cultivation practices and person-making more broadly. My argument highlights the limitation of Foucauldian governmentality in depicting person-making pursuits, notwithstanding its pivotal role in understanding social change and reproduction under capitalism. Anthropological applications of this model often imagine the person through value-laden snapshots from specific settings, thereby conflating the dynamic production of subjects with a fixed value system. While this Foucauldian application elucidates how power circulates across social realms through salient discourse, it downplays how individuals malleably perceive the multiple ethical prescriptions of their social worlds. This framework also risks disavowing the existential paradoxes that emerge through relevant discursive practices.

My analytical critique of governmentality is premised on a phenomenological analysis that attends ambiguity as a vital existential condition, accentuated under the moral complexity of industrial and post-industrial societies. I follow Simone de Beauvoir's (1962) seminal essay on 'ambivalence' in its attention to indeterminate aspects of the human condition, such as the dialectics of subject and object, agency and submission, factuality and becoming (in line with Sartre, 1966 [1943]), spirit and matter, singularity and sameness, to name a few axes. Clearly, the salience and significance of each of these pairs vary cross-culturally; de Beauvoir's recommendations for moral living, including her 'ethics of freedom', are notably inseparable from her own cultural perspective rather than offering a universally relevant model. Nonetheless, her theory serves as a general reminder for variations in individuals' standpoints vis-à-vis their social engagements, as well as their attempts to perceptively essentialise their position in denial of this dynamic flux. Ambiguity emerges from the plurality of ethical positions, as well as the futility of frameworks that seek to achieve coherence across social life, instead underscoring indeterminacy. Ambiguity, moreover, becomes an object of frequent reflection and intervention for people who draw on expertise that guides their person-making pursuits.

This chapter illuminates how this ambiguity of existence manifests vis-à-vis market-driven perspectives. Guo Feng's engagement with self-cultivation and her reflections on her ethical positions demonstrate how an abstract notion of self-reliant person-making may take different forms and valences through the nexus of material concerns, workplace hierarchies and familial roles. The variations are contingent on movement across social settings and tasks, along with the relational position that emerges through specific interactions. Following Henrietta Moore's (2007: 41) concept of 'multiply constituted subject', people respond to different cultural influences and powerful institutions in their becoming, as they 'identify with and take up different subject positions at different times'. Guo Feng, like most of my interlocutors, demonstrates how these layers intertwine, at times producing positive feedback in the reinforcement of market-driven trajectories, at times sequestrating priorities or domains and at times denouncing capitalist prescriptions altogether. These indeterminacies reveal the limitation of teleological paradigms for person-making and the crucial role of ethnography in depicting these processes in high resolution.

Pedagogies and agendas of self-cultivation in contemporary China

Self-cultivation (*xiuyang* or *xiushen*) has a long history in China. In rough lines, most Confucian schools of thought stipulated self-cultivation in tandem with the becoming of a person (*zuo ren*) who is morally accomplished through the fulfilment of social roles and perfections of key relationships across different life stages. Daoist and Buddhist schools expanded prescriptions for self-cultivation to ascetic practices that diverge from conventional lifepaths (Munro, 1969). In the twentieth century, these traditions have altered, transformed through the dominant political forces that coupled person-making with the construction of the new nation and later the communist revolution. Since the 1980s and the onset of economic reforms, self-cultivation has coincided with new material imperatives and competitive apparatuses.

In the past four decades, market-driven forms of self-cultivation have expanded from targeting immediate material imperatives to fostering new perceptions of wellbeing and social competency. Through my ethnographic work among young adults in urban China in 2015–16, I encountered individuals who attend numerous workshops and read expansive advice literature, while also engaging with bigger philosophical and political questions about education, ethics and social development. In the 1990s, many of the emerging practices of self-cultivation addressed the imperative of adjusting to the new economy. A genre of 'success studies' (*chenggong xue*) took over the shelves in bookstores, including translations of foreign texts and local guides on becoming rich and savvy. These texts promote an entrepreneurial and wealth-seeking spirit, which is often embodied in the authors' personae, shedding off more communal or socialist ethics (Davies, 2007). In addition, industries for extracurricular training have developed, fuelling a competitive market where people have sought to expand their skillset as well as gain instant training for specific jobs.

These processes have continued to expand in the 2000s, while being gradually supplemented with discourses about wellbeing and morality.

From the perspective of urban citizens, the demand for self-reliance had already become somewhat commonsensical, now seeking to accomplish a more balanced and wholesome sense of wellbeing. From the perspective of the state, this shift coincided with the aim of making Chinese citizens more emotionally resilient as they continue to increase their productivity, while signalling a 'civilised' and 'modern' nation. One key initiative has been a series of reforms in public education, known as 'education for quality' (*suzhi jiaoyu*), that set to foster more creative and independent individuals at the expense of disciplinary conformity and rote memorisation (Anagnost, 2008; Woronov, 2009). Another state-driven initiative that prompted the evolving model of citizenship has been the expansion of psychotherapy. In what is known in the scholarship as the Chinese 'psycho-boom' (Kleinman, 2010; Huang, 2013), the state established counselling services, public education curricula, entertainment programmes, self-help literature, and an examination system that accelerated counsellor certification.

Self-cultivation in China, thus, indicates a trajectory that resonates with much of the capitalist world in its turn towards self-reliant citizenship and emotional disclosure via commodified expertise. Yet these developments do not fully reflect Chinese citizens' range of concerns. This is exemplified in Heart's Secret, a privately run centre in the city of Jinan where I conducted fieldwork. Heart's Secret coordinates psychological workshops that focus on communication skills and emotional wellbeing. Licensed counsellors draw on insights from humanistic or positive psychology while inviting participants to express themselves more 'genuinely' and pay attention to their 'inner' emotional realm. This process is conceived by most attendees as conducive to the actualisation of their individual self as well as inducing self 'growth' (*chengzhang*). Participants, most of whom are in their thirties, appreciate psychotherapy and incorporate its main tenets in their worldviews. About two-thirds of them are also licensed counsellors, yet only a handful work in the field. Instead, they treat counselling as a backup career option, while some wish to foster skills helpful for their existing job and others simply see the training as a form of self-help (see also Zhang, 2020). The value of the workshops in relation to participants' everyday concerns is also indistinct and, at times, questionable. Many participants treat Heart's Secret as a refuge from the pressures of routine, including the lack of ability to identify their individuality through their obligations as employees, parents, spouses or filial children.

Thus, while participants in Heart's Secret embrace person-centred values, they also regard them as ethically alien to most of their relationships and tasks. These doubts mirror dilemmas at the level of state policy. In public education for example, despite the initial aspiration to reduce the significance of exams via 'education for quality', high-school and college entrance examinations continue to set the tone in the path to educational and occupational success. Similarly, the seemingly individualistic potentials of psychology have been conducive in China for authoritarian forms of governance and control (Yang, 2015; Zhang, 2020). These gaps between designated expertise and practice in China are not an exception to an otherwise coherence between forms of self-cultivation, everyday ethics and models of personhood under global capitalism, but rather illustrate the contingent relationship between these elements across people's social engagement. As Nicholas Long (2018: 90) recommends, when anthropologists examine the globalisation of expertise, they must note when and how people employ their learning, including how they sustain attachment to techniques that have a limited effect on their lives.

The wider setting of this chapter is Jinan, the provincial capital of Shandong in northeastern China. The prefecture of Jinan is currently populated by nearly nine million residents, among whom nearly one-third are rural migrants (Jinan's People's Government, 2020). Outside several coastal metropolises, Jinan is the biggest occupational and industrial hub in Shandong, even if it is still not among the 'first-tier' cities according to official standards in terms of size and economic development. Jinan is also known for its strong Confucian heritage due to its proximity to the hometowns of Confucius and Mencius, and the ongoing imprint of their doctrines in the region in different historical periods. Most residents, Guo Feng included, identify 'traditional' values such as filial piety, fixed gender roles, esteem for education and practices of 'saving face' (*mianzi*) to be particularly preeminent in this region. This somewhat fatalistic view reinstates for them the dilemmas about the application of new values and the prospects for social change.

Guo Feng's dilemmas

I first met Guo Feng in October 2015 during an afternoon seminar at Heart's Secret titled 'The Ideal Self' (*lixiang ziwo*). The instructor, a psychologist named Jiang Cheng, facilitated a discussion where he invited participants to reflect upon their expectations of themselves. He identified how fixed norms and responsibilities led participants to deny their individual desires and possibilities. Guo Feng had just joined the centre for a six-month membership. During this session, she talked assertively about the pressure she felt as a result of her father's ongoing criticism of her marital status. She mentioned his comments about her supposedly 'inflexible' attitude in her life choices and her failure to find a new husband. After inputs from fellow participants, Jiang suggested that Guo Feng recognises that she is a 'strong' and 'irregular' (*bu zhengchang*) woman. He added that she should engage more with psychology and through this discover what drives her behaviour and relationship patterns. Guo Feng was left quite perplexed; Jiang seemed to suggest that she accepts herself, and another peer further restated this message in optimistic tones, but she could not help but feel criticised for her character and temperament.

Guo Feng was a self-proclaimed 'nü hanzi' (literal meaning 'manly woman'), a popular term in China for strong-willed and somewhat masculine women, varying in its connotation from a neutral depiction of youthful tomboy dispositions to the condemnation of aggressivity (Baidu, 2021). Guo Feng, a tall woman who owned an apartment and drove a scooter for transportation, associated this term with her outspoken and friendly attitude along with her ability to smilingly adjust to different social circumstances. In this respect, she felt like a youthful 'outlier', not conforming thoughtlessly to gender conventions in terms of career choices and interpersonal demeanour. At the time I met her, she was contemplating getting her second tattoo, an uncommon sight in Jinan, with the English-language motto 'stay young, stay foolish', a reminder to maintain her unique style without being hindered by external pressures. She supplements this attitude with an increasing passion for travel. Through a travel group that catered to people her age, she had been on two journeys to west China and dreamt about going overseas. As a woman who had left an unhappy marriage and earns her livelihood in the private sector – working first in the marketing of an extracurricular school for young children, later in the marketing of a cinema complex – she perceived herself as embodying a timely spirit of self-development.

Psychology is one of various self-help methods which Guo Feng exercises to buttress her self-reliant approach. From the time I met her, she has been regularly reading advice literature and considering new techniques for self-cultivation. There was a period when she mostly read guides for triumphing in the private economy. Later, she decided to stop reading 'superficial' (*fuqian*) books of 'success studies'. She turned to listening to daily recordings of 'Logical Thinking' (*luoji siwei*), an online service that offers short lectures on practical and effective attitudes towards everyday problems by businessman and motivational speaker Luo Zhenyu (De Dao, 2021). She had also read Lao zi's *Dao de Jing*, Sun zi's *Art of War* and books in translation on 'rational thinking'. For her, this content moved beyond 'instant success' to expanding her horizons and fostering 'new ways of thinking'. As for psychology, Guo Feng saw a connection between market-driven competency and mental resilience which she hoped to address through her learning. Yet she has another reason for learning psychology: being more prepared to excel in her future romantic relationship. In her previous marriage, which lasted five years, she found herself in constant quarrels with her mother-in-law while her husband was passive. She does not want to reproduce this problem in the future and hopes she might become less 'stubborn' (*guzhi*), so she could eventually happily re-marry.

Guo Feng's endeavours coincide with market demands. In an era where most Chinese do not experience lifelong occupational security through the state sector, and are not aided by their work unit to find a spouse as was the custom in the past, women like Guo Feng must find their path more independently. These practical adjustments are accompanied by the celebration of an entrepreneurial ethos, which for Guo Feng is embodied in Steve Jobs and Chinese hi-tech tycoons. But for Guo Feng these entrepreneurial values do not reflect or produce a uniform social reality. Outside her career path, she finds less congruence between this ethos and her objectives, especially when facing increasing criticism from family and friends on her divorcee status. Market-driven attitudes fail to produce optimal outcomes in her career and cannot sustain a coherent framework for person-making across social life, thus producing a sense of 'inconclusiveness', as described by Cabrera Torrecilla (this volume), in the experience of social change. In light of this indeterminacy, it is often unclear to Guo Feng which aspects of her behaviour she should endorse and which she should reject. Her engagement in self-cultivation accentuates her unsettling self-examination, in addition to producing moments of excitement and 'complacency'. This duality intensified when the extracurricular school where she worked shut down in late 2015. Facing job interviews, including employers' suspicions that possible marriage plans would obstruct her professionalism, as well as implicit criticism about her character, her stress achieved new heights, which she shared with me:

> I went to the training in this tea business I told you about, I learned some new techniques, but I felt oppressed (*yayi*), having to be quiet. The owner told me later I lack the right temperament (*qizhi*), that I am not calm (*chenwen*) enough … I have friends around me telling me I should change my behaviour. I didn't have these thoughts for a while, now I am increasingly puzzled (*mimang*). In small private businesses I can fit maybe, but in foreign or state enterprises (*waiqi, guoqi*) one needs to be more enduring of unpleasant situations (*fuzhong*).

Guo Feng's 'puzzle' is a combination of market pressures and patriarchal values. Her independence and outspoken attitude are configured as the wrong 'temperament', despite their imagined liberating potential (see Hizi, 2018). More generally, Guo Feng's predicament, stemming from indeterminism, demonstrates how ambiguity becomes a meaningful existential condition that undermines any attempt to form a coherent ethical framework across social life, especially in the context of market-driven self-cultivation in China.

The process of becoming, for Guo Feng, is directed towards certain ideals and objectives. Yet, in line with de Beauvoir, there are always multiple forces that impact self-understanding and produce new lived priorities. In addition to navigating different cultural inputs, Guo Feng moves between different forms of agency, including acting upon the world proactively, dreaming of alternative life trajectories, protecting herself from negative feedback, and submitting to others' demands. These competing forces occasionally appear as irresolvable conflicts, and occasionally as co-existing possibilities within single and idealised enterprises.

Once, in a moment demonstrating her conflicting drives, Guo Feng stated that she dreamed of owning a store for handmade artefacts, which would allow her to live a relaxed and spiritual life. She used the Buddhist concepts of 'withdrawing from the world' (*chushi*) and 'experiencing the actual world' (*rushi*) in imagining a lifestyle of 'withdrawal from the world while engaging with the real world' (*yong chushi de xintai zuo rushi de shiqing*). She construed her market-driven desires through these concepts while expressing an ascetic drive to supersede contemporary materialism.[1] Thus, even within her entrepreneurial ambition, Guo Feng expresses puzzling dualisms of proactivity–passivity and matter–spirit. She could not fully demarcate herself in practice or symbolically as exterior to the seemingly corrupt norms of the actual world, comparable with the Serbian activists described by Steindl-Kopf (this volume), notwithstanding her ongoing self-development. Drawing on a neoliberal ethos, she also tries to produce space and time for pursuing values that extend beyond business and even individualised self-realisation.

Contingent subject positions amidst market expansion

The ethical positions of young people in China are subject to the pull of various cultural models, ideologies and model pragmatic requirements, as well as varying across social domains, moments and relationships. Individuals who are less explicitly affected than Guo Feng by the turmoil of the job market, such as many members of Heart's Secret who have more familial stability, pronounce market principles in moments that drastically counteracted in their view the gravity of their everyday engagements. Some individuals who work in the state sector comment on the static nature of their job; others emphasise the imposition of social networks that limit any potential for individualised expression (cf. Osburg, 2013); still others see their familial roles as their primary identity from which acts of self-cultivation are a temporary escape. As Brian Harmon (2014) notes, based on a study of feasting in Chengdu, the 'hegemonic' status of 'symbolic individualism' as a cultural ideal in urban China is not congruent with actual possibilities for individualistic perceptions and behaviours in social life. This chasm is relevant in China for various person-centred values and ethoses. Thus, even when dealing with powerful globalised market forces, an accurate depiction of reality requires attention to indeterminacy and nuance, as emphasised in de Beauvoir's (1962: 8–9) critique of 'doctrines' that discount complexity:

> At the present time there still exist many doctrines which choose to leave in the shadow certain troubling aspects of a too complex situation. But their attempt to lie to us is in vain. Cowardice doesn't pay. Those reasonable metaphysics, those consoling ethics with which they would like to entice us only accentuate the disorder from which we suffer. Men of today seem to feel more acutely than ever the paradox of their condition.

Much of the scholarship on changing subjectivities in contemporary China employs the concept of neoliberal governmentality as developed by Foucault. In the last two to three decades, this approach has become dominant in anthropology, particularly when examining economically changing societies shaped by global capitalist technologies. Foucault emphasised how subject positions premised on calculated 'productivity' and the self-management of seemingly inner resources have expanded via dominant institutions, while being reproduced through people's actions and priorities. It is a process where the 'freedom' of the market is shaped by state interventions that constantly prescribe behaviours and dispositions while directing individuals to configure them as means and objects of self-realisation (Foucault, 2010: 130.

These ideas are useful in anthropology since they allow room for exploring processes of institutional and moral change in everyday life without necessarily assuming specific endpoints in terms of policy implementation or individual accomplishments (or failures). In China, the applications of this theory do not preclude cosmological and political holdovers from earlier periods. Aihwa Ong and Li Zhang (2008: 7) argue that 'neoliberal forms of self-management' in China are 'actually helping to sustain socialist rule'. In their view, the fact that the state restricts citizens' actions and expressions through coercive measures (censorship, nationalistic campaigns) does not counteract the potency of neoliberal governance in other domains. Indeed, many ethnographies have illuminated how livelihoods and social mobility in China have become increasingly tied to the responsible acts of individuals and households (e.g. Anagnost, 2008; Otis, 2011; Woronov, 2009; Yan, 2008). These accounts spotlight spaces where market technologies predominate, or where they blend with other apparatuses without losing their command. Thus, while for some scholars the Chinese state's overt social engineering is in stark contrast with the 'neoliberal' model (Kipnis, 2007; Palmer and Winiger, 2019), others identify autocratic power as corresponding to Foucault's emphasis on state intervention.

My aim here is not to discuss whether China is 'neoliberal', a debate that extends beyond the Foucauldian perspective and my data, but rather to reflect on the analytical temptation to assert coherence through paramount theoretical paradigms. Clearly, if neoliberalism equates social actors' general attempt to enhance 'self-mastery' in unpredictable situations (Dardot and Laval, 2014: 271), then it could be easily applied to most of the world's population. Yet technologies that induce existential mastery over, or immunity from, quotidian immorality have been evident in myriad religious or semi-religious practices of self-cultivation in China and abroad (e.g. Yang, 2011: 28; Ewing, 1997). Moreover, these practices often emerge in strong relation to competing priorities. Therefore, the scholarly challenge is to depict how social transformations affect and are enacted by people without presuming a fixed hierarchy of values and/or clear-cut social trajectories (we should also remember that it is contingency that leads us to wide-ranging theories to begin with). Overall, both positivist discourses of personal empowerment and critical theories that equate existence to overarching social structure tend to 'leave in the shadow', in de Beauvoir's terms, complexity and lived paradoxes.

The different ways that Guo Feng embodies market-driven imperatives are in dialogue with various ethical prescriptions that are not shaped by the economy. In my descriptions above, she emphasises the oppressive side of family members and employers who require that she change her dispositions, but at other times Guo Feng also associates these demands with moral virtues. She is particularly concerned with becoming more filial towards her parents by supporting them, avoiding quarrels and realising the life stages of marriage and motherhood. Although the virtue of filial piety (*xiaoshun*) has undergone dramatic changes in China along with market-driven birth restrictions that shifted households' support towards the younger generations (Fong, 2004), the parent–child relationship is still reconfigured through expectations of filial piety, and moreover, young people's material success is often conducive to fostering this relationship (Yan, 2016). Accordingly, Guo Feng sometimes treats her career as a channel for filiality by becoming independent (in tandem with her fantasy about withdrawing from the world – being '*chushi*') and later supporting her parents financially. Thus, while she often complains that her father's criticism of her divorcee status and 'impractical' career direction is 'narrow-minded', she expresses understanding towards his 'justified' concern, notwithstanding her vulnerability.

Ethical positions are dynamic and relational, and the market economy tends to further induce these attributes. Yan Yunxiang (2017) conceptualises the process of *becoming a person* in China through the triple dimensions of self-interest, moral self-reflection and fulfilling ethical roles through relational and altruistic acts. Nan Lin's (1988) earlier study shows how these aspects may manifest differently in different spheres in China, whereby the family is a site for mutual sacrifice compared to the instrumentality of social ties outside the household. Ellen Oxfeld (1992) extends this argument by showing how these different priorities may co-emerge as competing values (or 'voices') within individuals' ambivalent evaluation of their and others' acts. In Guo Feng's reflections, her career and personal development coexist with the imperative of filial piety, taking various meanings and priorities at different moments, at times appearing as polar agendas and sometimes as goals that can be jointly realised through her resourceful approach. Rather than dividing different endeavours into discrete cultural inputs, Guo Feng's experience demonstrates how variants of subject positions constantly emerge, taking dominance in particular situations while also reconfigured in relation to alternative concerns. The valence of ethical stances also develops through dialogue with changing circumstances, as well as through actual conversations with people, as elaborated next.

Shifting positions in social interactions

Variation in standpoints and ethical priorities, in addition to depending on life situations (such as loss of job), emerge through dynamic social interactions. In interactions, Guo Feng embodies relational positions that can heighten existing concerns or enable her to expand her self-perception. As Katherine Ewing (2006: 99) suggests, *conversations*, which she discusses in the context of interviewing research interlocutors, are not ways of discerning and presenting fixed knowledge but rather 'a fluid zone of intertextualities', where speakers constantly create meanings and identities through associations, references and activated memories. Furthermore, even when interlocutors utter culturally circulated scripts, this act shapes their position and impetuses vis-à-vis specific interactions.

In my meetings with Guo Feng, my presence frequently elicited statements about Chinese cultural norms and their 'conservative' nature, along with personal ambitions with a cosmopolitan flavour. Almost every time we met, for example, she mentioned her 'shame' that she cannot speak English and that we must converse in Chinese. When other people were present – work colleagues, friends and even waitresses – she would emphasise this message to their ears with glimpses of amusement and embarrassment. In our conversations, in particular during the first two months of our communication, Guo Feng tended to stress the dichotomy she perceived between the seemingly open-minded 'foreign' culture and 'Chinese' 'conservativism'. For example, she regarded me as an ambassador of a mobile travel-driven lifestyle, whereas Chinese culture, according to her view, prioritised a more sedentary sense of security, notwithstanding the immense rural to urban migration in today's China (interestingly, Guo

Feng iterated an idiom by Confucian sage Mencius on the positive attitude towards travel, '*bu yuan qian li*', literally meaning 'not regard one thousand li as a long distance'). When I told her that my mother had been doing ceramics since she retired, Guo Feng reacted with wonder and similarly associated this fact with the ability of 'your people' (*nimen*) to transcend practical concerns and bypass fixed life trajectories.[2]

As our encounter prolonged, Guo Feng shared with me more diverse perspectives on values of person-making and the expectations of her social circles. Moreover, the fact that I was still somewhat secluded from her social entourage allowed her to share with me thoughts without fear of repercussion or criticism. One of the turning points was a meeting we had at a local antique market. She was surprised I chose to meet in such a 'messy' site, in her words, and moreover that I had visited this place several times before. She said that she would not have offered to meet me in this market due to our previous encounters in 'civilised' (*wenming*) spaces, such as workshops, cafés and shopping malls. Yet she shared her fondness for the place and recalled the childhood days she spent there with her father when he was collecting and selling old artefacts. Through these types of encounters, the ways she talked about what she saw as 'traditional' values gradually altered. If in our first meetings she incorporated long-standing concepts and idioms either in reference to 'conservative' tradition or through her configuration of market-driven and person-centred values, in our later encounters she embraced some of these mores as virtues. This is when she began pronouncing the merit of filial piety.

This interactive dynamic both accentuates specific perspectives through relational comparison or contrast and enables individuals to explore the various possibilities in their person-making trajectory, in line with Moore's (2007: 41) concept of 'multiply constituted subject'. This dynamism is often perplexing, but it also experientially configures indeterminacy less as a hazard and more as an ethical journey. For Guo Feng, while different characters represented different objectives (girlfriends and relatives were associated with her inability to find a spouse while workshop peers epitomised the priority of individualised emotional wellbeing), her interlocutors are not static symbols for certain worldviews; conversations also allowed Guo Feng to examine new opportunities in regard to her perceived expectations. This was evident even in her interactions with her father, the most intimidating figure in her life. While the frequent recountings of her conversations with him tended to be gloomy, sometimes their bond emerged in a more uplifting fashion, as she once shared with me:

> I went with my father to visit his brother in the countryside near Rizhao (east Shandong). I thought it would be another annoying (*naoren*) encounter, where my dad would get upset with me. But getting out of the city was good for us;

driving, talking, listening to a comedy skit on the radio ... Then in the evening we went for a walk near my uncle's house. Our talks weren't about the same boring topics. At one point, I even got to tell him about some of my business dreams.

Guo Feng continued by saying it made her hopeful to see she can connect with her father. She did not expect a breakthrough in terms of his demands, but she was looking forward to more moments like this.

Another time, I observed Guo Feng shift from a stressful to a more uplifting interaction during a dinner with work colleagues. I met her after an activity at Heart's Secret; she was frustrated that she did not blend well with the core members and ate alone during the lunch break. We headed towards a hot-pot dinner in a shopping complex nearby, where we met three of her colleagues. They were very responsive to her comments and jokes, which combined some self-mockery with remarks on a popular TV show, food and other colleagues. She seemed increasingly relaxed and assertive. 'They are good fellows, they make me smile, I should hang out with them outside work more often,' she later texted. In this way, Guo Feng tends to identify in her interactions her ability to impact others and her relational position vis-à-vis others. These interactions also accentuate or ease her pressures regarding her projects and status. Within the process of becoming under multiple moral inputs, individuals seek both to enhance their existential mastery and find opportunities to refashion themselves vis-à-vis ideals, qualities and personae. The predicament of ambiguity opens and closes ethical pathways while rarely experienced as a desired or sustainable condition.

Conclusion

This chapter has demonstrated how pursuits and prescriptions of person-making can be laden with indeterminacy, even as they follow trajectories of structural change. Young adults in China draw on multiple cultural resources as they configure how to enact themselves and which values to nurture in different situations. These individuals tend to frequently probe their ethical priorities – how to be a good employee, career person, spouse, child and parent, and reflect on their agency and wellbeing vis-à-vis different options. Their perceptions correspond with broader existential tensions that individuals experience globally, albeit in different valences, between their individuality and the social world (Jackson, 1998: 54), by which their singularity may be both fulfilled and denied through relational undertakings. Under the growing command of the market economy, individuals face ever more conflicting prescriptions of subject-making, where some of these requirements stem from norms external to capitalism, and where desires for independence do not merely reflect capitalist ideals but can seek to combat overwhelming pressures. Thus, capitalism and its associated practices of self-cultivation do not so much materialise into a clear telos of person-making as they reinforce existential ambiguity.

In their attempts to address and combat ambiguity, my interlocutors often accentuate, dichotomise and essentialise their ethical standpoints to prompt their agency or make their endeavours intelligible. This resonates with de Beauvoir's (1962: 45–8) description of the 'serious man', a character that committedly asserts the moral certitude of its acts, to the degree that it sees its enterprises as epitomising the highest virtue and necessity while every external or competing approach is cast as unjust. This laborious rejection of doubt in given moments, according to de Beauvoir, curtails life's potential. This critique is a constant reminder for any enterprise that involves aspiration and heightened purpose, including intellectual attempts to theorise the vicissitudes of social life by employing conceptual trajectories that make their findings 'significant' and communicable, while demonstrating their expertise. My argument clearly adheres to de Beauvoir's critique, yet my findings also show that this narrowing of meaning through objectifying the social reality is to some degree inevitable in interpersonal interactions. While these reductionist acts limit people's degree of ethical 'freedom', in de Beauvoir's terms, they allow people to make sense of their social worlds, expand and accommodate them, and constitute social institutions (see Lambek, 2015: 79). As anthropologists, it is essential to acknowledge multiplicity as an empirical condition and incorporate it in the narratives we produce, as well as to note how our interlocutors perceive and act upon them. Ambiguity thus emerges at once as possibilities and obstacles to social practice, prompting responses that tend to both suspend and reinforce its command on social life.

Notes

1 In Chinese philosophy, '*rushi*' and '*chushi*' present polar attitudes to life, the former often associated with Confucian ethics and the latter with more monastic or ascetic pursuits. One of the earlier descriptions of *chushi* appears in the poem 'Returning Home to the Countryside' (*gui yuantian ju*) of Tao Yuanming from the late fourth century CE which coincided with earlier Buddhist influences in China during the Eastern Jin Dynasty (317–420) (Tao, 2009). A dialectic of *rushi* and *chushi* is also associated with the work of twentieth-century philosopher and political reformer Liang Shuming (see Zhang, 2009).

2 The dichotomies that Guo Feng expressed circulate in China in various popular, business and intellectual discourses, reinforcing a modernist ethos that identifies the 'self-inhibiting' attributes of local cultural norms, particularly those pertaining to social hierarchies and familial roles.

References

Anagnost, A. (2008) 'From "Class" to "Social Strata": Grasping the Social Totality in Reform-Era China', *Third World Quarterly*, 29:3, 497–519.

Baidu, B. (2021) 'Nü Hanzi', Baidu.Com, https://baike.baidu.com/item/%E5%A5%B3%E6%B1%89%E5%AD%90/3263563 (accessed 14 June 2021).

Dardot, P. and C. Laval (2014) *The New Way of the World: On Neoliberal Society* (London: Verso).

Davies, D.J. (2007) 'Wal-Mao: The Discipline of Corporate Culture and Studying Success at Wal-Mart China', *The China Journal*, 58, 1–27.

de Beauvoir, S. (1962) *The Ethics of Ambiguity*, trans. B. Frechtman (Secaucus, NJ: Citadel Press).

De D. (2021) 'Siwei Zaowu (Thought Forces)', Beijing Mind Creation Information Technology Co., www.igetget.com/ (accessed 14 June 2021).

Ewing, K.P. (1997) *Arguing Sainthood: Modernity, Psychoanalysis, and Islam* (Durham, NC: Duke University Press).

Ewing, K.P. (2006) 'Revealing and Concealing: Interpersonal Dynamics and the Negotiation of Identity in the Interview', *Ethos*, 34:1, 89–122.

Fong, V.L. (2004) *Only Hope: Coming of Age under China's One-Child Policy* (Palo Alto, CA: Stanford University Press).

Foucault, M. (2010) *The Birth of Biopolitics: Lectures at the Collège de France, 1978–1979*, Trans. Graham Burchell (New York: Picador).

Harmon, B. (2014) 'The Crisscrossed Agency of a Toast: Personhood, Individuation and De-Individuation in Luzhou, China', *Australian Journal of Anthropology*, 25:3, 357–72.

Hizi, G. (2018) 'Gendered Self-Improvement: Autonomous Personhood and the Marriage Predicament of Young Women in Urban China', *Asia Pacific Journal of Anthropology*, 19:4, 298–315.

Hizi, G. (2021) 'Zheng Nengliang and Pedagogies of Affect in Contemporary Urban China', *Social Analysis*, 65:1, 23–43.

Huang, H-Y. (2013) 'Psycho-Boom: The Rise of Psychotherapy in Contemporary Urban China', PhD dissertation (Harvard University).

Jackson, M. (1998) *Minima Ethnographica: Intersubjectivity and the Anthropological Project* (Chicago, IL: University of Chicago Press).

Jinan's People's Government (2020) 'General Survey of Jinan (Jinan Gaikuan)' (Jinan, China: Jinan's People's Government), www.jinan.gov.cn/col/col129/index.html (accessed 15 April 2021).

Kipnis, A. (2007) 'Neoliberalism Reified: Suzhi Discourse and Tropes of Neoliberalism in the People's Republic of China', *Journal of the Royal Anthropological Institute*, 13:2, 383–400.

Kleinman, A. (2010) 'Remaking the Moral Person in China: Implications for Health', *The Lancet*, 375:9720, 1074–5.

Lambek, M. (2015) 'Both/And', in Michael Jackson and Albert Piette (eds), *What is Existential Anthropology?* (New York and Oxford: Berghahn Books), 58–83.

Lin, N. (1988) 'Chinese Family Structure and Chinese Society', *Bulletin of the Institute of Ethnology Academia Sinica*, 65, 59–129.

Long, N.J. (2018) 'Suggestions of Power: Searching for Efficacy in Indonesia's Hypnosis Boom', *Ethos*, 46:1, 70–94.

Moore, H.L. (2007) *The Subject of Anthropology: Gender, Symbolism and Psychoanalysis* (London: Polity).

Munro, D.J. (1969) *The Concept of Man in Early China* (Palo Alto, CA: Stanford University Press).

Ong, A. and L. Zhang (2008) 'Introduction: Privatizing China; Powers of Self, Socialism from Afar', in Li Zhang and Aihwa Ong (eds), *Privatizing China: Socialism from Afar* (Ithaca, NY: Cornell University Press), 1–19.

Osburg, J. (2013) *Anxious Wealth: Money and Morality among China's New Rich* (Palo Alto, CA: Stanford University Press).

Otis, E. (2011) *Markets and Bodies: Women, Service Work, and the Making of Inequality in China* (Palo Alto, CA: Stanford University Press).

Oxfeld, E. (1992) 'Individualism, Holism, and the Market Mentality: Notes on the Recollections of a Chinese Entrepreneur', *Cultural Anthropology*, 7:3, 267–300.

Palmer, D.A. and F. Winiger (2019) 'Neo-Socialist Governmentality: Managing Freedom in the People's Republic of China', *Economy and Society*, 48:4, 554–78.

Sartre, J.-P. (1966 [1943]) *Being and Nothingness*, Trans. Hazel E. Barnes (New York: Washington Square).

Tao, Y. (2009) 'Gui Yuantian Ju' (Returning Home to the Countryside), *Zhonghua Huoye Wenxuan: Gaoyi Nianji Ban* (China's Leaflet Anthology: High-School First Grade Edition), 11, 50–2.

Woronov, T.E. (2009) 'Governing China's Children: Governmentality and "Education for Quality"', *Positions*, 17:3, 567–89.

Yan, H. (2008) *New Masters, New Servants: Migration, Development, and Women Workers in China* (Durham, NC: Duke University Press).

Yan, Y. (2016) 'Intergenerational Intimacy and Descending Familism in Rural North China', *American Anthropologist*, 118:2, 244–57.

Yan, Y. (2017) 'Doing Personhood in Chinese Culture: The Desiring Individual, Moralist Self and Relational Person', *Cambridge Journal of Anthropology*, 35:2, 1–17.

Yang, J. (2015) *Unknotting the Heart: Unemployment and Therapeutic Governance in China* (Ithaca, NY: Cornell University Press).

Yang, M.M-H. (2011) 'Postcoloniality and Religiosity in Modern China: The Disenchantments of Sovereignty', Theory, Culture & Society, 28:2, 3–44.

Zhang, L. (2020) Anxious China: Inner Revolution and Politics of Psychotherapy (Oakland: University of California Press).

Zhang, W. (2009) 'Liang Shuming and Buddhist Studies', Contemporary Chinese Thought, 40:3, 67–90.

13

Ontological ambiguity: crisis, hyperfiction and social narratives in postmodern Japan

Angélica Cabrera Torrecilla

Introduction

This chapter argues that, within the period of postmodernity, fiction entered into everyday life through globalisation, speculative capital, technology, and the increase of non-places. Fiction frames reality as hyperfictional, leading to time-space alterations that put the self in a state of ambiguity, or what I call ontological ambiguity. I propose a critical study of Japanese postmodernity through recourse to hyperfiction, taking Yasutaka Tsutsui's (1934) novel *Paprika* (2018 [1993]) as an example, known internationally due to its eponymous anime-adaptation in 2006 by Satoshi Kon (Cabrera, 2019). Set in Tokyo, the novel tells the story of a group of scientists who develop a technological device allowing psychotherapists to enter patients' dreams to record and analyse them. A conflict arises when the device is stolen and used to hack into the dreamworld and the patients' subconscious to manipulate them. Dreams then materialise and appear in the form of a street parade. Consequently, the uncertainty of *not-knowing* how to differentiate between sleep and wakefulness ensues. A large-scale psychosocial crisis emerges, ruining the mental health of Tokyo, turning the city into a kind of non-place through the manifestation of a plane absent from an overall spatial and temporal significance in an anthropological sense. Through these events – the dream parade and the transformation of Tokyo – I develop a theoretical analysis of ontological ambiguity.[1]

Paprika can be read in allegorical terms as a criticism of the effects of postmodernity on the Japanese people. I use the liminality concept, defined as a transitional time which 'involves a destruction of previous norms' (Thomassen, 2014: 83), to unpack the sense of the unknown. Liminality enables us to examine ontological ambiguity, which I suggest has resulted from the transition to postmodernity. It defines the time-space disturbance that comes from the transformation of reality into hyperfictionality, affecting the way social narratives are constructed and leading to an ambiguous sense of self. Ontological ambiguity will serve as an analytical guideline to discuss links between ambivalence and apocalyptic narratives, social anxiety, dreamlike feelings, collective imagination and world-building. This guideline helps us to pay attention to the influence that hyperfiction exerts on everyday life, providing frameworks for rethinking complex situations in times of crisis. Throughout, I highlight a theoretical stance in which literature is entangled with anthropology (Caughey, 1984; Barber, 2007; Behar, 2009) and 'has proven to be one of anthropology's most enduring companions in thought' (Brandel, 2020: 1). The process of reading a world within a literary work opens the possibility of observing cultural projections and allowing for the promotion of an interdisciplinary perspective. *Paprika* shows how literature ponders different literary criticisms and anthropological concerns related to disturbances in the perception of time and place due to the cultural changes amidst postmodernity from a non-Western context: concerns – affecting social narratives – that can be grouped into multiple and related forms of ontological ambiguity, such as the sense of non-conclusion as an eternal-present mode of expression, and as liminal in-betweenness due to an impediment for defining spatial relations.

To fully understand what is meant by hyperfiction and ontological ambiguity in the context of this chapter, it is necessary to first contextualise the intertwining of economic and psychosocial crises in Japan between the 1970s and 1990s. During this period, abrupt changes had profound effects on the understanding of being and its reality, experienced through Japan's rapid political-economic shift after World War II: its fast postwar recovery, becoming an economic and technological power from the 1960s to the early 1980s, its transition from modernity to postmodernity in the 1970s, and its sudden economic collapse in the 1990s, as will be further explained. The experience of intense change was visible in Japan, above all, in the social perception of time-space, perceived as a constant hyper-acceleration without a clear narrative. Inspired by the French theorists Baudrillard and Lyotard, the contemporary cultural sociologist Masachi Ōsawa claims that Japan experienced a cultural discontinuity divided into two periods: the idealistic age (from 1945 to 1970) in which ideals came true in the real world, and the fictional age (from 1970 to 1995) in which socio-political ideals and the narrative of progress became fiction (in Tanaka, 2014: 45). This last age coincides with and describes Japanese postmodernity. Ōsawa illustrates the fictional age through the success of Japanese hyperrealistic spaces in the 1980s, such as Disneyland: spaces that opposed the harsh reality of social nonconformity during the 1960s, in which unions, students, leftist parties and women's organisations were in protest for improved democracy and social justice, and against the abuses of capitalism and authoritarian structures (Guarné, 2017: 18). These profound ontological changes marked the social crisis of the Lost Decade in the 1990s.

During the Lost Decade, not only did Japan's economic bubble burst, but new uncertainties materialised, stemming from globalisation, increased unemployment, and fictionalised environments such as the 'Electric Town' in Tokyo, the centre of modern Japanese popular culture. Released in 1993 during the Lost Decade, *Paprika* raises a pressing question of whether Japan's recovery from financial and social crisis is possible, or whether the country will continue to live in a kind of reverie where it is not possible to find a temporal order and structure in collective and individual terms. An ambiguous sense of reality is therefore depicted. On this basis, hyperfiction is understood as a non-diegetic space in which reality and fiction fade into a dreamlike state. Due to this overlapping conflict, ontological ambiguity, for its part, is entirely defined by a sense of liminality. Feelings of inconclusiveness without a coherent narrative take hold. The perception of time becomes altered, giving the impression of living in an eternal present that irremediably affects the sense of completion. The same happens with the sense of space when the indefinite status of places turns them blurry. In relation to hyperfictionality, then, ontological ambiguity can only be understood in the context of late capitalism because of the continuous fragmentation of the time-space order produced by the boom-and-bust nature of the capitalism affecting everyday lives. In general terms, ontological ambiguity is a state of indeterminacy resulting from times in crisis within post-industrial societies given by the blurring between the real and the fictional, or what I call hyperfiction. Thus, by destabilising the configuration of reality, crisis foregrounds ontological structure, namely, the discontinuity of being. This is why *Paprika* symbolically alludes to the loss of self, by confusing wakefulness with dreams and then by turning Tokyo into a transitory space of indefinite status.

In what follows, I outline a cultural-historical framework of Japan to contextualise *Paprika*, which is defined by a social perception of time as a critical state. This framework is inscribed in the anthropological literature on crisis and temporality (e.g. Nixon, 2011; Vigh, 2008). Then, I focus on Bjørn Thomassen's treatment of the liminality concept to analyse how different psychosocial and financial crises in Japan prompted transitional temporal adjustments that led to a sense of non-conclusion. In the second section I focus on the dream parade to consider Turner's proposal of the liminal as play and defamiliarisation and argue how the parade metaphorically reflects a meeting point between the local and the global, enhancing the sense of eternal present. In the third section, I focus on Augé's non-places and Ōsawa's fictional age theory. The literary motif of Tokyo's transformation by dream invasion allows me to compare it to a hyperfictionalised non-place.

This chapter concludes by showing that literature and anthropology can work together in capturing contemporary uncertainties. I believe that, in the study of the persistent social crisis derived from postmodernity, literature is a good tool for anthropology. First, it contributes to analysing how spatiotemporal disruptions destructure social narratives, leading to an ambiguous sense of self. Secondly, literature helps to catalyse ontological ambiguity by providing a structured – albeit fictional – narrative to overcome the context of crisis.

Ontological ambiguity as a non-conclusion: time perception before the Lost Decade

In Japan, the aftermath of World War II influenced a timeless apocalyptic imagination that permeated society and cultural expression (Tanaka, 2014: 41). This timelessness may be defined by the sense of living in a perpetual state of crisis, observed in two main ways. From a political perspective, the defeat implied the end of the Japanese empire and the subsequent restraining of its multiethnic ideology into a supposed essentialism of the Japanese character (*nihonjinron*) (Guarné, 2017: 9, 14).[2] The violence of the war reduced most territories to ruins, causing immediate death for thousands. The atomic bomb attack had an incomparable apocalyptic impact due to its seeming timelessness. At ground zero, a blinding destructive power instantly burned everything down, while many survivors experienced a slow, endless death due to radiation. Such a temporal dispersion of 'slow violence', perpetrated by an unclear articulated agency, affects the development of an integral answer to different social afflictions (Nixon, 2011). Not only is the past never fully prior, but 'the difficulty of narrating temporal duration is compounded by the difficulty of narrating physical scale' vis-à-vis a persistent event (Nixon, 2011: 216).

In this sense, the Japanese experience of crisis was of an ever-present apocalypse that never concluded because, in situations of critical unease and temporal ambiguity, narratives that uphold social dynamics are interrupted and, with them, the articulated experience of time fades. In other words, as an account of a progressive series of events, the development of a narrative and the experience of time are intrinsically interrelated, as noted by Ricoeur (1980). Thus, in order to make the present meaningful, it is necessary to close a narrative to decrease anxiety. Fiction studies theorist Frank Kermode states, 'to make sense of our lives from where we are … we need fictions of beginnings and fictions of ends, fictions which unite beginning and end and endow the interval between them with meaning' (Kermode, 2000: 190). This may explain why, amid seemingly inconclusive narratives, Japan found in fiction an imaginative way to conclude an apparent timeless critical reality.

The possibilities given by fiction helped the public to conclude with that sense of unfinished state brought about by the slow violence experienced during the postwar period.

The paradox of living with the anxiety of a timeless apocalyptic feeling and the challenge of overcoming it through creative mediums gives rise to a veritable *in-between*. The serene but disturbing sensation of the in-between speaks of a period of transition, that in anthropological terms is connected to the notion of liminality. Liminality is a concept developed by Arnold van Gennep (1909) on rites of passage in small-scale societies, in which 'the ritual subjects pass through a period and area of ambiguity, a sort of social limbo ... concerned with calendrical, biological, social-structural rhythms or with crisis in social processes' (Turner, 1974: 57, 85). Later, Turner (1974: 76, 77) considered that in mass society it is within leisure that one confronts human identities; thus the term liminality could be used in a metaphorical sense for speaking of social processes and historical social formations, like revolutions, insurrections or cultural changes 'characterized by freedom in form and spirit' by emphasis on play, art and leisure. Nevertheless, such experiences, according to anthropologist Thomassen, 'share very little of that *danger* and real peril involved in entering a liminal phase' (2014: 83, original italics). In this vein, Thomassen (2014: 2) emphasises that a key feature of liminality is transition: 'liminality lends itself to a wider application, as the term captures something essential about the imprecise and unsettled situation of transitoriness'. Liminality, then, stresses 'the importance of transitions in any society' by considering 'those brief and important spaces where we live through the in-between' (Thomassen, 2014: 3, 4). Following these two authors, liminality has a double strand. For Thomassen it explains how, in the case of Japan, the postwar's liminal condition is experienced as transitional temporal adjustments. Firstly, in trying to overcome the uncertainties derived from the apparently unfinished time of war. Secondly, because the transition from modern to postmodern Japan meant people had to adjust to a new temporal switch marked by economic, social and psychological changes. On the other hand, for Turner, literature can be a source of liminality as a potential alternative through which clarity emerges, as it helps to confront human identity, inquiring and reflecting on socio-historical crises.

Starting in the 1950s, widespread industrialisation and urbanisation gave way to Japan's fast economic recovery, the so-called 'economic miracle' (Guarné, 2017: 15). The exponential increase of corporate salaried employees, better known as *salarymen*, between the 1940s and the 1950s in large urban centres, speaks of the rise of a new middle class characterised by the standardisation of procedures that began to limit alterations in daily life (Vogel, 1971: 6–10). This means that, in essence, *salarymen* signalled a renewed experience of time based on regularities and patterns, such as train schedules, overtime, free time, working time, family time, and vacation. Additionally, large modern organisations associated with large private corporations that began to structure everyday life had to coexist with traditional small- and middle-sized organisations, forming a contradictory phenomenon in society that Japanese scholars refer to as the 'double structure' (Vogel, 1971: 6). The spread of these two phenomena from the 1950s raised epistemological questions about one's ability to *understand* crisis, which later was experienced as ontological uncertainty. These changes morphed with concerns over living in a non-conclusive time which, since the war, had not been overcome but continued to grow.

The 1970s, for many scholars, represented a cultural turning point, moving from modernity to postmodernity in Japan (Tanaka, 2014: 45–6). The baby boom gave way to a wealthier generation that shifted sociocultural trends from that of postwar reconstruction, which had been defined by constant work, scarcity, and 'the ghost of imperialism' (Guarné, 2017: 18–9). This new generation grew up in a land of plenty, with urban middle-class consumerism, comfort, luxuries and 'essential inessentials' laying the ground for a growing fascination with the 'soft, round, adorable, frilly, or fluffy [aesthetic] … [that] radiate[d] a dreamy, aspirational foreign style' (Alt, 2020: 110). The consumption of such a hyperfictional lifestyle begins to open up an understanding of how narratives were imbued with meaning via overlapping conflict between reality and fiction.

In considering this cultural turning point, it is interesting to note the psychosocial effects from the main institutional policies conducted during that decade, *kokusaika* (internationalisation). The Japanese government and large corporations supported *kokusaika* as a two-way plan: domestically to build internal idiosyncratic consistency, and internationally to export a particular image (Lozano, 2009: 37). *Kokusaika*'s main purpose was to export cultural products and narratives to make of Japan a homogeneous brand and model for internal and external perception and consumption, which was possible thanks to the fast pace of techno-economic development. Precisely by foregrounding the ontological issue, namely what it means to be Japanese (*nihonjinron*), this internationalisation policy was not received with such encouragement by Japanese society. This was because, firstly, technological acceleration created discontinuity between the past and the present, calling traditional and rural culture into question. Many in the countryside migrated to metropolises with stronger economies, leading to their becoming overloaded, stressed cities. Furthermore, reception was mixed because internationalisation led to mistranslations and distortions of their own culture. As a result, this policy implementation left many citizens in a growing state of ontological anxiety which, coupled with an apparent timelessness inherited from the postwar, led to a sense of in-betweenness that questioned their sense of belonging.

In spite of growing self-doubt, however, the welfare and progress of Japan was quickly consolidated, turning the country into the second-largest economy. During the 1980s–1990s, manufacturing and cutting-edge technology and techno-consumerism (Tatsumi, 2006: 52) became heavily interweaved with the social, cultural and economic circumstances that formed and consolidated the time period of postmodernity in Japan, notably during the Lost Decade. Considering Fredric Jameson's sociocultural analysis (1991: 4), postmodernity should be understood in a broad sense, not as an artistic style or a cultural movement, but as a cultural dominant, 'a conception which allows for the presence and coexistence of a range of very different, yet subordinate, features'. According to Jameson, the first signs of postmodernism globally began with psychological and social transformations at the level of the infrastructure (the economic system) and at the level of the superstructure (the cultural). Once the shortage of consumer goods caused by World War II ended, the development of new products and pioneering technologies drastically changed lifestyles, causing a generational breakout particularly influenced by the hegemony of the United States as a global way of life. This was followed by the 1973 oil crisis, moves away from traditional communism, the gold standard being abandoned, and the end of national liberation wars (Jameson, 1991: xx).

On that basis, if Japan rose from the war-ashes in 1945 to become a 'pioneering Tomorrowland' of economic power from the 1960s to the early 1980s, the end of that decade marked a turning point. In economic terms, the 1980s in Japan was energised by financial speculation and fictitious capital via 'a flow of money capital not backed by any commodity transaction' (Driscoll, 2007: 167). Thus, the previous meteoric bubble eventually burst in the early 1990s, declaring the end of corporate capitalism, 'Japan Inc.', and the birth of the Lost Decade. The causes of this collapse are found in the excessively ' "neoliberal" deregulation of capital markets', one of the main effects of which was a rise in unemployment and wage reduction (Driscoll, 2007: 169). As Matt Alt noted in reference to the Lost Decade:

> The name is no exaggeration. During the 1990s and the first decade of the twenty-first century, college grads who trusted that they, like their parents before them, would enjoy lifetime employment at top companies suddenly couldn't land jobs of any kind. A lexicon of new terms erupted to describe previously unthinkable new social ills: *hikikomori* ..., 'freeters' ..., 'parasite singles'. (2020: 10, original italics)

Japanese nationalist leaders through official discourse and mass media tried to justify the economic collapse not by drawing attention to the financial bubble, but by blaming newly emergent subjectivities and social ills, many related to technological affectations. This orchestrated moral panic responds to what Mark Driscoll (2007: 166) calls a neoliberal restructuration 'activated by political elites to justify crackdowns on workers, women, and imaginary "internal enemies" '. In essence, the Lost Decade highlighted the anxiety derived from the neoliberal demand for the fulfilment of the optimal socioeconomic performance amid crisis, which called into question the meta-narrative of societal ideals (here crisis converges with failure, see Heffernan, this volume).

The liminal condition given by the temporal displacement of 'the end' – namely, the impossibility of concluding a given narrative– inherited from the period of postwar crisis, was updated in an uncertain present felt as eternal. Indeed, 'instead of being a passing period of chaos [crisis] settles as a social state … acquir[ing] an air of social and existential constancy. When crisis becomes context it gains an oxymoronic permanence' (Vigh, 2008: 12). Hence crisis, as context, 'implies the inability to envision the future and it is, therefore, a time that can only be lived as uncertain' (Visacovsky, 2017: 7). When a narrative of a crisis does not conclude, its experience is of an unclear permanent present.

The eternal present: perception of time during the Lost Decade

It was against this background of the Lost Decade that science fiction flourished. It became the quintessential genre in Japan in the 1980s and early 1990s to describe a particular hyperfictional scenario in which technological growth and economic success promised a prosperous future, while rapid technological advance simultaneously put that future at risk. The Lost Decade was, therefore, a symbolic phenomenon depicted by popular culture manifestations in a feeling of existential political-economic concern and socio-technological dystopia. These dynamics of crisis became material for Tsutsui's *Paprika*. For the literary critic Takayuki Tatsumi (2006: 53), 'Tsutsui has relentlessly deployed his postsituationist poetics of "cho-kyoko" (hyperfictionality) to expose the conspiracy between reality and fiction that characterizes a late-capitalist age haunted by spectacles and pseudo-events.' Thus, *Paprika* captures Japan's liminal state, focusing on the emergence of hyperfiction and a convulsive experience of time. The feeling of living in an eternal present is highly linked with hyperfiction, since it depends on the emotional intensities given by technology, the commodification of all activities, hyper-connectivity, and globalised economics, that give facts an almost dreamlike character. The oneiric sense of reality is indeed at the centre of *Paprika*'s plot.

In *Paprika*, the Psychiatric Research Institute of Tokyo creates experimental devices for psychotherapeutic treatment, which work through the analysis of patients' dreams. These devices allow doctors to enter the unconscious through visual recordings. Although the use of these devices is controversial, among other things because they lack security restrictions, they are used for healing schizoid patients. Atsuko Chiba, the institute's lead researcher, administers this treatment under a childish female alter ego named Paprika. Atsuko must 'transform' into Paprika to give the dream therapy in order to ensure patients are not able to identify her and, ultimately, come to feel more comfortable in their recovery (Tsutsui, 2018). This character embodies the multiplicity inherent within the concept of ambiguity. Thus, although Atsuko and Paprika are one, the former considers the latter to be a fictional character whose work has real-world consequences through dream intervention. The climax of the story is reached when a newer device prototype, DC Mini, is stolen and used to hack into people's dream-worlds and subconscious to manipulate them. This psycho-terrorism soon leads to total confusion between sleep and wakefulness, especially when dreams materialise in the waking world, depicted as a dream parade, and bring states of wakefulness and sleep under critical examination as the city of Tokyo contends with crisis.

Paprika's characters try to determine in which of these overlapped dream-worlds the self *truly* exists. On the one hand, the infection of dreams symbolically reflects the accelerated global invasion suffered by people in Tokyo,[3] gradually but steadily replacing traditional Japan. Moreover, it parodies the values inherent in Japan, fostered by dominant discourse, such as cultural homogeneity,[4] respect, labour efficiency and technical quality (Lozano, 2009: 32). Finally, the mental disturbance symbolises the sudden economic collapse which had profound social effects (joblessness, low salaries, and social ills). In terms of ontological ambiguity, these scenarios project a new way of being and understanding that breaks with a stable narrative structure and thus describe an unstable self. The questioning of Japanese social homogeneity and the outbreak of globalisation into Tokyo boosted the feeling of an unending present. Indeed, it was a temporality of constant acceleration that made it increasingly difficult to promote a persistent narrative due to the rapid succession of events linked to successive socioeconomic crises.

Paprika's dream parade sequence is the novel's key moment in representing metaphorically this eternal-present feeling. The dream parade appears as a living web of global iconic representations which includes elements of traditional Japanese culture as well as foreign symbols of popular culture and global urban commodities, such as, for example, the Virgin Mary, technological devices, Buddhas, teddy bears, Japanese dolls, street and house furniture, the Statue of Liberty, and different kinds of monsters, among many others. All of them appear from the edges of Tokyo and march together to the city centre. Dreams are depicted in a quasi-monstrous way through their aim of invading and collapsing the time-space of Tokyo. Tsutsui makes use of the dream parade to express postmodern social anxiety: a credibility crisis among the authorities, seen as incapable of preventing economic or psychosocial calamity, such as the effects of the internationalisation policy, techno-consumerism, high levels of unemployment, or the bursting of the financial bubble. The allegory of the parade to frame the liminal state of a critical transitional period becomes more significant when its cultural origins are traced, to understand the role of play and spectacle in culture.

During the Edo period (1603–1867), *misemono* (shows, carnivals) were an important part of urban culture, where supernatural figures proliferated. These monsters and exotic grotesqueries, *bakemono* or *yōkai*, were exhibited in spectacles clearly charged with a political significance, and thereby became a popular means of expressing social agitation and discontent. For the Japanologist Gerard Figal (2007: 23), 'in the wake of the Meiji Restoration [1868–1912] – catastrophic change itself was often portrayed as a monster to be feared'. By the mid-nineteenth century *bakemono* had become more than just cultural productions. It is worth considering the so-called 'monster riots' in Osaka (Tsutsui's hometown), which broke out on the northern border of the city as 'the direction from which demons appeared from the world beyond the borders of human settlements' (Figal, 2007: 32). Among other complaints, these riots compared the fear of the new rulers and the increasing number of foreigners to dangerous monsters. *Bakemono* appeared in Tokyo with special delight and new social implications, as Tokyo became the symbol of modern Japan and the centre that gathered together the production and discourses of peripheral regions (Figal, 2007: 24).

Just as monster parades inundated the period before and after the shift of the Meiji Restoration (1868–1912), *Paprika*'s dream parade can be seen as invading Tokyo as a metaphor of the outbreak of the Lost Decade. The importance of fiction in describing a factual reality has been explained by anthropologist Kazuhiko Komatsu (in Figal, 2007: 22), who states that there is a 'fundamental link between "times of crisis" and the prodigious appearance of monsters in narrative, visual, and performative art'. In this sense, fiction catalyses crisis as its counter-narrative for representing the uncertainty of an epochal shift (see also Piyarathne, this volume). This is much in line with Turner's (1974: 60) framing of liminality as the stage in which 'people "play" with the elements of the familiar and defamiliarize them'. Defamiliarisation, in this sense, is a relevant technique since it generates 'a critical angle on one's given historical predicament' (Figal, 2007: 163). Thus, play as defamiliarisation may be interpreted as the key component of liminality within society; it allows interaction with different sociocultural possibilities and enacts different potential realities; play, in a liminal sense, is the interaction produced amid transformation (Lie, 2002: 7).

The dream parade acts as a reference to Tokyo as a meeting point between the local and global that matches play and liminality. It is a sort of carnival where the identities of actors who occupy the procession, namely the local-global icons, appear unclear, defamiliarised, losing their definition or precise meaning. The dream parade mirrors Tokyo's mutating urban space in which its ever-changing components (objects and people) are trapped in a continuous present that does not want to elapse. The parade portrays the assimilation of postmodernity – from the fictional environments of global consumerism to the undefined transnational identities of places or their inhabitants. The liminality of fictional environments, therefore, leads not only to epistemological problems (the modes of knowing reality) but ontological problems (the modes of experiencing reality; for further discussion of the relationship between epistemology and ontology, see Alimardanian in this volume). Hence, the notion that Japan was transformed spatially and conceptually, from inside and outside, takes on resonance. This is why the in-depth repercussions of such changes and the overall state of living in a seemingly eternal present were best observable in Tokyo, the world's most populous metropolis. In this sense, rather than referring to a 'familiar place', Tokyo suddenly became a hyperfictional space. In the next section, I explore the effects of ontological ambiguity on the experience and connection to non-places and communicational spaces, specifically in the mega city of Tokyo.

The ontological ambiguity of non-places: Tokyo as a hyperfictional megalopolis

Along with New York and London, Tokyo was considered among the first global cities by urban studies theorists. These cities were seen as possessing large networks of flowing capital, people and culture, leading to liminal communicative spaces defined by an in-between time premised on the effects of technological, social and political change: the transitional time between work and home, or the waiting span amid activities, both outline the interval in which people consume public spaces, visually and materially (Lie, 2002). Just as in the postwar context technological acceleration standardised the tempo of daily life, in the Lost Decade context it voids many of them. Precisely because the in-between time lacks narrativity, it heightens the feeling of living in an eternal static present. It is argued that in Tokyo the effects of becoming a global city were more manifest than anywhere else (Segers, 2008: 13). Unlike New York or London, Tokyo did not officially appear on the world grid map until 1853, when Japan ended its isolationist foreign policy with the Meiji Period (1868–1912). But until the end of World War II, the country was 'largely powered by farmwork [where] service industries, and blue-collar labor ... was an aspirational image' (Alt, 2020: 80). By comparison, New Yorkers and Londoners were historically engaged with global flows, industrialisation and consumption. Consequently, their transition from modernity to postmodernity was experienced gradually, in contrast to urban Japan's explosive change (Tanaka, 2014: 46).

The category of global city with respect to Tokyo, therefore, opened the way for deviations from what is considered 'the local' for its inhabitants. Thus, the radical change of the city transforms not only the temporal perception as previously discussed, but also the very notion of home through places becoming transitional spaces between the local (historic city) and the global (tourist city). For Henrietta Moore (2004: 76), this 'sentiment of dysfunction' comes when globalisation breaks with theoretical assumptions about wholism, 'but without us being able to tell how the parts could be fitted back together again'. In reference to *Paprika*, while the dream parade illustrates the local–global condition as analysed, the transformation of Tokyo into a showcase of dreams depicts it as a dysfunctional transitional space. It no longer appears as a fictionalised city in which all the elements come together, but as a fictionalised non-place. For French anthropologist Marc Augé, non-places can be understood as postmodern transit points (such as hotels, supermarkets, refugee camps and transport networks) where taken-for-granted communication and expression is suspended, favouring abstract exchange, isolated entities, and ephemeral encounters (Augé, 1995: 78).

It is exactly this kind of image that Tsutsui describes in *Paprika*, as the 'new' Tokyo (a synecdoche of postmodern Japan) is invaded by wonderlands where dreams come true, such as the theme park of Disneyland. All of these, in Augé's terms, could be considered non-places full of self-referential iconographies and ephemeral experiences of consumerism separated from the continuity and embeddedness of everyday life. In *Paprika*, Tokyo becomes a non-place because local and global cultural elements (in the form of the dream parade) are exchanged ahistorically, and thus location loses common reference in an anthropological sense. Consequently, time and space are blurred, transforming places into transitory spaces like the kind of oneiric world described in *Paprika*. Considering that non-places not only intertwine fiction and non-fiction (turning into a hyperfiction) but also cloud the specific cultural context of a city or a country, ontological ambiguity describes how it is no longer possible for a community to identify themselves with their own narrative in a different and unique way. Providing the theoretical grounding for non-places, Michel de Certeau (1984) distinguishes between place and space, with the former demarcated as geographically fixed and established. The demarcations of space are flexible and symbolic, and since space is determined by its users, it is in constant change and interaction through its locatedness. Space is, above all, a lived/practised place. In this sense, places become communicational spaces (geographical, physical or neither of the two), created by consumption and interaction (in Lie, 2002: 4).

In terms of liminality, Tokyo's indefinite status of intermediality is metaphorically represented in *Paprika* by how a technological device allows the superposition of two places, the psychological one (dreamworld) and the physical one (wakefulness). In other words, Tokyo is completely transformed into a factual oneiric space, namely, a sort of communicational space where the constant flux between sleep and wakefulness has no frontiers at all. The fantastic visual codes of dreams come true in wakefulness through the comforting of goods consumption that allows people to escape from the real-life crisis. In real Tokyo, fiction is everywhere. Thus, the liminal status of Tokyo's non-place quickly exceeds its spatial condition by affecting its people. The constant flux between reality and fictionality given by the rapid advent of technology and global mass media renders not only the identity of Tokyo undefined, but also that of its inhabitants. This was particularly true for young people who were seriously affected by the widespread reach of electronic devices and virtual spaces within the city. Especially during the Lost Decade, technology became – in fictional settings – a powerful weapon capable of manipulating the very nature of the self (natural or artificial), revealing a real anxiety of an ontological nature. This is seen, for example, in the famous fictional narrative works such as *Akira* (1982–90) and *Ghost in the Shell* (1989–97). But it is also the case in *Paprika* through using the DC Mini device, which allows the dreamworld to be invaded, while confusing fiction and reality and provoking a psychosocial crisis over Tokyo.

From a critical perspective, this aligns with the thesis of the 'fictional age' proposed by Ōsawa in his book *The End of the Fictional Age* (1996). Within this age metanarratives and ideals do not define the real world. On the contrary, they become impractical in describing what the real world is, and thus ideals are sought only through fiction. But fiction can certainly be a key component of liminality as Turner understands it: the defamiliarisation of a crisis gives rise to the possibility of finding a narrative structure that helps to represent the world. In sum, the impossibility of distinguishing wakefulness from the oneiric in *Paprika* echoes the profound time-space alterations suffered by the *real* dynamics during Japanese postmodernity. These dynamics include the crisis of a seemingly unfinished time inherited from the postwar period, the eternal-present narrative defined by the bursting of the financial bubble at the birth of the Lost Decade, and hyperfiction as a liminal in-betweenness due to local-global interaction and technological advances within Tokyo's transformation. The rich plasticity of ontological ambiguity as seen in *Paprika* describes a phenomenon that needs to move across all these topics and connect them in different ways by considering the contradictory developments of technology and culture, the global and the local, tradition and modernity, and the fictional and the real.

Conclusion

This chapter has explored ontological ambiguity as an analytical guideline to problematise the hyperfictional sense of living amid crisis, showing how literature can help to explore this feeling in anthropological terms. Reference to *Paprika* exemplifies in detail hyperfictionality in the context of postmodernity. Among the many concerns addressed by Tsutsui, four stand out: the socio-political distress caused by the economic collapse of the 1980s, forced by remarkable temporal uncertainty; the local-global meeting point as an acute contradiction among the inner and outer psychosocial self; a temporal experience of permanence or inconclusiveness related to the drastic social transformations; and the dreamlike experience motivated by the persistent conspiracy between the real and the fictional. All create a liminal in-betweenness through which to expose social distress in apparent compliance, understood through ontological ambiguity. In close relation to Turner's liminal thesis, therefore, works like *Paprika* are latent systems that re-dimension critical historical events, being potential alternatives for inquiry and reflection from which clarity can arise.

The discussion about the rise of postmodernity in Japan and its profound transformations in temporal and spatial perception emphasises the importance of non-Western perspectives to broaden the study of its complexity and multidimensionality. Japan reveals itself as a strategic point for understanding postmodernity's long-term effects upon other societies, especially since its cultural manifestations have had the capacity to transcend domestic borders, becoming and exerting a powerful influence in the global postmodern imagination. Hence, *Paprika* proves to be a fruitful case study that effectively mirrors through Japanese society how postmodern sociocultural life has been reimagined and moulded by fiction(ality). It also underlines the role that information technologies, mediascapes, consumer culture, and digital environments have had in the process; hence, raising questions about the growing conflicts generated by the dialectics between technology and culture, the global and the local, the East and the West, the traditional and the modern and, above all, the blurring between the fictional and the real.

As a literary work of anthropological significance, *Paprika* manages not only a mediation between factual and fictional reality to depict an accurate psychosocial truth but, more importantly, points out that, within postmodernity, fiction has already entered the everyday world via globalisation, technology, speculative capital, or non-places. Certainly, all of this is now fully visible more globally (see Cabrera, 2023). To a large extent, fiction has altered or dislocated reality's time-space, trapping the self in a hyperfictional sense of living. Ontological ambiguity allows anthropologists to grapple with ambiguity and explain the context of a crisis in these terms: the difficulty of finding narrative coherence is related to temporal structures that oscillate between the real and the imaginary. The proliferation and continuous growth of hyperfictional spaces since the 1970s require narratives that allow people to give a narrative structure to crisis, helping them overcome feelings of in-betweenness inherent in postmodernity.

Notes

1 This chapter was possible thanks to the support of the Postdoctoral Fellowship Programme (DGAPA), at The National Autonomous University of Mexico. This research is part of the Project PID2021-122897NB-I00 funded by MCIN/ AEI /10.13039/501100011033 / FEDER, EU.
2 According to Blai Guarné (2017: 21), the 'nihonjinron discourse provided the forms of historical imagination necessary to navigate the difficult conciliation between the immediate past and the reality of the present' (my translation).
3 For the specialist in foreign affairs Takashi Inoguchi, the Japanese governance system was not prepared to deal with the convulsive changes of globalisation emergence in 1985 (Segers, 2008: 67–85).
4 In a 1986 speech, Prime Minister Yasuhiro Nakasone stated that, in the face of cultural heterogeneity and class conflict that plagued the United States, Japan's singularity warranted its success.

References

Alt, M. (2020) *Pure Invention: How Japan's Pop Culture Conquered the World* (New York: Crown).

Augé, M. (1995) *Non-Places: Introduction to the Anthropology of Supermodernity*, trans. J. Howe (London: Verso).

Barber, K. (2007) The *Anthropology of Texts, Persons and Publics* (Cambridge: Cambridge University Press).

Behar, R. (2009) 'Believing in Anthropology as Literature', in A. Waterston and M. D. Vesperi (eds), *Anthropology off the Shelf* (Chichester: Wiley-Blackwell), 106–16.

Brandel, A. (2020) 'Literature and Anthropology', *Oxford Research Encyclopedia of Anthropology*, Web. 25 April. DOI: 10.1093/acrefore/9780190854584.013.85.

Cabrera, A. (2019) 'Allegories of Japanese women in Paprika by Tsutsui Yasutaka and Kon Satoshi', *Electronic Journal of Contemporary Japanese Studies*, 19:3, 10.

Cabrera, A. (2023) 'Privacidad y Consentimiento en Dispositivos Neuro-tecnológicos: Un Estudio Crítico desde la idea de Biocapitalización', in P. García, A. Rivera and P. Santamaria (coords), *Neuroética y Biopolítica. Pensar la Subjetividad en la Época de la Tecnociencia* (Mexico: UNAM).

Caughey, J. (1984) *Imaginary Social Worlds* (Lincoln: University of Nebraska Press).

de Certeau, M. (1984) *The Practice of Everyday Life* (Berkeley: University of California Press).

Driscoll, M. (2007) 'Debt and Denunciation in Post-Bubble Japan: On the Two Freeters', *Cultural Critique*, 65, 164–87.

Figal, G. (2007) *Civilization and Monsters: Spirit of Modernity in Meiji Japan*, 2nd edn (Durham, NC: Duke University Press).

Guarné, B., ed. (2017) *Antropología de Japón: Identidad, Discurso y Representación* (Barcelona: Edicions Bellaterra).

Jameson, F. (1991) *Postmodernism or the Cultural Logic of Late Capitalism* (Durham, NC: Duke University Press).

Kermode, F. (2000) *The Sense of an Ending: Studies in the Theory of Fiction*, 3rd edn (Oxford: Oxford University Press).

Lie, R. (2002) 'Espacios de Comunicación Intercultural', 23 Conferencia Anual de la Asociación Internacional de Estudios en Comunicación Social (Barcelona: AIECS), 1–42.

Lozano, A. (2009) 'Genealogía del Tecno-Orientalismo', *Inter Asia Papers*, 7, 1–64.

Moore, H. (2004) 'Global Anxieties: Concept-Metaphors and Pre-Theoretical Commitments in Anthropology', *Anthropological Theory*, 4:1, 71–88.

Nixon, R. (2011) *Slow Violence and the Environmentalism of the Poor* (Cambridge, MA: Harvard University Press).

Ōsawa, M. (1996). *Kyokō no jidai no hate (The End of the Fictional Age)* (Tokyo: Chikuma shōbō).

Ricoeur, P. (1980) 'Narrative Time', *Critical Inquiry*, 7:1, 169–90.

Segers, R.T., ed. (2008) *A New Japan for the Twenty-First Century: An Inside Overview of Current Fundamental Changes* (New York: Routledge).

Tanaka, M. (2014) *Apocalypse in Contemporary Japanese Science Fiction* (New York: Palgrave Macmillan).

Tatsumi, T. (2006) *Full Metal Apache: Transactions Between Cyberpunk Japan and Avant-Pop America* (Durham, NC: Duke University Press).

Thomassen, B. (2014) *Liminality and the Modern: Living Through the In-Between* (Farnham: Ashgate).

Tsutsui, Y. (2018) *Paprika*, 2nd edn, trans J.C. Álvarez (Girona: Atalanta).

Turner, V. (1974) 'Liminal to Liminoid, in Play, Flow, and Ritual: An Essay in Comparative Symbology', *Rice Institute Pamphlet – Rice University Studies*, 60:3, 53–92.

Vigh, H. (2008) 'Crisis and Chronicity: Anthropological Perspectives on Continuous Conflict and Decline', *Ethnos*, 73, 5–24.

Visacovsky, S.E. (2017) 'When Time Freezes: Socio-Anthropological Research on Social Crises', *Iberoamericana – Nordic Journal of Latin American and Caribbean Studies*, 46, 6–16.

Vogel, E.F. (1971) *The Salary Man and his Family in Tokyo Suburb*, 2nd edn (Berkeley: University of California Press).

Afterword: sitting and being with ambiguity

Mahnaz Alimardanian and Timothy Heffernan

Curtains up

Both the playfulness and seriousness of ambiguity have been a great source of inspiration in many plays mirroring life on stage. From the tragedy of hesitation and search for certitude in Shakespeare's *Hamlet* to the tragicomedy of waiting and indeterminacy in Beckett's *Waiting for Godot*, the magic of ambiguity has drawn attention to ethical and existential dilemmas in these plays.

The power of dramatic text was not unknown to Simone de Beauvoir, whose existential ideas have been explored in this volume, particularly in relation to the notions of freedom and of constraint (see Marshall, this volume). She used the medium of creative writing to elucidate her ideas outside of essays, composing several dramatic, literary and audio works. These works fictionally, though no less critically, explored abstract philosophical theory as grounded in lived experience. De Beauvoir explored this connection in the complex web of her characters' lives. Her relationship to theatre, using it as a practical device to present philosophical ideas, was expanded to the work of other existentialists in what she referred to as 'existentialist theatre'. The questions raised in these works provided an imagination to *think* about the person in philosophical terms and philosophical ideas on existence in the passage of everyday life (Gilbert, 2012; Holveck, 1999). The power and magnitude of theatre to transform actors and spectators were also not lost on Victor Turner, alongside performance studies scholars such as Richard Schechner (1985). Turner (1987) was interested in theatre's ability to comment on the ambiguities of human life and relationships 'acted out', so to speak, in social processes; and remarked on theatre's ability to offer social critique. Similarly, Michael D. Jackson, whose work in anthropology has drawn on continental philosophy, including existentialism, has stressed the role of creativity as intervention into human life, utilising creativity in writing. For each of these writers whom the contributors of this volume have explored and sometimes critiqued, the experiential and the creative have been used to bring the focus of ambiguity to the centre of anthropological inquiry.

And yet, as shown in this volume, ambiguity can mean different things to different people, look and sound quite diverse, and manifest or be experienced in a wide range of modes and forms. Tolerance for ambiguity, for instance, can be socioculturally tuned (for example, Hossain's chapter on contending with island erosion), and thresholds for marking ambiguity can be politically constructed (for example, the political action of Māori checkpoints amid the COVID-19 pandemic, in Clifford's chapter). This can all be influenced by the philosophy of life to which an individual or collective is committed to define connections and interrelationships, or similarities and differences. Curiously, ambiguity and its effects are not always visible, intelligible or translatable and may even be muted, taken for granted or ineffable. The magic of ambiguity is in its living force of being and becoming, as espoused by de Beauvoir, a force that can break the chains of constraints or create new ones. Ambiguity has been taken as a concept, state, situation or feeling in contemporary life, which the book has underscored as a quality of being, becoming or possessing many things at once (or none at all); a quality that presents challenges and opportunities to people while also representing a conundrum for doing and writing ethnography. This is important as there is a freedom inherent in ambiguous phenomena for exploring and even disassociating from what would normally be expected in a given situation, and this freedom can work in both generative and destructive ways as life unfolds. Contributors have thus shown how the complex and slippery nature of ambiguity does not limit analysis, nor is there always a need to define ambiguity in any strict sense or use a single definition or treatment. The core argument, therefore, has been the utility in *sitting and being with ambiguity in all its forms and modes of expression*, thus demonstrating the power embedded in this constituent force of life.

As a feature of life as well as what emerges amid disruption and disjuncture, ambiguity can be entertained and embraced by people to drive transitions and transformations. It can be constructed, increased or utilised to make sense, form opinion, or pursue certain agendas. If anthropology's main goal is to study what it means to be human, in the broadest sense, a primary observation from this volume is that the study of ambiguity holds tremendous promise for continuing to expand and extend this mission. Centralising ambiguity shifts the analysis away from undermining life as calculated or searching for predictabilities to what is in stock for social and political actors, ordinary citizens or everyday people to create meaning in life. The collection demonstrates the richness of ambiguity in sharpening the analysis of situations, events and phenomena, be they political or sociocultural, in attempts to understand and respond to a world.

The chapters present a collage of navigating, imagining, framing or criticising ambiguity under the light or shadow of something unknown, unfamiliar or uncertain. In this way, ambiguity is the essence of being and becoming (Heffernan and Alimardanian), the source and the elementary force of dynamism between certainty and uncertainty (Alimardanian); it is 'a basic feature of the world' (Rosner), and 'the fundamental existential circumstances of human social, ethical and political action' (Marshall). Its core tenet is the ability to throw into disarray the epistemological and ontological sureties that give life its sense of forward or controlled momentum. Through examinations of human crisis and natural hazards, economic tensions, the provision of public health, policymaking, political activism and of personhood, ambiguity has been explored via several registers that explicitly engage, rather than eschew, this lack of surety.

Throughout the volume, ambiguity has been analysed in association with knowledge, experience, sense-making, temporality, belonging and the cultivation of the person and the self, which we recapitulate by extending our theatre-experience metaphor, to bring this volume to a close.

Scripts

The presence of ambiguity demonstrates how possessing knowledge, or engaging in knowledge production, is very different from *knowing a world* through being and experience. Being in the world and making existential and ethical sense of this is the mysterious interplay between living knowledge and experience that cannot necessarily be reduced to each other, with Alimardanian pushing our understanding of what lived experience is and how it develops. Yet it is this interplay that produces numerous possibilities and contingencies, which shape each other amid moments of certainty and uncertainty. Ambiguity is immanent in and fundamental to the circulation of knowledge and experience, certainty and uncertainty, and what is explored as ontology and its double (non-ontology). Focusing on knowledge production in times of crisis, Rosner, Marshall and Heffernan demonstrate that the mere *accumulation and evaluation of information* does not render the world more knowable, nor does it reduce ambiguity. In the context of crisis, attempts to understand situations and the presence of false messages in one's environment highlight knowledge deficiency in the process of crisis and crisis-response. Rosner enquired into the utility of contingency in the making of knowledge during the US response to COVID-19, noting that the inability for people to control the contingencies of the pandemic means that an open, discerning mind is required by the public, media and academic community when sorting through the plethora of facts and information being generated. Open-endedness is a complicated position to entertain during times of uncertainty and yet is fruitful in encouraging new ideas and associations to be made that address feelings of not-knowing when little can be known as crisis unfolds. Conversely, facts and information are powerful tools during crisis, especially for politicians and policymakers, as Marshall has shown with the climate crisis in Australia, as powerbrokers manipulate discourses to affect political narratives and voter support and promote self-interest. Intolerance to ambiguity can create dogmatism and diminish problem-awareness and ethical concern. Sitting with ambiguity requires open-mindedness: Rosner and Marshall argue for embracing ambiguity by being open to mystery, and not rushing for closure. Indeed, Rosner sees the answer in plasticity of mind, and Marshall suggests revisiting our relationship with the human and nonhuman world as an ethical project for creating and sustaining meaning.

A similar trend of the failure and ignorance of the nation-state is recognisable in recovery after the global financial crisis as a temporal disruption to daily life (Heffernan). Individual recovery journeys in Iceland after mass miscalculations and shocks to the economy involved a sense of despair and failure which grew into a search for a new personal and collective ethics by reshaping the moral landscape, similar to activists' work explored in Serbia (Steindl-Kopf). Both chapters show how new sense-making capacities and meanings are created. Heffernan particularly explored this through a method for gaining a 'thick description' of ambiguity through interviews and timelining to record the nuances in crisis and recovery narrations. This enabled a view to temporality, with social experiences of time being affected by periods of prevailing uncertainty amid the desire for certainty. In times of temporal disruption, whether in the economy or, as explored by Puszka and by Hossain, in health or the environment, it is ordinary citizens and local players who, relying on their social networks, embrace risk and seek to create new opportunities for carving out a life. Governments increasingly adopt not-knowing in such cases to avoid blame and manage risk. In the face of governments doing very little to curb or adequately address crisis, people rely on what can be known through lived experience to create meaning and often utilise the knowledge held by multiple agents within diverse social worlds, reconciling this with local knowledge. The dynamism of certainty and uncertainty in embodying chronic illness on Yolŋu Country in Australia and living with natural hazards on a *char* village in Bangladesh demonstrate how ambiguity and its associated temporalities create new ways of understanding without aiming to resolve unpredictability. The effects of uncertain health conditions, as well as uncertain climate conditions, pushes life towards accepting flux, creating alliances, and expanding worldviews and social connections. People make sense of their socio-political environments and recast relationships through deploying strategies and engaging in life-affirming political and economic projects. Rather than attempting to reduce uncertainty by calculating probabilities, social actors employ techniques (ignorance and alliance, Puszka) or local wisdom (natural hazards as 'an act of God', Hossain) leading them to sit and to be with ambiguity in temporal disruptions.

Actors

In later chapters, contending with ambiguity moved from dealing with disruption and unclear temporalities to ways of framing and manipulating opacity and enigma. Overlapping, competing and contradictory phenomena and the multiplicity of diverse publics' interpretations of these were shown to be coordinated by political actors and activists to bring about change and reform.

Social activists (Steindl-Kopf) and policymakers (D'Aloia) nurture their views through perceptions of what needs to be changed or improved. Otherness and bringing forth 'an otherwise' are the keys to conceptualise what is perceived to be absent, or needs to be enhanced in these contexts. Bike activists in Belgrade imagine and articulate this in the form of an Other Serbia, and policymakers in Ecuador explore this in the form of an alternative economic model to capitalism. In these stories of transformation, life takes its own course of action, and nothing is urgent or under risk in contrast to a state of emergency, as seen in the pandemic experience in Aotearoa New Zealand (Clifford). Bike activism in Belgrade and COVID-19 checkpoints in Aotearoa New Zealand are sites of ambiguous political situations. This is particularly expanded to a visual scene of ambiguity in the case of Māori iwi checkpoints where the nation-state is faced with its own limits through the presence of ambiguity, and how people on society's periphery can use this to their own advantage. The exploration of how Indigenous communities, long seen in Aotearoa New Zealand as distinct political units on the nation-state's edge, highlight the plasticity of the nation-state and authority subversion. Checkpoints undermine the sovereignty of the Crown and come to represent Indigenous sovereignty. The lockdown was enforced by the state, but it was iwi who initiated the checkpoints, demonstrating the perplexity inherent to claims of sovereignty held by the Crown and Indigenous authorities. Sitting and being with ambiguity can have a snowball effect: attracting new ways of responding and mobilising change while at the same time being a site of great tension.

In a journey of self-realisation and person-making, the fluidity of belonging drives the journey of being and becoming. One may find comfort, resilience and hope in the act of searching or taking an in-between position. Whether such a journey is informed by the legacy of colonialism on one's identity and claims to belonging (Hutchings, Clifford), is impacted by a history of state–citizen interaction through political activism (Heffernan, Steindl-Kopf), or is an exploration of alternatives to anchor sense- and meaning-making (D'Aloia, Hizi, Cabrera Torrecilla), there is power in sitting and being with ambiguity to create and sustain autonomy. Commonly, the presence of an 'otherwise' through a focus on modes of thinking, acting and being that might bring forth a renewed or wholly different way of being puts the action into perspective. Alimardanian explored such a phenomenon as one of the attributes of non-ontology where the idea of an impossible world (lost, forbidden or non-existent) defines the existing one. 'Otherwise' is a destination to move towards (e.g. an Other Serbia) or to stay away from (as in the 'good-life fantasy' in Iceland). It can be explored via magical realism (Hutchings) or be analysed through a dreamscape (Cabrera Torrecilla). It can further be marked by desire and belief in alternatives and imagining other ways of being, such as an alternative economic model to capitalism (D'Aloia) or a 'foreign culture', seen through the meshing of tradition and neoliberal thought in contemporary China (Hizi). To this end, when competing forces, such as communism, neoliberalism, and local philosophies of thought, muddle one's sense of identity and values, as seen on person-making in contemporary China involving Confucian principles, collectivism, filial piety and neoliberal self-help workshops, hybrid practices for personal growth are part of transformation and pieces of an ethical journey through disjuncture.

An 'otherwise' is not always conceptual or projected into the distant future, it can also be objectified and materialised. For instance, Cabrera Torrecilla engaged with the uncanny and dreams as affecting people's sense of self and connection to place, referencing older forms of monster riots into cities and the 'invasion' of Western globalisation into Japan. Piyarathne further looked to an otherwise through subversion and public uses of humour, as in the Grease Yakā scandal, being the projection of Sri Lanka's politics and societal relations in a post-independence crisis involving political mistrust, fear, terror, violence and claims of government corruption. Journalists and cartoonists, as social analysts and critics of life on the ground, illustrated the Grease Yakā scandal as a cry for political reform. In this story of social crisis and anxiety through political satire, cartoons are used to discuss an emerging moral panic while at the same time gently ribbing politicians about their own political failings and corruption. Sitting and being with existential ambiguities can find a home and refuge in humour and the personal and collective sentiments can work hand in hand with imagination in a time of social crisis and transformation to depict an otherwise.

The use of cartoons in social critique as an act of observation is important in conceptualising the study of ambiguity: from whose point of view does the ambiguity stem? Rather than being perceived by social actors alone, ambiguity can be identified by a range of social analysts. This is critical for an anthropology of ambiguity since ambiguity is not only something that is perceived, experienced and shared with others – sometimes there is no ambiguity from the collective or individual point of view (in the case of 'added value' for D'Aloia, checkpoint legitimacy for Clifford, and activists' expressions and actions for Steindl-Kopf), rather it is the ethnographer as observer who senses ambiguity or interprets something as ambiguous. The distinction is important for the analysis of ambiguity, positioning the ethnographer as a social analyst for whom ambiguity is an analytical tool to navigate and observe the complexity of expectation, explanation and experience. Hutching used reflexivity in concert with well-publicised attacks on racial and ethnic identities to shed light on the ways that the ambiguity perceived in a person's appearance and heritage can be subverted to question hegemonic norms.

Last scene

To conclude the present study of ambiguity, three key observations from the chapters are offered, namely: the power in *sitting and being with* ambiguity; ambiguity creates a field of openness, timelessness and plasticity; and the 'feedback' from this openness has value in social analysis. Beginning with the power of sitting and being with ambiguity, rather than striving for remedy, ambiguity can hold the inconsistencies of people's lives or those encountered in the field, without needing to ameliorate these inconsistencies. There is a generative, constructive *and* destructive, positive *and* negative element to ambiguity which, as highlighted in this volume, could be identified with social actors and utilised in a range of ways to build up one's experience of life, fundamentally altering existence, or creating new or revised conditions for the improvisation of the self and for societies broadly. In many situations, the tendency is not to resolve ambiguity but to embrace it. Sitting and being with ambiguity is a situation to experiment with life expression.

This experiment is marked by indecision and inclusiveness and is the result of ambiguity creating fields of openness, timelessness and plasticity. Ambiguity is the source of being and becoming, and the moving force behind the dynamism between knowledge and experience on one level, and certainty and uncertainty, and ontology and non-ontology on another. Emerging from encountering, dealing and engaging with opacity, enigma or unpredictability, this field of openness, timelessness and plasticity is captured through reflexivity (Hutchings), the pairing of interviews with timelining exercises (Heffernan), and through the melding of cultural analysis with literature (Cabrera Torrecilla) and cartoons (Piyarathne) – bringing to the fore not simply calls for an 'otherwise' state of individual and collective being but also highlighting the non-linearity of experience and temporality.

This has led us to see feedback in ambiguity as having value in social analysis. Feedback is in many ways linked with the concept of ambiguity, as messages are disrupted by poor signal strength or receptivity. Yet this volume has shown how feedback, in its many forms of informational deficit or process disruption, can be useful for feeding-back about how knowledge and experience are endured, thus contributing to understanding the way that meaning is made, remade and manipulated. An anthropology of ambiguity, then, is one that takes seriously the ways in which people communicate and make sense of the world, including paying attention to notions of avoidance, ignorance, rejection, absence, failure and other similar forms to embrace inconsistencies as a source of meaning-making in human life and in the process of ethnographic writing. This sometimes includes paying analytical attention to nuance, contradiction, or negative forms of engagement, noting there is value in exploring what is ambiguous without overdetermining it, and therefore emphasising a sense of life, being and becoming.

Anthropology, in attempting to create a cohesive narration of human life, or of arguing fundamental qualities and units of existence in a shared humanity, often aims to highlight consistency and cohesiveness. In this volume, contributors engaged with inconsistencies to see where they take the ethnographer in analytical and theoretical endeavours as well as exploring processes of transition and transformation. This, we argue is essential in scholarship engaging with humankind and claiming to value and analyse lived experience through qualitative research.

References

Gilbert, D.A. (2012) 'Simone de Beauvoir on Existentialist Theatre', *Sartre Studies International*, 18:2, 107–26.

Holveck, E. (1999) 'The Blood of Others: A Novel Approach to The Ethics of Ambiguity', *Hypatia*, 14:4, 3–17.

Schechner, R. (1985) *Between Theatre and Anthropology* (Philadelphia: University of Pennsylvania Press).

Turner, V. (1987) *The Anthropology of Performance* (New York: PAJ Publications).

Index

EU authorised representative for GPSR:
Easy Access System Europe, Mustamäe tee 50,
10621 Tallinn, Estonia
gpsr.requests@easproject.com